Education
for the
Slow Learners

Prentice-Hall Psychology Series
Arthur T. Jersild, *editor*

PRENTICE-HALL INTERNATIONAL, INC.
London · Tokyo · Sydney · Paris
PRENTICE-HALL OF CANADA, LTD.
PRENTICE-HALL DE MEXICO, S.A.

G. ORVILLE JOHNSON

Professor of Special Education

Syracuse University

Education
for the
Slow Learners

PRENTICE-HALL, INC.

ENGLEWOOD CLIFFS, N.J.

1963

Preface

The necessity for providing adequate and appropriate kinds of educational experiences for all children has been steadily becoming more and more acute. Today it has reached a point where educators are most anxious to arrive at a satisfactory solution. The need for the solution has, in a sense, been forced upon the schools by legislation, general public clamor, and world events. There is a widespread demand that there be an elimination, or at the least a reduction, of numbers of the sociological problems precipitated by inadequately and inappropriately trained persons. In addition, government, industry, substantial segments of society, and vocal lay leaders are demanding a huge increase in the number of technically trained people.

Educators, in a sense, are responsible for much of the furor that is being directed against them. Education should and must reflect the philosophy of the society in which it exists. Unfortunately, however, it has in many ways actually encouraged lay persons to define the specific kinds of experiences and methods that shall be required to best educate future citizens to take their appropriate roles in this society. Not only have educators been hesitant to assume responsibility in these, their legitimate areas of functioning, but too often they have aggressively sought responsibilities that do not belong to the school, thus exposing themselves to criticism in these other areas as well. Examples of the latter are excursions into the realms of Public Health, Welfare, Mental Hygiene, Physical Correction, and Law Enforcement. Delinquent behavior in the schools, for example, is often kept quiet and law enforcement agencies are not notified of the very incidents which fall within their special area of jurisdiction.

This book attempts to define the problem presented by the slow learners from an educational point of view. Principles will be de-vi   Preface

fined along with descriptions concerning their application as possible
approaches to arriving at a solution to the problem. In many instances, the slow learners are a broader and more complex sociological problem than they are often considered to be by many educators.
Community agencies, other than the schools, must help the slow
learners. Among the agencies that must become involved are Welfare, Family, Juvenile, Religious, and Red Feather or Community
Chest. These agencies should coordinate their efforts through Central Councils. The school has its specific, unique contribution to
make, but if its efforts are to be most effective and lasting, it must
cooperate with these other agencies.

It is often stated that the school has become involved in many
inappropriate activities because other agencies have failed to assume
their responsibility. Further, the school has the facilities, rooms, and
personnel to provide the essential services. Where the school does
assume inappropriate services several things are apt to occur. First,
personnel required for educational activities may be "stolen," and
as a result guidance, diagnostic, remedial, and other essential programs suffer. Second, additional personnel may be employed by the
school to keep up legitimate services as well as illegitimate ones. In
either instance, due to the non-educational activities in which the
school is engaged, the school budget does not truly reflect the costs
of education. This, in turn, usually has a detrimental effect upon
salaries, employment of essential educational personnel, and the provision of necessary facilities directly related to the educational programs. Finally, the schools are heaped with abuse and criticism for
their imperfect handling of problems with which they should never
have become involved.

The solutions to most sociological problems are not easy ones.
Many of the problems related to social and community adjustment
of the slow-learner are not readily accepted by appropriate agencies
because they are among the most difficult ones they have to solve.
Often, the wrong agency will assume the responsibility for a problem. Only if the school carefully and clearly define its role and
refuses to assume the responsibilities of other agencies will these
other agencies be forced to accept their true functions. The school
will then be able to effectively carry out its own responsibilities.

The solution to providing the kinds of educational experiences
required by each child cannot be achieved quickly. It often requires

a complete rethinking of curriculum and school organizations. Changes made for one child affect not only that child but all the children of the school. Furthermore, program planning cannot occur at one level only and be effective. It must be planned for the school life of the individual, starting when he enters school and continuing until he is ready to leave school. Planning should not stop at the time he or his parents decide he wants to leave school or when he may legally discontinue his formal education.

The very magnitude of the problem often makes it difficult to discern its component parts. The multiplicity of problems usually results in numerous discrete efforts providing piecemeal solutions, such as a science curriculum, reading instruction, planning a unit to include slow learners, and so forth, without ever really coming to grips with the total problem. Even when the problem is recognized and understood in its entirety, the results are usually just as meager, since the general attitude is then one of, "How can we deal with a problem as complex as this one?" Often, nothing is done because everyone is waiting for an "authority" to show the way. In order to arrive at a solution, the problem must be understood and a method of attack planned that is realistic in terms of the facilities and personnel available or potentially available.

This book will help the administrators, supervisors, and teachers of a school system to (1) better understand the slow learners, (2) better understand the total scope of the educational problems they present, and (3) be able to organize a systematic attack on these problems. Since each school and school system is unique, the general information, principles, and methods of attack will have to be applied in such ways as to be appropriate for that setting. There is no simple "cook book" solution to the problem.

A second fundamental concept developed and presented is that of clinical education—not just for the educational deviates but for all children. The special educator has recently been called upon to aid in the educational planning for the slow learners. The slow learners are not usually considered a part of the group of exceptional children with whom the special educators concern themselves. The special educator, however, brings to the problem a clinical educational approach that makes him highly qualified for participating in the planning of solutions. He will advocate a clinical educational approach designed in reference to the characteristics of each child

—individualization of instruction. This does not necessarily mean teaching one child at a time. Grouping, however, occurs where a number of children present problems and levels of ability that are so similar in nature that they can be helped to find solutions with common instruction.

Most of the ideas presented in this volume are the result of numerous conferences, workshops, and study groups in which the author has participated during the past decade. The method of arriving at a satisfying solution for both the school and the children has gradually evolved from these work sessions. It has been put to test, with promise of success, in a number of school systems of various sizes. Many communities are now in the process of developing, expanding, and refining extensive programs for slow learners. The author is truly appreciative of the invaluable experiences he has had with them as these programs were planned, organized, and put into operation.

Contents

ix

part II   School Organization for the Slow Learners

part III   Instruction for the Slow Learners

Education
for the
Slow Learners

Introduction

The fundamental problem related to the provision of appropriate and satisfying school experiences for the slow learners is in the area of curriculum development. Yet, of the hundreds of articles and pamphlets related to the education of the slow learner, few have approached the problem in this way except in a fragmented fashion.

As one observes the operations of schools in general, it appears that educational thinking in the area of curriculum has become stereotyped to the detriment of children who do not fit into the "average" or "normal" part of the population. Curriculum, traditionally, has been evolved in a number of different ways, but whatever methodology has been used, a general curriculum, theoretically applicable for all children of a specific area or academic developmental level, has usually been the result. These curriculums may be developed by teacher committees for use within a specific school, or may be "guides" developed by state departments of education that find wide acceptance by the schools throughout the state. In many instances, textbooks determine the curriculum. The content and organization of a text thus determines what is taught and the order in which it is taught. This is true for reading, arithmetic, social studies, science, health or any other textbook series the school may select.

The basic curriculum must then be adapted or modified where an attempt is made to meet the educational needs of those children who do not conform to the tight little compartment of normalcy. In most instances the basic curriculum for any grade or subject is accepted as the foundation or starting point for "curriculum adjustment." Curriculums for the gifted children then consist largely of this basic material supplemented or "enriched" by extensions consisting of more reading and information about the same subject. Seldom do these programs also include instruction in the skill areas needed to increase competence and efficiency.

The concept of "watering down" the curriculum for the slow learner is generally derided by educators as being unacceptable in principle. However, when one observes instruction and examines many of the articles published in professional periodicals related to the slow learners, it is difficult to come to any other conclusion but that this is what is usually done for them. At the elementary level in a traditional school they are unable and not expected to read as much or understand as much as the rest of the class. The modern elementary program, using the experience-unit approach, achieves the same results of reduction of quantity and content in a somewhat different fashion. Since the slow learners are unable to read and thus derive adequate benefit from the materials assigned to the class, books and materials written for a lower level of competence (and also with simpler concepts) are provided them. True, they participate with the rest of the class in the discussions, but to what end? The secondary schools have tended to deal with the problem in a somewhat different fashion—repeat the subject until they either pass it or quit school.

The basic assumption underlying this type of curriculum application appears to be that the basic, essential skills and content for all children at all grade levels have been defined. There should be no difference in the educational requirements of children with varying abilities, experiences, or backgrounds who may also reside in quite different areas and communities. Thus, the educational needs of slow learners, average, and superior children are the same. The educational needs of children residing in a preferred suburb, city slum, metropolitan center, rural area, mountain region, or southwest desert are assumed to be identical. Put in this way, no educator would subscribe to "total" identity of education.

Curriculum, then, must be examined and specific curriculums defined upon a different and more fundamental basis. A curriculum to be meaningful, appropriate, and effective must reflect three things. First, the curriculum must reflect the characteristics of the child or group of children for whom it is designed. This means that the person or persons responsible for the curriculum must be intimately familiar with the children or have had sufficient experience with children having similar problems as to be aware of their basic characteristics. Second, the curriculum must take into consideration the educational, vocational, and social prognosis of the individuals. Only in this way will provisions be made to ensure that they have the kinds of experiences that will enable them to most adequately meet the demands of the society and economy in which they will be living as adults. This does not mean educating for the future in the narrow sense of the term. This cannot be done even if desired. It does mean, however, that the present experiences provided the child should give him the kind of basic background and foundation upon which he can continue to build. It means that he will have the necessary tools and skills to make appropriate adjustments as they are required. Third, the curriculum should reflect the environment of the individual in order that he will learn to live as effective a life as is possible within that environment. This is the life he is living, the life he understands. The mores that are not of his culture will have little or no meaning to him. He can, however, learn to improve his life within his environment and eventually make changes in that environment to better it.

The broad principles outlined above are impossible to put into immediate action due to their extent or scope. Most teachers and administrators recognize them as being essential and could list them as readily as they can list the four objectives of education (personal, social, economic, and civic) listed by the Policy Committee of the National Education Association in the late 1940's. But, there is a huge gap in many instances between listing principles and objectives and organizing for the achievement of them. Because it is difficult, if at all possible to directly achieve such all-encompassing objectives, little or nothing has been done. The very magnitude of the problem becomes so overwhelming that it consequently tends to be ignored. What is required is the breaking up of the total problem into segments that can be dealt with in an organized and systematic fashion. Since the segments can be solved, when the solutions for the segments are combined, the total problem can be solved.

What then are the organizational steps that might be used in planning an attack on the problem of providing educational programs for slow learners? First, the school personnel must agree upon their basic, broad educational objectives for the school. It is essential that these objectives be thoroughly understood and accepted by the various members of the faculty. They must also be in harmony with the objectives of the society in which the school is placed and which supports that school. In those instances where a small segment of the general society has undue influence upon a specific school or school system, the educator must take the lead to prevent those purely local or provincial biases from unduly effecting the program of that school. Exemplary of broadly stated general objectives were those recommended by the Policy Committee of the National Education Association.

After the broad educational objectives have been agreed upon, it is necessary to ask the question, "What do they mean in relation to the program of the Primary School, Elementary School, Junior High School, Senior High School?" After the general objectives of education have been listed and defined, it is essential that they be interpreted in relation to the developmental levels of the children at these various education levels. Thus we arrive at a second set of general objectives reflecting and in harmony with the over-all general objectives but applicable primarily to children at one particular developmental level. Following this, a more comprehensive list of specific objectives must be developed for each of the four education levels. While the program thus far is still outlined in terms of objectives, it is possible to determine what is expected to be accomplished at the primary, elementary, junior, and senior high school levels toward the achievement of the broad educational objectives originally selected.

The "break-down" of general and more specific educational objectives for the various developmental levels must not be done in complete isolation from the considerations being carried on by other groups. It is essential that the primary teachers be thoroughly familiar with the objectives of succeeding levels, the high school teachers must know the kinds of experiences the children have had prior to coming to them, and the elementary and junior high school programs must be planned taking into consideration previous and succeeding experiences.

After the more specific objectives have been developed, the experiences that can and must be provided to accomplish these objectives can be defined—this is the curriculum. Curriculum must be thought of in two ways, however. The development outlined appears to be most applicable to a horizontal or levels approach with the growth or development present only in terms of succeeding levels. Curriculum can and must also be planned vertically. Thus, objectives and experiences are defined for various skill and content areas that cut across or continue through 2, 3, or 4 levels. This is true of such skill areas as reading, arithmetic, spelling, and such content areas as science, health, social studies and so forth. The curriculum can be thought of as a combination of vertical and horizontal organization with the experiences selected or defined for any one level or time being essentially a cross section of the vertical (skill and content) curriculums.

It should, therefore, be possible for any teacher at any specified time to be able to define (1) where each child is in regard to each and all of the skill and content areas, (2) what the present experiences are contributing to the achievement of the goals of that area, and (3) cross-sectionally what these experiences are contributing to the school level as well as the over-all, general, broad objectives of the program for this child.

Figure 1 shows graphically the kind of organization for planning previously described. It will be noted that the total school is involved in defining the broad philosophy and educational objectives. Then each developmental level must work through the same process of

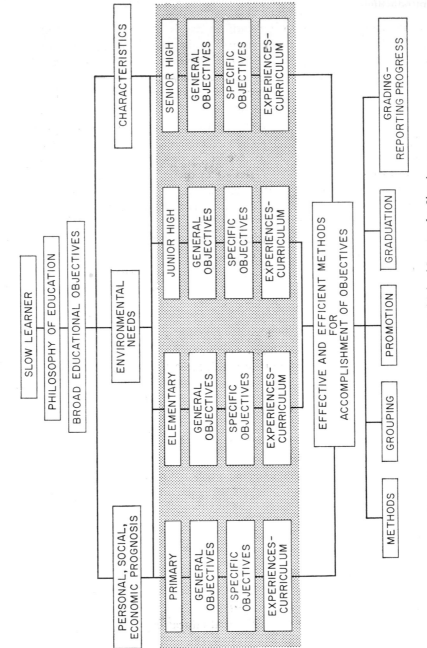

Figure 1. *Organization for Planning a Total School Program for Slow Learners.*

first defining the general objectives for that level, second, developing the specific objectives, and third, listing the experiences appropriate for the accomplishment of these objectives but always in harmony with the characteristics of the children, their environmental needs, and their personal, social, and economic prognosis. The vertical structure of the skill and content area curriculums then become an overlay upon this organizational structure.

The problems regarding the slow learner of which classroom teachers are most aware and to which they address most of their questions (e.g. methods, reporting progress, grouping, promotion, and graduation), then can be seen in their proper perspective. Once this perspective is established and understood, the fundamental principles involved in providing appropriate answers can be applied and the problems become no greater than those faced daily when the concern is the "average" or "normal" child.

The chapters following will consist of an elaboration and more detailed explanation of the preceding outline. Principles will be presented and discussed, and examples of application will be included. Only an approach upon the basis of principle, however, is appropriate since each school, each school system, and each community must plan a program for its own children if the program is to achieve its objectives—to be of greatest value to the children.

part I

The Problem of
the Slow Learners

1

Description of the Problem

The children who are included in the lowest quartile, intellectually, of the population are steadily demanding more attention from psychologists, educators, and various social agencies. No matter what the problem being examined, whether it is learning, adjustment, or social behavior, this portion of the population is sure to be involved as a factor to be evaluated. They are problem learners in school because of their limited rate and level of development. They are adjustment problems because of the innumerable failure and frustrating situations they encounter while they are growing up

—situations that under present conditions they can do little or nothing about. They are behavior problems, but not just because of their inability to meet the demands of their environment. The majority of the group are raised in the slum areas of the community, where certain kinds of deviate behavior is not only condoned but in many instances actually encouraged.

The composition of this 25 per cent of the population is heterogeneous, as are the problems presented. Intellectually and educationally they form at least three broad and rather distinct groups. These are the mentally deficient, the mentally handicapped, and the slow learners. The mentally deficient are severely retarded. They compose approximately 0.5 per cent of the total population. Between 3 and 4 per cent of the population is mentally handicapped. These persons are potentially educable to a limited degree and capable of working on unskilled and semi-skilled jobs. The remainder of the lowest quartile are slow learners. About one-fourth of them come from adequate homes and are making a reasonable although somewhat difficult adjustment to the traditional school and instruction. The remainder, 14 or 15 per cent of the population, comprise the group around whom the various problems are centered. It is this group of children for whom more appropriate educational programs and experiences must be developed.

Thus, the problems of curriculum planning and organizing the programs of the school to include instruction designed to meet the needs of the slow learners have become of major importance to educators and society in general. The awareness of the problem and consequent pressures for a solution have grown steadily since World War II. As time has passed, rather than arriving at answers to the various questions that have arisen, educators have found the problem becoming more and more intensified as more questions to which they have few answers are raised both within the profession and by individuals and groups outside the profession.

Most educational administrators have been made painfully aware of the need for some kind of solution to the problem. Motivation for a desire to do something stems from many stimuli. Parents request guidance and differentiated programs for their children who are having difficulty completing the general educational requirements. Civic groups are asking whether special programs are being provided various groups of "problem" children. Researchers are pointing out that an unreasonably large number of children are not completing their public school education. Their reports often imply that the fault lies with the schools and their lack of adequate programming and instruction. Teachers are demanding to know what should be done with certain children under current promotional policies—children who are academically incapable of benefiting from the educational experiences provided in the next class, grade, or school.

What is the answer? Where is the solution? Study councils have organized to attack the problem usually with inadequate time or resources. Too often the personnel assigned to participate have had insufficient influence or authority to try out new approaches and their chief administrators have not been sufficiently interested or knowledgeable to follow their recommendations. Visits have been made to other school systems with the hope that in a single day sufficient information will be gained to warrant the transplanting of the program observed to existing programs, preferably with a minimum of disruption. Teachers conferences have been held in the hope that some speaker in his 45-minute address will be able to provide a blueprint. Only rarely has a community resorted to research—research through which they have attempted to clearly define their problems, to establish an hypothesis, and to test a solution or a number of solutions with adequate controls and evaluation.

The teacher who is daily facing the children is fully aware that a major problem exists. He knows from personal experience that the provision of meaningful experiences for the slow learners is one of our most acute problems. While he may have relatively little understanding of their characteristics and consequent educational needs, he is still aware that their attitudes and behavior indicate that the educational experiences being provided at the present time have little value or meaning. He is, nevertheless, expected to provide them with as adequate an educational program as is provided the majority of the children. At the very least, he is expected to "keep them quiet" so that they do not interfere with the other pupils or disrupt the discipline of the room and school.

Since the teacher is unaware of the characteristics and limited learning ability and potential of the slow learners, his primary efforts are usually in the direction of "bringing them up to grade level." He devotes a disproportionate amount of time preparing special help activities. He may also use too large a portion of the instructional time in remedial activities. For the slow learners, these activities are usually a waste of time, since they literally are intellectually incapable of keeping up with the normal stream and achieve at grade level unless a retention policy is used extensively.

Innumerable articles have appeared in professional periodicals, but they have done little to indicate a solution to or clarification of the problem. Rarely do they provide the basic help, information, or guides required to develop educational programs for the slow learners. Articles concerned with the specific solution to a specific problem in a specific setting have little or no general value unless (1) the situation can be duplicated or (2) principles can be evolved that have general application. As a result of the limited treatment of the problem, these articles have tended to confuse and discourage rather than clarify and point out directions toward solutions.

One of the greatest deterrents to any positive action has been the lack of definition and a commonly accepted terminology. In fact, the present use of terms has tended to confuse the issues. The reader is too often required to carefully evaluate the descriptive material contained in an article or book before being able to determine the specific group of children with whom the author has worked or to whom he is referring. Where this careful evaluation is not done, the reader may accumulate a great deal of information that has little or no meaning for the group in which he is interested but to whom he applies it indiscriminately.

DEFINITION OF TERMS

Numerous terms have been used by various groups when referring to persons with retarded intelligence. Such descriptive terms as *slow learner* and *mentally handicapped* have been used interchangeably. They have been used as descriptive terms by some persons and to refer to specific groups with restricted degrees of mental retardation by others. Many parents, and clinical psychologists and teachers when talking with parents, use the term slow learner when referring to marked degrees of mental retardation to soften the impact of the diagnosis. The term slow learner is obviously more socially acceptable than such terms as mentally deficient or feebleminded.

Authorities have also used the term slow learner to refer to groups of children with varying degrees of intellectual ability. To some it means those children who do not keep up to grade level in their academic work, regardless of cause. Thus, in their concept the slow learners may have average or above average intelligence. To others, slow learners are that group of intellectually retarded children who only have a potential academic learning ability of second to fourth or fifth grade level. These children, in most states and larger communities have special class placement made available to them. Some states use the term slow learner in their educational regulations to pertain to children of any level of mental retardation. Other states, such as Ohio, use the term to refer to the educable group, previously discussed, who require special class placement.

It is obvious that there is no universally accepted terminology. Certain terms, however, are gradually coming to have relatively broad acceptance by substantial numbers of educators. For purposes of mutual understanding between the readers and the author, the most common educational usage will be accepted. To further reduce confusion, these terms will be defined and used consistently whenever reference is being made to a specific educational group.

Mentally retarded

The term mentally retarded is ordinarily used as a descriptive term including all children with any significant degree of mental retardation. As a result, it gives no specific indication of the individual's potential or level of academic ability. It includes children with mental ability from a level so low that no academic skills can be learned to levels approaching normalcy allowing the individual to potentially achieve from sixth to eighth or ninth grade level. About 20 per cent of the general population has some significant degree of mental retardation that prohibits them from learning academic skills at the normal rate and to the same degree of understanding and proficiency that is ordinarily expected from most children.

Mentally deficient

The mentally deficient compose approximately 0.5 per cent of the general population. They are the persons whose degree of intelligence is such that they are usually considered uneducable in terms of learning academic skills or insofar as school programs have been traditionally conceived. In the past, relatively few mentally deficient children were found in the public schools. Only a few of the largest cities, such as New York and Detroit, have provided a limited number of classes for them. They were excluded upon the basis of their lack of intellectual and academic potential. Many of them also have physical anomalies that set them apart from the general population, such as Mongolism. Since World War II, the parents of these children have become active, organizing into local, state, and national organizations. The result of their activity has been that a majority of the states have now included provisions for mentally deficient children within their educational legislation. Public school classes for these children are no longer rare although there will never be large numbers of them since the population is small—only approximately $3\frac{1}{2}$ per 1000 school children.

The mentally deficient persons are not only defective in terms of their intellectual development. Physically, in addition to the anomalies and stigmata often present, they also tend to be somewhat retarded. This applies to their motor development as well. As a group they weigh somewhat less, are somewhat shorter, have a poor body carriage and muscular development, and a greater number of physical defects than is found among persons of comparable age in the general population. In addition, they are socially and economically defective. They are incapable of making their way in society independently. They require lifetime supervision and direction by their parents, relatives, or private or public agencies. Some mentally deficient persons have demonstrated the ability to produce to a limited degree within a protected work and social environment, but even under optimum conditions they can never become entirely socially and economically independent.

Mentally handicapped

Approximately 2 to 3 per cent of the general population is mentally handicapped. Unlike the mentally deficient, the mentally handicapped are relatively normal in their physical and motor development. A mentally handicapped person cannot be recognized by merely looking at him; identification requires a psychological diagnosis. The mentally handicapped attain a maximum mental growth between approximately 7 years–6 months and 11 years. Their grade achievement should be from second to fourth or fifth grade level.

Mentally handicapped children, however, deviate intellectually so significantly from the normal that a special class has been found to be the best educational placement for them. They are educable. This fact has been recognized by the majority of the states. In these states the State Departments of Education usually encourage local communities to make special class provisions for the mentally handicapped by providing supplementary state funds for their support.

The mentally handicapped can learn the basic academic fundamentals and can learn to use and apply these skills in situations in which they are needed. In addition, mentally handicapped children have the potential of becoming adequate social and economic members of society. They can learn to get along in the community independently, to travel about the community, and to support themselves by obtaining and holding jobs.

Slow learner

The slow learners compose the largest group of mentally retarded persons. Among the general school population, 15 to 17 or 18 per cent of the children can be considered slow learners. Since they are a very large group and since they do not deviate as markedly from the average as do the other groups of mentally retarded children, special educational provisions have not been considered essential. They do provide one of the largest and most intense, continuing problems facing the general classroom teacher. They confront every teacher, with the possible exception of those teachers who instruct only advanced academic senior high school subjects. In an average community where the school serves children from all cultural, social, and economic levels, a class of 30 unselected children can be expected to contain 4 or 5 slow learners.

These percentages and numbers are not true for all communities. Preferred suburban communities where executive and professional persons reside will have very few slow learners. In these communities it is not at all unusual for the mean or average I.Q. of the school children to be 110, 115, or even 120. The sub-cultural areas of large metropolitan communities where the children receive little psychosocial stimulation present quite a different picture. The mean I.Q. of the children attending some of these schools is 85 or 90. Fifty per cent or more of the children can appropriately be designated as slow learners.

The most obvious characteristic of the slow learners is their inability to "keep up" with the rest of the class in their rate of academic growth. For example, they learn to read approximately one year later than the majority of the children. Their rate of reading development is then about four-fifths to nine-tenths of a year during each succeeding school year. They start late and continue to fall farther and farther behind as they become older. What is true for reading is also true for other skill areas and the content areas as well. They grasp new skills and concepts more slowly than is expected for children in general. Their maximum mental growth ranges from 11 years to 13 years–6 months. They form the group of children who receive the majority of the grades in the lowest quartile. They often drop out of school before graduation. Deviate, antisocial, unacceptable behavior in the classroom and school is not rare.

It is this group of slow learners to which the discussion of this volume will be directed.

HISTORICAL REVIEW OF THE PROBLEM

The slow learners have always been with us and probably always will be. The problems presented by their reduced learning rate and eventual level of intellectual development depend upon the demands made upon them by society. The slow learners have not always been an educational problem in the American public schools. In fact, the problem only dates from about the turn of the last century.

The education of the Colonial and post-Revolutionary War period was characterized by the relatively few educational opportunities available. Large numbers of persons never attended school or they attended sporadically and for only short periods of time. Available funds were small, teachers were poorly trained, and textbooks and materials extremely inadequate. During this period, education was the responsibility of the individual and the local community. It was by no means universal. The characteristics of the various schools differed widely, but almost all of them had as their primary purpose preparing the individual to eventually enter college.

Gradual changes were taking place, particularly in the secondary school during the early part of the nineteenth century. The Latin Grammar School whose primary emphasis had been Latin, English, and mathematics was unable to adjust to the demands for a broader curriculum more in keeping with the characteristics of the developing American society. As a result, these schools steadily declined in importance.

During this period the academy reached its greatest development and the present day high school began to form. The academics were, for the most part, local, independent institutions, unsupervised by state regulations. The academy was designed to meet the demands of the large and growing middle class. Its purpose was to prepare students to take their places directly in trade and commerce with a lesser emphasis upon preparation for college. The academy provided greater freedom of choice of subjects, made provisions for girls, and in general greatly broadened the educational programs and opportunities. They were, however, by no means the free, public-supported high school of today, being privately controlled and charging tuition. As a result, they declined over a period of time and were gradually replaced by the publicly controlled and supported high school.

During the nineteenth century, the United States was becoming much more highly industrialized. With industry came a movement from rural to urban areas, causing greater concentrations of population. Industry also provided a more prosperous economy. The combination of money and concentration of population effected the building of more and better schools with greater diversity of courses and more adequate supplies, materials, and equipment.

Other important movements in the social areas began to make themselves felt during the latter part of the nineteenth century. One of the most important of these educationally was a growth in the feeling of social responsibility for children. This resulted in a number of legislative acts that furthered the development and expansion of educational facilities and programs. The primary acts were the child labor and compulsory school attendance laws. The attitude that childhood is a period of growth and development, a time to learn and prepare to become a citizen who could contribute to the welfare of the society was reflected in these acts of the legislatures. These acts markedly affected the activities and training of all children and brought the educational problems of the slow learners to the forefront for the first time.

Very few slow learners were enrolled in school while the Latin Grammar School and the academy were the primary secondary schools. The slow learners not only were unacceptable to the educators responsible for these schools but were seldom enrolled for any period of time in the lower level or elementary schools. They presented an educational problem of little or no magnitude. The early rural economy neither provided a great deal of opportunity for an education for all children nor placed a high premium upon education. It was not essential in maintaining oneself in the society and economy of the day. It was, therefore, common to find many illiterates, short school years, irregular attendance, and children with a wide span of ages and schooling within a single school room. One teacher taught children with a wide range of ages, abilities, and grade levels. The curriculums were designed to provide instruction in the "fundamentals." In this way the child could acquire competencies in those skills and areas necessary for enrollment in the next school level (from the elementary school to the Latin Grammar School or the academy, and from the Latin Grammar School to a college). Or, upon leaving the academy, he was prepared to enter business or commerce. The curriculums were not designed for the slow learners and they were not encouraged to participate. In actual practice quite the opposite occurred. They were usually encouraged not to participate—not to attempt to continue their education. They either quit or were dropped from the class rolls.

With the advent of the compulsory education laws during the latter part of the nineteenth century and with their enforcement starting in the early part of the twentieth century, the slow learners began to enter the schools in numbers. By this time quantities of well-graded academic materials were becoming available to a group of better trained teachers. It became immediately obvious to the schools that numbers of children were enrolling that were apparently incapable of learning as rapidly as the majority of the children.

A CHANGING PROBLEM

An outgrowth of the early development of the American schools has been the primary emphasis upon the acquisition of academic knowledge and skill and preparation for college entrance. The function of the early schools was to provide the colleges and universities with students who had reasonably advanced academic competencies and skills. The public school of the early twentieth century maintained this same basic objective despite the change that was occurring in the school population. Little or no account was taken of the fact that a smaller and smaller proportion of the children were continuing on into college or going into commerce or trade. Little was planned specifically for the growing number going directly into unskilled and semi-skilled industrial occupations. That the classical or even the business education would in reality be of little or no value to them seemed unimportant.

Perhaps this emphasis was caused by natural inertia and resistance to change. Perhaps it was easier to accept the way of doing things as they had always been done, making only the minimum, essential adaptations required. Perhaps society accepted this as "education" and essentially demanded it for their children. Whatever the reason, primary emphasis was placed upon the acquisition of academic skills. Children remained in a grade until they had accomplished the work-level established for that grade. Little or no account was taken of the social and emotional requirements of the children.

As a result, the slow learners often spent two years in the first grade because they could not read satisfactorily after their first year in school. They also spent two years in some of the future grades as they gradually fell behind in their academic skills due to their slower rate of intellectual development. Under the 8 years elementary school and 4 years high school organization, children had only to repeat two grades to have reached a chronological age of sixteen by the time they had finished the eighth grade. Since sixteen years of age was the maximum compulsory school age in most states, the slow learners could, and usually did drop out of school by the time they had completed the eighth grade at the most. In this way the public high school was rather effectively isolated and protected from the problem presented by most slow learners. Those few slow learners who entered the secondary school were either effectively discouraged from continuing by successive failures or had a tremendous amount of drive that partially made up for their lack of intelligence and enabled them to participate to some degree. They studied intensively, memorizing as much of the material as possible, and occasionally were even able to graduate with marginal grades and promotions.

Gradually several forces within American society began to make themselves felt in education. A changing philosophy of education and the demand for greater democratization of the secondary school have been responsible for a number of present day school practices which in many instances have tended to make the educational prob lem of the slow learners more rather than less acute. At the very least, these practices have tended to spread the problem over both the elementary and secondary levels rather than continuing to confine it to the elementary school. It might be said that it is now a *total* school problem.

It has been observed that during the early days of American education the secondary school had as its primary responsibility preparing students to continue their education in the colleges and universities. A formal academic preparatory program was therefore completely justifiable. As time went on and a new philosophy became felt, the situation in the high school changed dramatically. Instead of the majority of the high school students continuing into higher educational programs, the secondary schools were providing the terminal educational programs for 6 to 7 times as many students as were continuing their education. This presented a distinct problem in a democratic society. The existing public school programs, organizations, and curriculums were in fact only meeting the needs of a small fraction of the children. This is a challenge that has been met with only partial success.

A number of other changes, however, have also occurred. One, additional content was added to the elementary school curriculum. Previous to this time the emphasis of the elementary school had been to provide the students with competencies in reading and arithmetic and to help them live more effectively in society. Such content areas as science, geography, history, and health were added and expanded to provide the student with a better understanding of his environment.

Two, the instruction became less formal. Curriculums were less apt to be planned and applied on a day by day basis with specific reading and comprehension requirements at each level. Teachers began to pay greater attention to individual differences, particularly at the elementary level. The knowledge acquired from the studies in child psychology and the resulting better understanding of children had definite influence.

Three, a tremendous increase in subjects was apparent in the secondary school. The high school no longer devoted itself almost exclusively to grammar, mathematics, and languages but began to include the natural and physical sciences, social sciences, wider selections of mathematics, English, and foreign languages, commercial subjects, art, music, home economics, and various kinds of manual and industrial arts. With the introduction of new subjects and the expansion of course offerings in the traditional subject matter areas, the high schools had an opportunity to organize curriculums to meet individual needs much more adequately. Thus, many of the students for whom high school was the terminal education level could receive experiences that would be of direct value in making their future economic adjustments. Many communities have even gone so far as to offer specific vocational training through the organization of technical high schools. The organization of an extensive vocational school program also encouraged persons who had left school or were about to leave school to learn a specific skill or trade.

Four, the distribution of time between the elementary school and the secondary school was equalized by reducing the elementary school to six years and inserting an intermediate or junior high school between the elementary and high schools. Psychological study concerning child development indicated that preadolescents had problems that were unique and the creation of this new school level was the educator's attempt to provide for them more adequately. Most states took the easy way in determining the certification requirements for teachers of these new schools. Teachers previously certified to teach in the high schools were now provided with secondary (junior and senior high school) certificates. As a result the junior high school rapidly took on the characteristics of the senior high school with all its rigidity, emphasis upon grade standards, and subject matter centered curriculums. In the expanded secondary school there was little awareness of or desire to understand and provide for individual differences, particularly in the direction of children with below average intelligence.

This change in school organization and structure brought the program of the slow learners to the attention of the secondary school to such a degree that it could no longer be completely ignored. The majority of the slow learners, even under an achievement promotional policy, eventually reached seventh or eighth grade. With a policy of social promotion they reached these grade levels at a somewhat earlier age and continued on. The secondary schools were now "inheriting" numbers of slow learners who had to be taught for one, two, or three years. As long as the slow learners arrived in the secondary schools in these increased numbers, they presented a problem that could not be ignored, for the simple reason that there were now numbers of children who were slow in their intellectual development rate. They were often unable to acquire the knowledge and skills taught in the classes in which they were placed. The dilemma: "How often can one require a child to repeat a class?"

The problem of the slow learners now faced the secondary schools as it had been facing the elementary schools for three or four decades. Unfortunately, this situation did not act to the benefit of the slow learners. If anything, the move of expanding the secondary schools from four to six years acted to their detriment. Two grades (seventh and eighth) in a school oriented to providing for individual differences at least on an instructional if not a curricular basis had been taken away from them.

Five, the secondary schools have made some attempts to provide for individual differences, but seldom in the way of basic program change. These attempts have not involved the training of teachers or the use of instructional personnel who have the understanding or orientation that is found at the elementary level. Instead, additional specialized personnel have been added to the staff. Guidance personnel, counselors, psychologists, and student deans are often employed. Their job is to determine the nature of individual problems that arise (learning, emotional, behavioral, and so forth) and help both the students and the faculty. This aid may be in the way of psychological counseling, guidance in the selection of appropriate courses, vocational counseling, helping organize remedial and special instructional programs, and working with teachers to help them better understand student problems. Unfortunately, these kinds of personnel (well-trained) are limited in number. In addition, much of the good they can potentially do is largely dependent upon the attitudes of the faculty in general and the school administration as well as the programs available. Finally, the solutions recommended seldom are in the form of necessary, sweeping curriculum and educational objectives changes.

THE EFFECT OF MODERN CONCEPTS OF EDUCATION

The factor which probably caused the problem of providing educationally for the slow learners to become really acute at both the upper elementary and secondary levels was a changed philosophy of education. In practice, this change has become more apparent in the elementary school but certainly is responsible for many of the considerations and decisions of the secondary school as well. It is reflected in increased content and educational experiences, in instructional methods, in ways of grouping, and in promotional standards and policies. Other factors which have affected the educational provisions for children are a greater understanding of child growth and development, methods of diagnosis of psychological and educational problems, increased knowledge of how people learn, and that children have differing needs, abilities, and methods of solving problems. Much of the educators' heightened awareness is based upon a greater knowledge of individual differences.

As the content of the elementary school expanded and greater emphasis was placed upon the social and physical sciences, somewhat less time and emphasis were placed upon instruction in such skills as reading, language, grammar, writing, spelling, and arithmetic. At about the same time, different methods of instruction were introduced into the elementary school. The result has been that the secondary school personnel and numbers of influential lay persons have accused the elementary schools of not performing their instructional duties effectively. Too many pupils are appearing in the secondary schools with poor abilities in the basic skills areas. All available evidence indicates that children with average and superior intelligence are more competent in these areas than children were a generation ago. However, the number of slow learners without the ability to achieve the same level of competence is increasing in the secondary schools. This makes it appear that a less adequate job is being performed at the lower grade levels.

The principle of social promotion entered the elementary school as a result of the growing awareness of child development, greater knowledge of the varying characteristics and needs of individual children, and a desire to do more to help children grow into effective adults than merely teaching them a few discrete facts and skills. Children grow and develop socially, physically, and intellectually at differing rates. Initially children are selected for admission to school almost exclusively upon the basis of chronological age. As a result, the children in first grade form a relatively homogeneous group insofar as life age is concerned. But this initial group of children is quite heterogeneous in their individual social, emotional, and mental development. Following a highly structured program with promotion based upon acquisition of academic skills, a child would remain in a grade until he had achieved proficiency in the skills expected to be acquired at that grade level. In this way, grade groups were kept relatively homogeneous on the basis of academic achievement but were quite heterogeneous when considered on the basis of chronological age and social maturity. The slow learners, remaining in a grade until they achieved the academic skills required for that grade level had little or no opportunity to progress beyond the elementary school. In terms of academic instruction, the elementary school teacher under this promotional program had few problems because all the children were at relatively the same academic level.

The changing philosophy of the modern school brought about important changes in promotional concepts and methods. No longer is the acquisition of academic skills regarded as the single, fundamental objective of education. At first the philosophers and psychologists pointed out the need for changed objectives. Their recommendations were accepted by the educator and gradually put into practice. Today the new objectives and educational practices are rather universally accepted by educators and by many parents. The four most commonly listed are self-realization, social relationships, economic competency, and civic participation.[1] The former objectives of acquisition of the various academic skills for the sake of the skills themselves or as preparation for further academic training are no longer obvious on the surface. The academic skills are taught and are of value only insofar as they contribute to the total welfare of the individual.

The acceptance of a philosophy emphasizing the values and needs of the individual within the society required a re-evaluation of methods practiced within the public schools and major changes in some schools. One important change involved promotional practices. While homogeneous achievement grouping presented relatively few instructional problems to the teacher in regard to content and method, it deprived children who were academically retarded, regardless of cause, of the many personal, emotional, educational, and social experiences that would be of greatest value to them. With the inclusion of personal and social values as major educational

[1] Educational Policies Commission, *Policies for Education in American Democracy* (Washington, D. C.: National Education Association, 1946).

objectives, promotional policies changed to what is now usually referred to as "social promotion."

Social promotion is a procedure whereby a child is advanced through the school with *his* social group. In actual practice it is seldom followed to its ultimate conclusion wherein every child is placed in a group having relatively the same social interests and degree of social maturity. Usually a child who is having difficulty with his school work is evaluated by the teacher and either promoted or retained according to whether or not the teacher thinks he would derive the greatest amount of benefit from promotion with the present group or retention and having his next educational experiences with a younger group of children about to enter that grade.

An examination of social promotion as practiced by a number of school systems reveals many interesting and rather incongruous practices. For example, while occasional retention seems to be acceptable, occasional acceleration appears to be strictly taboo. A bright child apparently cannot develop socially more rapidly than his chronological peers, but a dull child can develop more slowly. Also, although the concept of social promotion and only occasional retention of a slow child has been practiced for approximately three decades, it has not yet been universally accepted by teachers and principals. As a result, some school systems have found it necessary to institute a rule that no child may be retained more than twice during his elementary school years. Regardless of the problems that have arisen as a result of the practice of promotion without requiring the acquisition of a specified minimum level of academic proficiency, it has resulted in the slow learners being advanced to higher grades than in the past before they leave school.

Social promotion has also presented many instructional problems to the educator. Class groups are no longer homogeneous in regard to the level of academic skills of the children but rather in terms of social interests and maturity. This means that a teacher will have to provide instruction at several grade levels to a heterogeneous group of children if each child is to receive instruction that will be of the greatest value to him. No grade is composed almost exclusively of children achieving at that grade level but of children achieving below, at, and above grade level. Single level instruction only provides for some of the children. The others will derive little or no benefit either because the instruction is below their achievement

level and consequently provides no challenge or is above their
achievement level and is consequently beyond their ability to understand.

The elementary schools have faced the problem of the slow learners since the turn of the twentieth century. They have been steadily
enrolling them in greater and greater numbers. At first the problem presented by these children was primarily one of physical and
social maturity because of the promotional policies then being followed. It was difficult to provide them with both instructional materials at their ability level and social and physical activities that
would be of value and interest because of their small numbers within
each class. Other factors, however, acted to offset the slow learners
being physically larger and older than all of the other children. One
of these was that the literacy level was lower and school opportunities were fewer than today so that the premium placed upon academic learning was not as high. Older, normal children were also
enrolled in lower grades. Another factor was the waves of new immigrants entering the country. The children of these people were
enrolling in the schools of the metropolitan areas particularly and
were receiving their first educational experience—at least in the
English language. Having a major language handicap, they were
required to enroll in lower grades than their abilities would warrant.
This helped to increase the number of overage pupils and presented
another kind of educational problem to the teacher so that the
plight of the slow learners was not so obvious.

The slow learners in rural areas probably fared the best. Schools
were widely separated with many children attending only sporadically and for short periods of time. Because teachers worked with
multiple grade levels and students had widely deviating levels of
academic progress, the slow learners were able to fit into the educational picture naturally rather than as deviates.

The situation gradually changed as education became more
universal and schools more common, immigration reduced, and educational philosophy and consequent policies changed. In many ways
the elementary schools were prepared to meet this problem and to
arrive at a fairly workable solution. First, the training provided
elementary teachers was and is designed to aid them to better understand children's problems and provide an atmosphere conducive to
the individual's greatest growth. The elementary teacher is not a

specialist, in regard to subject matter, but rather a generalist competent to provide instruction in all the basic academic skills and content areas. He has been taught the basic psychological laws of
learning, how to apply them, and methods that have been found to
be applicable to the majority of the children. Second, the elementary
school did not inherit any specific objective or purpose of education
from its forebears but had an opportunity to grow and develop as
educational objectives and philosophies changed. Facing no precedent to be broken away from, it was thus in a good position to meet
the new problem of heterogeneous ability grouping.

THE PROBLEM TODAY

The problem of the slow learners as it exists today is quite different at the two major levels or divisions of the school—elementary
and secondary. The solution, however, is basically the same at both
levels except that the elementary schools have come much closer to
achieving it than have the secondary schools. The modern elementary schools using interest and experience units, individualizing
instruction to the level of the child, forming small instructional
groups within the classroom, and concerning themselves with fundamentals in the skills, content, and personal relationship areas have
had much of value to offer the slow learners.

The downward 2-year expansion of the secondary schools plus the
widely practiced policy of social promotion has brought the problem
of the slow learners to the forefront in the secondary schools during
the past two or three decades. The secondary schools, however, have
not been as prepared to cope with the problem as have the elementary schools for a number of reasons. In actuality, little has been
done of a substantial and effective nature toward the achievement
of a solution to the problem since it was first presented. It is fully
as acute today as when it first appeared.

The thinking of teachers, administrators, and the general public,
and the resulting practices of the secondary schools hark back to the
Latin Grammar School and early academy. Curriculums are geared
primarily to the average and superior students. Objectives are to
prepare students to continue their formal education in institutions
of higher learning or take a productive place in society, primarily in
business. States require minimum numbers of courses in civics, history, English or grammar, and physical education. Specific school

systems require additional courses in these areas and in the areas of mathematics and the physical sciences. Courses in these areas are assumed to provide the student with the information and under- standings he needs to live a personally fuller life and to participate more intelligently in community, state, and national affairs. Beyond the basic core of subjects, a student ordinarily has the choice of college preparatory, general education, commercial, fine arts, or home economics and industrial arts courses. In some relatively rare instances, courses of study and schools are devoted to vocational skills and training.

Despite the rather wide diversity of courses available at the sec- ondary level, seldom has a curriculum been designed specifically for the slow learners. The early, inherited objectives of the secondary schools have influenced the training programs for teachers and ad- ministrators as well as curriculums and course offerings. The usual secondary teacher tends to be a highly trained specialist in a specific subject-matter field. Most of his training has been designed for the purpose of attaining information, content, and understanding of his field of major interest. Relatively little time has been devoted to the basic understanding of the learning process or to help him to better understand the learning and emotional problems of the stu- dents. The average secondary school teacher is provided with tech- niques of instruction in his particular field—techniques that have been found to be of value for the majority of the students. These techniques are too often applied indiscriminately with the class ex- pected to "catch on" and keep up. Those that cannot or do not keep up are failed, upon occasion given some supplementary help, or placed in a "slow" section of that course in the future.

The secondary school teacher then complains that students are no longer provided with the basic academic skills at the elementary level. They enter the secondary schools unprepared to derive maxi- mum benefit from the instruction. They cannot read, they cannot write, they cannot spell, they do not know their number combina- tions and tables. Many secondary teachers even say that the attitudes of the students have changed. They not only are poorly prepared but are uninterested in school and learning. They resent having to apply themselves and prepare the necessary assignments. They have been entertained so long by a "sugar coating" method of instruction at the elementary level that they do not know how to study.

The secondary teachers and administrators that make statements such as these have failed to recognize the change that has taken place in the population attending the public schools during the past half century. They have failed to recognize that numbers of students now entering the schools are intellectually incapable of achieving at the level traditionally expected in the high schools. They have failed to understand or accept the newer philosophies of education and the necessary changed or broadened objectives of the school.

The problem of the slow learners will not go away or solve itself if it is ignored long enough. While it has been ignored the problem has continued to become more acute. Whether teachers and administrators like it or not, the slow learners must attend school for ten or twelve years, depending upon the compulsory attendance laws of the state. They must remain in school no matter how little they may apparently learn, no matter how discouraged they may become, no matter what the extent of their academic failures may be.

A few abortive attempts to arrive at a solution have been made by some schools for varying lengths of time but never with noteworthy success. Two of the most common methods have been homogeneous grouping and special help or remedial programs.

There are a number of basic reasons why neither of these methods has received wide acclaim for its success and both have failed to demonstrate that they are of any great value. Homogeneous grouping, as it has usually been practiced, consists of dividing a large group of children into a number of smaller, class-sized groups, homogeneous insofar as academic achievement level is concerned. How homogeneous the classes are and the number of sub-groups formed depends upon the size of the school and population available. In this way slow, average, and fast-moving classes are formed and the instruction can theoretically be geared to the ability of the whole class rather than just the middle of the class.

Many modern educators object to homogeneous grouping primarily upon a social basis stating that this method deprives children from having the opportunity to associate with *all* the other children. This is undemocratic, it is an unnatural life situation, and gives bright and average children no opportunity to learn to understand slow children and appreciate the contribution they can make. It also provides the slow children with no opportunity to appreciate his relative relationship with bright children or to benefit from the intellectual stimulation they provide. Furthermore, the classes with the slow children often have a stigma attached to them, thus destroying much of the value they may have. The attitudes of the children enrolled in these classes toward themselves and the attitudes of other children toward them all act negatively.

These are all sound reasons, as things now stand, for the rather general attitude of dislike for homogeneous grouping. It has been discussed by most faculties, tried by some, and after relatively short periods of time usually abandoned. These reasons do not, however, provide the basic answer to why this method of grouping has not achieved its purpose. First, the children are usually placed in their respective groups on the basis of scores obtained on academic achievement tests or the combined scores of group achievement and intelligence tests. These intelligence tests, being unduly influenced by achievement level (particularly reading), add little to the determination of selective placement. It is still primarily a placement based upon demonstrated achievement. Since there are many reasons for children's failure to achieve, the so-called slow groups actually became heterogeneous. Many kinds of learning and adjustment problems are usually present. The teacher neither understands the problems nor is capable of coping with them in most instances. A diversity of unique problems requiring differentiated programs of instruction are often housed together, with no provisions made for either helping to correct them or for the teacher to understand them. The only resource the teacher can resort to is his basic orientation which results in minor changes and adaptations of the instruction provided the average and superior groups. The instruction provided the slow learners when they were in heterogeneous classes with all levels of children had proved to be unsatisfactory to all concerned. This type of homogeneous grouping has proved to be little if any better, and when one analyzes the situation there is no reason to expect this practice to succeed. Rather, one might expect quite the opposite to be true since by bringing all the problems together, particularly when they are of a diverse nature, they often tend to be emphasized to a greater degree and tend to precipitate latent behavior that had not been previously overtly present.

Second, the curriculum, content, and methods of instruction in homogeneous grouping are usually the same for all groups and are not specifically applicable to the slow learners. The method by which it operates in practice is that the basic curriculum is planned for the large, middle group of pupils. Some supplementary or "enrichment" activities are provided the children in the advanced group. A "watered down" or thinned out version of the same basic materials and experiences is provided the children in the slow or retarded group. The textbooks used are usually identical despite the fact that the children in the slow group cannot read them or derive any consequent benefit from the contents.

The basic assumption underlying this method of solving the problem of the slow learners is that their educational needs differ in degree rather than kind. All they require is some special help, remediation, or a sufficient amount of pressure to insure that they will apply themselves diligently. It is assumed that the basic content of the course, as generally taught, is written so that all the children of a specified age will comprehend and understand it with the same facility and to an equal degree. Furthermore, it assumes that the knowledge and experiences provided are those of most basic value to all persons and required by all persons in order that they be able to lead personally fuller and more satisfying lives. It is also felt that these experiences will consequently contribute to the development of a child's greatest ability to work for the welfare and advancement of the society in which he is living.

These are dangerous assumptions to make. An attitude of this type tends to drug the teacher or administrator into a self-satisfied feeling of security and uncritical acceptance of what is being and has been done. Because commonly accepted practices, methods, and content have been used and found of value for the majority of the children for a number of years, or even decades, it does not necessarily mean that they are the best or of the greatest value for the majority of the children today. This is to say nothing about the group of slow learners who are apparently deriving minimal benefits despite the extra time and efforts expended by many teachers. In a heterogeneous group, this extra teacher effort may well be to the detriment of the group as a whole since the time must be taken from them. The slow learners are not remedial problems although there are slow learners who can benefit from some remedial help. The slow learners cannot "catch up" or even "keep up" by doing more homework or receiving additional instruction.

Regarding curriculum, little scientific evidence is available concerning the value of many of the specific skills and concepts taught. Much of what is taught today has been inherited from the past and continues due to tradition. It has been included because of pressures exerted by specific interest groups, or added following discussions and workshops conducted by "authorities" in the field. The curriculum is then taught through the use of methods that are often superior to the content since they are more often based upon good psychological principles of learning and instruction.

Unfortunately, the characteristics, problems, and needs of individuals are often not recognized or considered. Planned programs for slow learners who form a substantial minority group within the schools are too often nonexistent. The kinds of experiences that will be of the greatest value to them are seldom recognized, nor are provisions made to include them in the instructional program. Before a comprehensive program can be developed for the slow learners, a complete evaluation of the school curriculums must be made with the specific characteristics, background, and potential of the slow learners kept clearly in mind at all times. An adaptation of a traditional curriculum with the prayerful hope that it will solve the problem will never do the job. *The program must be planned and designed specifically for the slow learners.*

SUMMARY

The problem of providing appropriate kinds of educational programs for slow learners has a number of facets that must be understood before solutions that have meaning and value can be proposed and accepted. It is a lack of thorough understanding of the problem and an inability to clarify it rather than a lack of recognition of its existence that have caused educators to fail to arrive at an acceptable, long-lasting solution.

One of the primary factors that has confused the issue is the problem of terminology. To various persons the term slow learner has meant different things. Remedial problems, emotionally disturbed children, behavioral deviates, children uninterested in school, the mentally handicapped, as well as the true slow learner have all been referred to as slow learners at various times. These children are all slow in their performance of academic subjects but most of them are better described by other, more accurate terms than slow learner.

The concept of the slow learner to be used in this volume is predicated upon a psychological assessment of the quantity, amount, or rate of intellectual development of the individual. The slow learners are retarded in their intellectual development. Their retardation is not as great as that of the mentally deficient (trainable or severely retarded) or the mentally handicapped (educable). Their retardation is severe enough, however, to cause them to have marked difficulty in a school program planned for and taught to children with normal or average intelligence. As a result of continuing dissatisfying experiences in school, numbers of other problems are common to slow learners—discipline, lack of interest, inability to adjust socially, and so forth.

The educational problem of the slow learners had its inception at about the turn of the twentieth century. It was at this time that the compulsory education laws were passed by the various states and began to be enforced. Since that time the problem has steadily increased in intensity and seriousness as the nation has moved from a rural to a predominately urban society and a higher and higher premium has been placed upon the obtaining of an education.

The slow learners can benefit and profit from an education. They can learn, but they can derive little value from programs designed for average and superior children. They can derive little benefit from programs that are based upon the Latin Grammar School and the academy of the nineteenth century—programs designed to prepare students to enter college or the commerce of the day.

Relating the problem to the various school levels, it appears to be more acute at the secondary than at the elementary level. This is due to differences in school organization, differences in teacher training and orientation, and possibly differences in the length of time each level has been faced with it. The problem of providing for slow learners in the secondary schools dates back only two or three decades. It was partially precipitated by a change in school organization (from 8-4 to 6-3-3). The inception of the practice of social promotion has also been of importance.

There are many factors that have created the problem as it exists today. Educators are for the first time beginning to look intensively at the various aspects of the problem. Hopefully, as more is understood concerning the causes and the characteristics of the children concerned, a willingness to attack the basic issues, regardless of history or precedent, will develop. Only then will a fundamental study and planning of the greatest need—curriculum—occur.

SELECTED RELATED READINGS

"A Study of Slow Learning Children," *Pittsburg Schools,* 15:1–51, September, 1940.

Bloom, I. and W. I Murray, "Some Basic Issues in Teaching Slow Learners," *Understanding the Child,* 26:85–91.

Bolzaw, Emma L. and Elizabeth L. Keltz, "What Shall We Do for the Slow Learner?" *American School Board Journal,* 133:37–38, November, 1956.

Doll, Edgar A., "Varieties of Slow Learners," *Exceptional Children,* 20:61–64, 86, November, 1953.

Dunn, Lloyd M., "The Slow Learner—An Overview," *N.E.A. Journal,* 48:19–21, October, 1959.

Educational Policies Commission, *Policies for Education in American Democracy,* Washington, D. C.: National Education Association, 1946, 277 pages.

Edwards, Newton and Herman G. Richey, *The School in the American Social Order.* Boston: Houghton Mifflin Company, 1947, 880 pages.

Engel, Anna M., "Challenge of the Slow Learning Child," *Educational Leadership,* 11:151–55, December, 1953.

Featherstone, William B., *Teaching the Slow Learner.* Bureau of Publications, Teachers College, Columbia University, 1951, pp. v–viii.

Gahimer, H. S., "The Problem of the Low Ability Student," *Education,* 62:172–79, November, 1941.

Meade, Mary E. and Raymond A. Green, "What Program of Education for Slow Learners?" *National Association Secondary School Principals Bulletin,* 35:17–32, March, 1951.

Mones, Leon, "What Programs for the Slow Learner?" *National Association Secondary School Principals Bulletin,* 33:47–58, May, 1949.

Nickel, Kenneth N., "Better Education for Non-Academic Pupils," *North Central Association Quarterly,* 31:352–84, April, 1957.

Smith, Donald E., "In Behalf of the Slow Learner," *Peabody Journal of Education,* 29:154–56, November, 1951.

U.S. Office of Education, Department Health, Education and Welfare, *Teaching Rapid and Slow Learners in High Schools.* Bulletin No. 5, 1954, 97 pages.

2

Characteristics of the
Slow Learners

The slow learners have been victims of a great deal of misinformation and many misconceptions regarding their characteristics and educational problems. Numerous types of problems and specific behaviorisms have been attributed to them based upon the hearsay evidence and unscientific observations of a few naive or biased observers. Basically, the slow learners seen in the public schools are children with similar physical, intellectual, educational, and emotional characteristics as most children. Their general appearance and reactions are much the same as those of children in general. It is impossible to distinguish them by merely looking at them or even by giving them a thorough physical examination. This is probably the cause of many of their difficulties—they appear to be so "normal," so "average." Consequently, the casual observer and the unaware educator do not recognize or realize their deviations and resulting problems.

PHYSICAL CHARACTERISTICS

A popular misconception about slow learners is that they are "big (or beautiful) but dumb." Conversely this concept leads to the belief that large, athletic persons are not too bright. They are often characterized as the "big, dumb football [or] basketball player" type. They are more often than not thought of as the persons who are outstanding athletes, but who have great difficulty in maintaining their eligibility. They cannot do the required academic work without special help and even then often would not pass were it not for the sympathetic teacher or the pressures exerted by the coaches and school administrations who desire winning teams at any cost. It comes as a distinct shock when an All-American football player is also a Phi Beta Kappa or a Rhodes Scholar, or a professional baseball player is pointed out as a doctor, lawyer, or college graduate.

Physically, the slow learners are probably slightly below average in size, build, and motor ability. This statement is based upon knowledge available in the general area of mental retardation. Unfortunately, there is no comparable evidence related to slow learners *specifically*. It is true that there is some small, positive correlation between physical and motor development and level of intelligence. But the correlation is so small that for a group as near the middle or average of the total distribution of intelligence as the slow learners, no significant deviations can be expected or have been found. Any tendency toward a deviation from the norm should be in a negative rather than a positive direction. This would make the slow learners, as a group, somewhat smaller and more poorly coordinated than the population in general rather than the reverse.

Upon examining a group of slow learners, one would find among them some who are tall, short, and medium in height; fat, thin, and average in weight; and having good, poor, and average motor coordination. They deviate widely one from another. Individually they would extend from one end of the physical and motor development scales to the other. The majority of the slow learners are clustered near the center of the distributions in much the same way as the general population.

Unlike the popular concept, as a group the slow learners do not tend to be "big but dumb" or "beautiful but dumb." They do not tend to become the outstanding football players, basketball players, or weight men on the track team. One should not expect the proportion of slow learners having the necessary physical attributes and motor skills required of a proficient athlete to equal the proportion one would find in any unselected group of students. As a result of the small correlation found between intelligence and physical development and motor skills, one would expect to find a slight preponderance of students with average or superior intellectual ability with the necessary physique for successful athletic competition. Following the findings of Terman's studies,[1] one would actually expect to find a disproportionately large number of children with superior intelligence who have superior physical and motor development.

It does not necessarily follow that a smaller proportion of slow learners will attempt to become members of an athletic team or squad. Again, just the opposite is probably true. Children with superior intelligence tend to have a wide diversity of interests so that many who are capable of participating in competitive athletics devote their time to such activities as music, art, physical sciences, or some hobby. The slow learners do not have the same broad interests and are prohibited or discouraged from entering many fields in which they may have some interest because of their intellectual inability to participate effectively. In many areas of athletics, however, physical and motor rather than mental or intellectual skills are at a premium. They thus provide some slow learners with an opportunity to excel in a socially acceptable activity without being unduly penalized by their limited intellectual capacities. The slow learners cannot ordinarily make meaningful contributions in the academic areas so physical activities help some of them to fulfill this need.

There are, however, some limitations imposed upon the slow learners in regard to the kinds of athletics in which they can participate effectively and the manner in which they may be able to

---

[1] Lewis M. Terman and Others, *Mental and Physical Traits of a Thousand Gifted Children* (*Genetic Studies of Genius*, Vol. I [Stanford, California: Stanford University Press, 1925]), 648 pages.

participate. For example, they may be able to become a member of a high school football team, playing certain positions and under optimum conditions, depending upon the kind of football played and the level of the competition. Under certain conditions the player next to him can direct the slow learner's movements and indicate his assignments. The more complicated, highly organized team games are not particularly appropriate for slow learners. They may have the physical requirements but usually lack the intellectual ones. Physical activities involving less organization or even of an individual nature, such as track or golf, are more applicable.

PSYCHOLOGICAL AND EDUCATIONAL CHARACTERISTICS

The slow learners are, by definition, slow in their rate of intellectual development and retarded in their level of intellectual development, as compared to the normal child, at any specified age. They, therefore, deviate widely from the general student population in this facet of their growth—probably more widely than in any other area. This differential rate of intellectual growth effects their growth in other psychological and educational areas. Due to retarded learning ability, adjustment problems, grasp of academic instruction, and so forth are all affected directly or indirectly. By the time the slow learners come to the attention of the educator it is difficult to determine which characteristics are innate and which ones are acquired. They have had both attributed to them for so long that many educators think that they are all inherent and that little or nothing of a positive nature can be accomplished in dealing with them.

Intellectual growth and ability

The definition of the slow learner is based upon a psychological evaluation of the rate and extent of intellectual growth and development. Their rate of growth, as previously indicated, is between three-fourths and nine-tenths that of the average. This means that the extent of their growth or amount of intellectual ability at any one time is also in the same proportion as compared to the normal learner. Since the definition or conception of the slow learner is founded upon a comparative intellectual basis, it was impossible to adequately define or diagnose them prior to the advent of the intelligence test.

The measurement of intelligence dates back only to the beginning of the twentieth century, and only became a popularly accepted concept following World War I. Binet, a French physiologist interested and familiar with measurement of physical characteristics, was requested by the Paris schools to develop an instrument or method of measurement that would differentiate educable from non-educable children. The schools found they had numbers of children enrolled who were not benefiting from the instruction. It was necessary to determine which of these children were intellectually incapable of learning a sufficient amount to define them as educable so that they could be excluded from school. Then other causes for inadequate performance could be looked for in the non-learners who still remained on the school's rolls. Binet with his colleague Simone developed a scale of intellectual tasks. They determined which ones the majority of the children at various age levels could perform, and when the items were administered to a child, his performance could be compared to the average performance of children his age. It could thus be determined whether he could perform these intellectual tasks as well, better, or more poorly than most children. Using a ratio comparison method, a decimal relationship called the *Intelligence Quotient* was arrived at. Since the development of this original scale, most intelligence tests have used the same basic method of measuring intelligence, although some tests (such as the Wechsler Scales) have used a different method of determining the I.Q.

The schools have need of an instrument that will predict, with some degree of accuracy and reliability, the rate and level of academic achievement that should be expected of a child. With this information, the schools can not only select those children who can profit from formal instruction, as was the desire of the Paris schools in making their original request of Binet, but in being provided with this information can provide better counseling services. Students can be better placed in programs more nearly designed to meet their needs than the general program provided all children in the past. Binet himself made successful use of this diagnostic information in the organization of programs for the educable mentally handicapped.

Educators and psychologists soon realized the value of Binet's work. Goddard and Terman in the United States made translations of Binet's original scale and by adding and deleting items and restandardizing it on a population of American children provided American educators with a comparable scale. Terman's first revision was published under the title *Stanford Binet* in 1916. It became widely accepted by both psychologists and the public and was the general standard for intelligence scales for about 20 years. This was followed by the *1937 Revision* by Terman and Merrill. The latest revision was published in 1960 but does not include the extensive restandardization provided in the *1937 Revision* of the 1916 scale. Since Terman's original work, many intelligence tests have been published. Generally these have not only followed the pattern originated by Binet but many of them have even been standardized against the work done by Terman on either the 1916 or the *1937 Revision* of the Binet.

The first population to be tested on a large scale (aside from the populations of children available in the public schools) were the recruits of World War I. Special paper and pencil tests that could be administered to groups of subjects simultaneously were developed for this purpose. The results of this testing program were studied intensively and discussed widely in both positive and negative terms. Much of the furor that developed was caused by newspaper reports of test excerpts taken out of context and read by an uninformed public who knew little or nothing about the basic assumptions underlying intelligence testing.

The eventual outcome of this work, however, was to provide a tremendous impetus toward additional test development and construction and the use of standardized tests of all kinds. This, then, became the major effort of psychologists for many years following the initial translations of Binet's work. This work proved valuable in two ways. First, a number of different kinds of intelligence tests have been developed, the characteristics of which will be discussed later in this section. Second, more information concerning intellectual characteristics and behavior of individuals and groups became available than ever before.

There existed during much of this period a relatively common acceptance of the belief that the intelligence tests could provide all the answers to all questions concerning intellectual behavior. It was expected that the results of these tests could predict academic achievement and account for success, or lack of it, in industry, commerce, and even emotional adjustment and ability to establish social relationships. As psychologists and educators look back on the attitudes and beliefs of this period, the general feeling is that persons holding them were certainly poorly informed and naive.

One does not have to look back two or three decades, however, to discover these same beliefs, practices, and lack of knowledge. There are in the schools today many teachers and administrators who would find it very difficult to define an intelligence quotient and explain the value and what appropriate use can be made of it. The frequency of use of intelligence tests varies from school to school. Some schools never administer them because of a belief that the results are of no value; other schools use them freely with complete confidence in the results for the planning of all programs for all children. When some teachers or administrators are informed that a child's I.Q. is relatively low, they feel that this isolated piece of information alone is sufficient to explain the child's problems related to academic learning as well as the resulting adjustment problems that he displays in school. On more than one occasion children have been seated in the room according to the score each received on an intelligence test with no regard being given to other pertinent information that was available. Uninformed teachers, thus will organize instructional groups and establish achievement criteria with inadequate information inappropriately used.

Because of the inappropriate use of test data, many school psychologists and guidance counselors have encouraged school administrators to organize pupil personnel files in the central office. Often teachers who should have easy access to this information for planning purposes can only obtain it with difficulty, and if the materials are not going to be used, what is the purpose in obtaining them? The fault lies initially in the teacher preparation programs. Prospective teachers need to be made aware of the kinds of standardized tests available, how to administer appropriate ones, and the value as well as the limitations that must be placed upon the results. Rather than withholding useful information from the teacher because he does not understand it and consequently does not make correct use of it, inservice programs should be instituted to teach the meaning and use of test information. Various instruments for the purpose of measuring intellectual growth have been developed more rapidly and disseminated more widely than the knowledge of their values, limitations, and proper usage. The tests and their results have too often been indiscriminately placed in the hands of unprepared persons with no further instruction than those contained in the brief descriptions and directions contained in the manual for administration and scoring—directions which in many instances are not read completely and carefully, or followed accurately.

Before the development of diagnostic tests, particularly intelligence scales, it was impossible to select slow learners and differentiate them accurately from children having other kinds of problems that also showed up as retardation in achievement. Present day instruments may leave much to be desired, but persons having a potential use for them need to learn more about them. Before an adequate intellectual description of the slow learner can be given, a basic understanding of intelligence and its measurement is essential. The more psychologists have learned about intelligence the more they have become aware of its complex nature. It is impossible to adequately measure and describe the intelligence of an individual using any single instrument that has been thus-far devised. Certain instruments predict behavior in specified areas better than others. But to completely evaluate, describe, and predict behavior is impossible with the instruments presently available. This does not mean psychologists and educators are left in a hopeless position, because much valuable information can nevertheless be obtained.

It is also necessary to have a basic understanding of the theories and concepts of intelligence and an understanding of what intelligence tests test before the intellectual characteristics of slow learners can be understood. Prior to the twentieth century a widely accepted theory of intelligence was expressed by a group known as faculty psychologists. Their theory describes the total intellectual behavior or abilities of an individual as being made up of a group of discrete parts or faculties. They further theorized that these faculties could be trained or improved by instruction, study, and practice. As the faculties were strengthened, the individual became more intelligent. Certain areas of study were thought to improve the faculties and were consequently included in all programs—Latin, Greek, rhetoric, logic, philosophy, and so forth. In studying these courses the individual not only learned the content and skills required for adequate performance in them but at the same time became a totally educated person. He would be able to participate effectively in all intellectual activities. A course or courses in logic would help him to attack any problem logically and mathematics taught not only numerical and quantitative relationships, it also taught how to attack problems in general in a systematic, step-by-step fashion. Similar broad state- ments could be made concerning the other selected subjects.

This theory is far from dead today. It still has strong advocates, although some of the original subjects or areas of study have changed and other variations have been made. It does not, however, have the same position of importance and influence it once held. At one time educators reflected the thinking of faculty psychology in the devel- opment and extensive use of didactic materials that were unrelated to the experiences required in daily living. These materials have almost vanished from the educational scene.

Most educators turned from the faculty psychology theory to a more acceptable philosophy reflecting newer knowledge concerning human behavior. This theory or philosophy has been largely credited to Dewey although a number of persons have been involved in its development. Since its original exposition, the various inter- preters of Dewey have added their personal refinements. Other changes and adaptations have also been made, with the inclusion of new ideas and new information as educators have become more familiar with the importance of the psychologists' research findings relating to human development, learning, and adjustment. Today most educators recognize the need for a diversity of experiences for children that relate to the context and situation in which they will be used or which are familiar to the children. In addition, the past experiences the learner brings with him to the learning situation must also be taken into consideration if the program is to have value to the individual. Advocates of a modern philosophy of edu- cation further emphasize that learning is an active process in which the learner must participate. He can not sit passively by and, like a sponge, absorb knowledge. Neither does he learn through a process akin to osmosis.

Psychologists have developed numerous theories of learning. They have attempted to establish these theories by supporting them with the results of studies and research. In this way much has been learned about the way in which learning takes place and the condi- tions that will affect learning. Laws of learning have been formu- lated. All this information is of tremendous importance to educators.

What, then, is the intelligence test expected to do? It is expected that it will provide a measurement of an extremely complex phenomenon and that it will give a quantitative value to this measurement so that the intelligence of one person can be compared to the intelligence of a society of persons. The educator anticipates knowing how well the individual will be able to perform in school as compared to other children. He needs to know the child's present ability level today and the growth that can normally be expected to take place.

The intelligence test is not designed to test the *innate* or *real* intelligence of the individual. By a sampling technique it tests the manifestation of that intelligence. Samples of the individual's behavior are observed—problem solving, information, vocabulary, and so forth—in order to determine how much he has benefited from the experiences he has had as compared to the amount learned by children in general who have had the same or similar experiences. Most intelligence tests are, consequently, culturally loaded, but this is good. The basic desire of the educator is to determine how well the child can cope with the problems present in his environment and from this make some prediction concerning how effectively he will be able to do so in the future. Thus, most intelligence tests are designed in reference to the characteristics of a specific culture and are inappropriate for use in a different culture.

The following are only some of the many facets included in an over-all measurement of intelligence to obtain a complete description of an individual's intellectual behavior: how effectively and accurately he perceives the various factors in the environment that stimulate his several senses; how well he remembers; how well he is able to apply his knowledge and deal with both the concrete and the abstract; and on and on. As a result of the complexity and nature of the factor being tested (intelligence), as well as the only partial understanding that is presently available concerning it (as reflected in the numerous theories), it is not surprising that many different group and individual tests of intelligence have been developed over the years. These tests contain many similar and even identical items as well as some quite different items and performances required of individuals being tested. As a result, they may be testing different things or different aspects of intelligence, and in different degrees. Yet, almost universally they arrive at numbers that are given the identical name—intelligence quotient or I.Q.

The psychologist and the educator familiar with the testing of intelligence know that one must know the name of the test used, the group upon whom the test was standardized, and the basic statistical analysis that was applied to the original standardization data before any credence can be placed upon derived I.Q. It is also necessary to know the basic characteristics of the test, the kinds of items contained in it, the conditions under which the test was administered, and the reactions of the individual toward the test, the administrator, and toward the general test situation.

There are two basic types of intelligence tests—verbal and non-verbal or performance. Each of these can be subdivided into two sub-groups—individually and group administered. In addition, there are some tests, both individual and group, that provide the examiner with both a verbal and a non-verbal score. Verbal tests are those tests where the examiner directs the subject verbally, or the subject reads the directions and responds accordingly, usually also in a verbal fashion. Non-verbal, or performance tests, are not always non-verbal in the strictest sense of the term. On both the individually and group administered tests, the examiner often gives the subject oral instructions but the subject responds in a non-verbal fashion by doing something such as performing a non-verbal task by arranging pictures or objects, putting together a puzzle, and so forth. A few tests of a complete non-verbal nature have been developed particularly for children having communication problems such as deafness. Here the directions are given by pantomime and the subject responds by a non-verbal performance. These tests may also be used with hearing children who have quite adequate oral communication skills.

It is not a rare thing to find a variation of 10, 15, or 20 points in I.Q. between verbal and performance test scores obtained from the same individual. Upon occasion the difference may be even greater. Which score, then, is the I.Q.? Actually, they both are. The I.Q.'s on the two tests merely have different meanings—meanings that are important in making a psychological diagnosis of the person if there is an understanding that the tests are really testing something more specific than what the general term intelligence implies. The comparative results obtained from two different verbal or two different performance intelligence tests may agree fairly closely. This is particularly true for children who achieve a score near the central tendency or mean of the test, an I.Q. of about 100. Deviations are more apt to occur for children who score one or more standard deviations from the mean or middle scores. These differences in scores may be attributed to a number of factors. First, the subject may have been feeling different or approached the test situations differently. Second, there may have been differences in the groups used in the initial standardization of these tests. Third, different statistical methods may have been used in analyzing the data collected for the standardizations thus giving different characteristics to the distributions of scores from the two tests. Whatever the cause, it is most unsatisfactory and inaccurate to attempt to make comparisons of I.Q.'s obtained from two different sources.

Educators have been bombarded with discussions, lectures, and articles concerning intelligence. When the educational problems of a child are under discussion, someone will invariably inquire, "What is his I.Q. score?" or "How did he do on an I.Q. test?" Both questions indicate a lack of understanding of intelligence tests and intelligence testing. There is no "I.Q. score" but there is an intelligence quotient. There is no "I.Q. test" but there are intelligence tests.

The intelligence quotient, as originally conceived by Binet and his followers, is a quotient derived in the true arithmetical sense. The term *quotient* is taught in the elementary school and is the answer or solution of a problem in division. When used as Binet used it, it represents a ratio of a person's tested intelligence level or score to 100, with 100 being the average.

The intelligence quotient, again following the Binet approach, is derived by dividing the individual's measured mental age (M.A.) by his chronological age (C.A.), carrying the answer to two decimal places and then multiplying the resulting quotient by 100 to make it a whole number and thus easier to read. Most tests of the Binet type and most group intelligence tests do not provide the examiner with an I.Q. directly. They do not measure an intelligence quotient. Rather, these tests provide the examiner with some measure of the individual's mental age (M.A.), and the I.Q. is then either calculated or found by looking it up in a prepared set of tables.

Some persons who have developed tests or scales of intelligence have not agreed with the commonly accepted concept of mental age. They feel that it is quite inaccurate to conceive of children of different ages capable of having identical mental ages. (A child of 12 with a mental age of 6 years certainly is not a 6-year-old and perceives things differently than 6-year-olds.) They have by-passed the mental age in calculating the I.Q. Standard scores may be used instead. The I.Q. is then determined by using the appropriate table that takes into account both the individual's chronological age and his obtained test score. Thus a specific test score has different meanings and different values for persons of varying ages in much the same way that a specific mental age results in different values (in terms of derived I.Q.'s) for persons of differing ages.

Other basic assumptions usually made concerning the mental age and intelligence quotient are that the average I.Q. and distribution of I.Q.'s are relatively the same for various ages, that under normal conditions the I.Q. of an individual remains fairly constant within a restricted known range for that particular test, and that in general the mental age increases or grows at a known rate for most persons until they reach an age of approximately sixteen years, at which point it has achieved maximum growth and will, therefore, remain constant for a number of years. As a result, the mental age theoretically provides information concerning the level of whatever mental growth or development has occurred to date and is measured by the particular instrument at the time of the examination. The I.Q., being a quotient or ratio of the mental and chronological ages, is an index of rate of mental growth. It is usually assumed that the I.Q. is fairly constant and this assumption is accurate if no dramatic changes occur in the individual's psycho-social environment. The I.Q. can then be used to determine the approximate level of mental development (M.A.) at any future chronological age.

For example, a four-year-old child is found to have a mental age of 3. Using the formula for deriving an I.Q., it is found that:

$$I.Q. = \frac{M.A.}{C.A.} \times 100$$

$$I.Q. = \frac{3}{4} \times 100$$

$$I.Q. = 75.$$

To project this into the future, assuming no marked changes in the individual and his environment, it is possible to predict the approximate mental ages for any desired chronological ages. Thus,

$$I.Q. = \frac{M.A.}{C.A.} \times 100$$

$$75 = \frac{M.A.}{8} \times 100$$

$$M.A. = 6.$$

The M.A. will be 6 years when the child is 8 years of age.

$$I.Q. = \frac{M.A.}{C.A.} \times 100$$

$$75 = \frac{M.A.}{12} \times 100$$

$$M.A. = 9.$$

The M.A. will be 9 years when the child is 12 years of age.

The relationship or lack of relationship between the results of various kinds of intelligence tests, indicating that they apparently measure different aspects of intelligence, has been briefly discussed earlier. The educator is primarily interested in how well a child can perform academically—the level at which he is capable of performing and his ultimate potential in acquiring academic skills. He is interested in an instrument that gives a score that provides the most information concerning the intellectual activity required for satisfactory school performance. The verbal intelligence tests, while far from perfect predictive instruments, perform this task more satisfactorily than any other instrument presently available.

The slow learners are those children who score between approximately 75 and 90 I.Q. on a verbal intelligence test. Translated into comparative intellectual growth terms, this means that they are developing at a rate between three-fourths and nine-tenths that of the average rate. At any specified age they should, on an average, be expected to be performing at from three-fourths to nine-tenths the level of the normal child. This does not mean that they can perform a fraction less of the *same* tasks expected of normal children who are their chronological age peers. It means they are actually capable of performing at a fraction less or on a lower level than that group.

Careful observation of the slow learners shows that general intellectual slowness is evident in all phases of their development. Their pre-school development is characterized by this same slowness in maturation, although it may go completely unnoticed due to lack of general understanding of the specific things pre-school children can and should be able to do by specified ages. If it is observed, it may be considered insignificant because it is not sufficiently great. This same slowness follows throughout school (where it is obvious due to carefully defined achievement levels) and into adulthood. Slow learners are often described as being unable to carry on reasoning and thinking activities as deeply or as comprehensively as the normal learners.

The interests of slow learners are not as wide or varied as are those of normal children. Furthermore, their level of understanding is more superficial and limited. Observed in classroom settings, slow learners are not as discriminating, able to judge or abstract, develop initiative, direct their own activities, or detect and correct their errors wth the same ability as normal children of the same chronological age. They require more guidance and help in understanding their mistakes.

When the slow learners are first noticed, they are already retarded intellectually as compared to the norms for their age level. If they are truly slow learners and not children with remedial or primary emotional disabilities that interfere with test performance, they will never catch up to their age group. Rather, the reverse is true. They continue to grow intellectually at a somewhat slower rate. The discrepancy between their mental ages and their abilities and those of normal children continues to increase. In addition, the problem of understanding them is complicated by the fact that they do not form a completely homogeneous group even insofar as intellectual development is concerned. As a 6-year-old, the slow learner with an I.Q. of 75 has a mental age of 4 years-6 months and one with an I.Q. of 90 has a mental age of 5 years-5 months. At ten years of age, the slow learner with an I.Q. of 75 has a mental age of 7 years-6 months and one with an I.Q. of 90 a mental age of 9 years. At 15 years of age, the mental ages are 11 years-3 months and 13 years-6 months for slow learners with I.Q.'s of 75 and 90 respectively.

Educational growth and ability

The slow learners, testing on a verbal intelligence test between 75 and 90 I.Q., create a most difficult educational problem—one that is seldom solved to the satisfaction of the slow learners, the community, or educators. They are not sufficiently retarded to be committed to an institution or placed in special classes, nor are they (as a group) capable of profiting satisfactorily from the offerings of the regular class. They furnish the bulk of the children who by the age of 12 to 15 are 2 to 4 grades retarded.

Children with I.Q.'s of 80 will eventually attain an approximate mental age of 12 years-6 months. It has been found that these children usually spend two years in the first grade and probably repeat one or two additional grades during the time they are in school. By the time full mental growth has been attained, they are capable of average seventh grade work. The slow learners on the extreme of the continuum with I.Q.'s of 90 are close enough to the average to make normal or almost normal progress throughout most of their school life. This is particularly true for the elementary grades and junior high school. If they happen to be among the older children in the grade (i.e., their birthdays fall during the beginning of the school year) their chances of regular progress are even greater. In the course of their schooling they may become retarded one or even two years but the majority can expect to graduate from high school if they have sufficient drive.

It is widely accepted among educators, partly because of some research but primarily due to extensive personal observation, that a minimum amount of mental ability is required for the acquisition of specific skills. Assume, for descriptive purposes, that the skills and concepts are placed on a relative continuum of difficulty, the easiest being taught first and the more and more difficult being taught successively later. Assume further that skills and concepts are taught at the earliest possible grade and age level at which the majority of the children can understand them and derive maximum benefit from them. Reading, for example, requires a minimum mental age of 6 years plus if a first grade child is to have success. A slow learner with an I.Q. of 75 does not have a mental age of 6 until he is 8 years of age but one with an I.Q. of 90 has a mental age of 6 years when he is 6 years-8 months of age.

The slow learners are retarded in their rate of intellectual growth and development as reflected by I.Q.'s between 75 and 90. The mental retardation is reflected in school by academic retardation. They do not and can not learn academic skills at the chronological age at which these skills are taught to most children. They are capable of learning many of these skills at a later date when they are older and when they have achieved sufficient mental maturity. Some skills and concepts they will never be capable of learning completely because mental growth will have ceased before the required intellectual developmental level has been reached. In terms of planning and providing appropriate programs for the slow learners, these children cannot be conceived of as remedial problems or "late bloomers" who will eventually catch up if given sufficient time.

Planning an instructional program for slow learners requires an understanding of the relationship between learning and developmental rates in children.

Many statements concerning the learning rate of *slow learning* children are undoubtedly made by persons who (a) are unfamiliar with the basic concepts involved in an understanding of the learning process, (b) have failed to differentiate immediate and sequential learning, or (c) lack an understanding of child development. Often they have not differentiated in their own thinking between learning and development, using the terms interchangeably. As a result, articles concerned with development rate have appeared where the author has used the term "learning," and in other writing, the author has used a reverse of the terms and concepts involved. This has resulted in a great deal of confusion on the part of readers. The confusion on the part of authors has thus been compounded to the extent that numerous dogmatic statements appear in print concerning the learning abilities (or disabilities) and characteristics of *slow learning* children that are erroneous in light of interpretations that can be made concerning the findings reported in the learning studies (with the mentally retarded).

When concerned with child development and rate of development in general, one may be referring to the growth rate of an individual or group in one or more of a number of somewhat discrete and only distantly related areas—physical, mental, academic, social and so forth. The *slow learning* group for education purposes is defined (as the name implies) upon the basis of retarded or slow intellectual development. This is reflected in the theoretical meaning of the IQ which, on most standardized intelligence tests, is a ratio showing the relationship between intellectual growth and number of years lived. The individual's present intellectual behavior upon a selected sample of tasks is compared to the average responses of a large sample of the population of the same life age.

Thus, a child with an IQ of 75 has an intellectual developmental rate three-fourths that of the average or normal. A child with an IQ of *87* or *88* is developing intellectually at *seven-eighths* the rate of the average or general population. It will, consequently, take this individual from one-fourth to *one-eighth* times longer to "pass through" a specified developmental growth period than is required for the "average" or normal child. Assuming each of three children has an intellectual developmental level (mental age) of 6-0 years, the normal child will achieve one year of intellectual growth in one chronological year, and after a one-year interval will have an intellectual developmental level of 7-0 years. During the same period of time, the child with an IQ of 75 will have grown intellectually 9 months, and the child with an IQ of *87* or *88* . . . $10\frac{1}{2}$ months. The child with an IQ of 75 will require 1 year and 4 months and the child with an IQ of *87* or *88* will require 1 year and $1\frac{1}{2}$ *to 2* months to develop intellectually the one year that the normal child accomplished in a 1 year period of time.

The IQ, therefore, does not provide the observer with an evaluation of the present intellectual power or ability of the individual but is rather derived from this knowledge plus a knowledge of the individual's life age. On such standardized instruments as the *Stanford Binet,* the intellectual developmental level (mental age) may be derived from a knowledge of the developmental rate (intelligence quotient) and life age (chronological age).

Learning is dependent upon a number of variables of which intellectual developmental level is an important one. This factor will largely determine the maximum complexity and level of learning that can possibly take place at any specified time. Thus, in comparing the learning ability (level, rate, and so forth) of two groups of children at the same intellectual developmental level, and assuming the same degree of readiness to learn in terms of background experiences, attitudes, desires, quality of instruction, and so forth, one would expect that they would learn the skill or concept in the same period of time. Although the two groups (normal and *slow learning*) may differ significantly on such developmental factors as life age, physical and motor development, or social development, as long as they are equated for intellectual developmental levels, experiences, and previous learnings to insure equal readiness, they should have similar patterns of learning, require the same amounts of practice, and retain equal amounts of the material learned.

The preceding statement should hold true in terms of immediate learnings within the intellectual abilities of the subjects included within the respective group. In the case of learning studies, it should hold true for the younger, normal subjects and older, *slow learning* subjects of the same mental age. This statement would not apply, however, to a sequence of learning activities (such as learning to read, which actually consists of many discrete learnings). Where sequential learning is properly placed in terms of an intellectual developmental scale and each successive learning activity requires (1) greater intellectual maturity as well as (2) previous learning, then the concept of intellectual rate of development as well as the concepts involved in learning must be incorporated into planning for the learning of the entire, total sequence.

The subject with normal or "average" intelligence will learn the sequence in a specified period of time. The subject developing more slowly requires that successive learning be spaced farther apart, thus extending the sequence of learnings over a longer period of time, but no more practice time in learning a specific skill or concept and consequently no more total instructional time to learn the entire sequence should be necessary. The only additional time devoted to skill instruction for the slower group should be in terms of additional review to overcome the factor of forgetting.

Proper application of these concepts can have great implications in regard to classroom instruction and curriculum planning for *slow learning* children. It essentially means that the teacher of these children can devote approximately *one-sixth* of her time to concepts and experiences of a "special" nature while still taking no time away from the instruction of "basic skills" usually considered to be essential as tools that will enable the individual to make continuing adjustments independently.[2]

SOCIAL AND EMOTIONAL ADJUSTMENT

There is no evidence from research and reported studies that the slow learners as a group have any specific emotional and behavorial characteristics. They have the same basic wants, needs, and desires as all children. Like all persons, they have need for feeling that they belong, that they are intrinsically of value, and that they are accepted and a part of a group. All children have a need for affection

[2] G. Orville Johnson, "The Relationship of Learning Rate and Developmental Rate," *Exceptional Children*, 26:68–69, 1959. Italics indicate words changed from the original text. Changes consist of substitution of the terms "slow learner" or "slow learning" for "retarded" and "mentally handicapped" and insertion of IQ's and fractional parts appropriate for slow learners.

and understanding—to feel they are accepted, basically for what they are. They need to be able to contribute to the activities of the group, to contribute something that is of value and is worthwhile, and that will be accepted as a valued contribution by the group. Gesell [3] believes that the slow learners should be regarded as definitely normal persons. They are only different in that their intellectual abilities are somewhat below the average. They can make their way in the world quite satisfactorily in the sphere in which they normally operate.

While the slow learners have the same basic emotional needs and characteristics as all children as well as the same basic methods of achieving them, they have much greater difficulty in making satisfactory adjustments to these needs because of their limited intellectual capacities. It is common to find many more discipline problems among the slow learners than among the children comprising the rest of the general school population. This is relatively easily accounted for when one remembers that in many instances little or no attempt is made to provide a curriculum designed in reference to their peculiar needs and characteristics or to adapt the methods of instruction in relation to their intellectual abilities to learn.

As a result, the school situation is a continuous succession of frustrations for the slow learners. They enter first grade at the same age as other children. During this first year the majority of the children become competent readers at the first grade level. The slow learners do not become competent readers during this same period of time. Some of them remain non-readers, some learn to recognize a few words by sight, and some become poor first grade readers. Children themselves feel that they are attending school to learn the basic academic skills. This attitude can be easily observed by any teacher who asks a number of first graders, "Why do you come to school?" The response will almost invariably be, "To read" or "To learn to read." Educators have much broader objectives for the school, believing that the basic objective of the school is to help the child become a better adjusted individual who, as a result of his school experiences, will be able to lead a personally fuller, more satisfying life and also make a greater contribution to the society of which he

[3] Arnold L. Gesell, *The Retarded Child: How to Help Him* (Bloomington, Illinois: Public School Publishing Company, 1938).

is a part. Children's objectives are much simpler and much more concrete.

Emotionally, slow learners are very similar to normal children. Such characteristics as excitableness, oversensitiveness, repression, shyness, and apathy are frequently attributed to this group of children, but it should not be concluded that they inevitably possess temperamental or emotional difficulties. Their attitudes are largely the result of past experiences which in too many instances have not been of positive value or of a satisfying nature. For the individual slow learner the degrees and intensities of his emotions undoubtedly show the same variations as are found in a normal child although they may have a somewhat different content and be based upon somewhat less abstract values.

The basically important educational objectives, in terms of the adjustment of the child, are not the educators' but the children's and the family's objectives. These are also reflected in the questions asked of children by parents. "What did you learn in school today?" "Can you read me a story now?" If, then, the educational objective of the children and their parents is the acquisition of basic academic skills, the slow learners are frustrated as a result of their inability to attain this objective as do other children. Their first academic experiences are frustrating and dissatisfying. Within a short period of time the slow learners tend to feel they are not a part of the total group. If they are retained in each grade until they have achieved competency in the academic skills required for that grade, they soon become older and larger than the majority of children in the class. As a result they have little in common with the other children, either socially (as a result of greater chronological age and more experiences) or physically. If they are promoted as the result of a social promotion policy, they are unable to make suitable contributions to class projects and discussions because of their lack of academic ability and lack of general comprehension, knowledge, or information.

The primary problem here is not just that slow learners exist, but rather that they are a relatively small number of children who deviate from the large group in an area of work or experience that is of fundamental importance to them in this situation. The same factors operate when an occasional community is found where the majority of the children in school have somewhat superior intelligence and the children with "average" intelligence form a minority group. The problem is usually one of an existing discrepancy from the middle group or average. The greater the individual deviates from the middle group the less chance he has of being able to make an adequate personal adjustment in that situation. Instruction is usually planned for and taught at the level of the majority of the children—the children forming the large middle part of the group. Consequently, children comprising a deviate group are less apt to receive instruction appropriate to their needs and abilities.

Since the slow learners cannot, under the usually accepted social promotion procedures, derive satisfactions from their academic achievements in the classroom, they become frustrated. They begin to feel apart from the total group in that they are not performing the same kinds of tasks or contributing to the total experiences of the class to the same degree as the rest of the children. As a result, they, like any children under similar circumstances, react to their frustrations. Some tend to withdraw from the group and refuse to participate actively in the class programs or even contribute insofar as they are able. Others, and this group makes up the majority, tend to become aggressive in their attempts to compensate for their inability to participate.

The slow learners that become aggressive in their behavior soon become known as the discipline problems in the class and in the school. Within the classroom their behavior takes the form of rebellion against doing required assignments, rebellion against the authority of the teacher and accepted modes of classroom behavior, creating disturbances and distractions, and in general disrupting the classroom discipline and routine. They thus not only interfere with any learning they might achieve personally but also prohibit other members of the class from deriving maximum benefit from the instruction.

Behavior of this type is not acceptable to persons responsible for classroom discipline or control—the teachers and administrators. Nor is it usually approved by the majority of the children. The slow learners then tend to select as their friends others who are having similar problems and displaying similar behavior. A group develops where action contrary to that generally considered desirable is highly approved. This behavior is often ascribed to poor judgment in the selection of friends and associates. It is said that slow learners are easily influenced and easily led. Then, with the teacher as a leader, why do inappropriate behaviors develop?

These attitudes, resulting in lack of attention in class and refusal to apply oneself to school-centered learning activities, have additional detrimental effects upon the acquisition of academic knowledge and skills. By high school age, or even before, a substantial proportion of the slow learners attempt to avoid almost all printed matter except pulp magazines, comic books, and certain sections of the daily newspaper. All of these have little or no value relative to either academic achievement or to the gaining of general useful information. With the emphases found in some of these materials the reverse is more likely to be true. Value systems may be extolled that introduce or strengthen ideas that are harmful to the individual, ideas that may tend to interfere with his learning to become an effective, participating member of the community. As the slow learners progress toward adulthood, they tend to concentrate more highly on the present or immediate goals than the normal adult. They appear to be less able to project into the future; they feel insecure and the unknown becomes threatening. Consequently, they ignore the future or attempt to do nothing about it.

Upon leaving school, and this more often than not occurs as soon after the slow learners reach the compulsory school attendance age limit as possible, they usually settle down in the community. Here they seek employment and when they find it, it is likely to be in some unskilled or semi-skilled area. Furthermore, their participation in civic affairs is at a minimum level. Unless something positive is done for the slow learning children of today, the educator will continue to be faced with the same kinds of problems in their children tomorrow. This deviate behavior should be anticipated because it is a part of the value-system of the social group from which most slow learners come. It has been found that they usually come from homes that are lower than the average in economic and social conditions. The cultural conditions are meager. The psycho-social environment places little emphasis on academic learning—on schooling.

It is apparent, that the overt, aggressive behavior characterizing so many slow learners in the classroom also often carries beyond the classroom and into the total school, community, neighborhood, and home. Many slow learners become bullies, particularly when placed with younger, smaller, more immature children. When outside the classroom they attempt to compensate for their classroom failures through a display of physical prowess and aggression toward other children. They may become members of preadolescent and adolescent gangs—and for good reason. They are seeking to become members of a group—to be accepted by a group. If the gang moves in the direction of destructive, socially unacceptable behavior, they must go along. The slow learner may even become a leader in some of the gang activities in order to receive the approbation of his peers.

The school is not solely responsible for the many antisocial acts that are perpetrated by slow learners. Slow learners are not just retarded in the acquisition of academic skills and proficiencies but are also less intellectually capable of understanding the need for proper behavior than other children of their age. With inadequate home and neighborhood examples in the majority of the cases, organized community effort to teach appropriate attitudes may be essential. Yet this effort is seldom made except through the efforts of voluntary agencies such as Association Houses, religious groups, and so forth. By expecting a level of behavior higher than the individual is capable of achieving and which he has never been taught, society has also added to the frustrations of the slow learners, helping to push them farther along toward delinquency.

This does not abrogate the school's responsibility, however. That the schools are not meeting the needs of the slow learners is attested to by the fact that a large number of them become truant and an even larger number drop out of school as soon as they are able under the compulsory attendance laws. In most states school attendance is compulsory until age 16. Yet, 16 is too young for most persons to obtain satisfactory, adult employment. As a result, there are two or three years during which the drop-out is at "loose ends," unable to secure adequate employment and unwilling to continue in school to become better prepared for life in the social and economic community.

Those states and communities that have attendance laws requiring persons to remain in school until a later age need not feel smug. The laws in and of themselves are of little or no value unless some positive program has been put into practice designed to provide the slow learners meaningful experiences during this added time. Otherwise, only more and stronger resentment is built up toward a school or society that continues to restrict their activities. Experience with the next lower intellectual group (the mentally handicapped) has indicated that where meaningful programs are provided, the compulsory attendance laws are unnecessary. The holding power of these special classes has become considerably stronger than the holding power of the school in general.

These ages (the teens) are a time of stress for the adolescent approaching adulthood. He desires independence of action—independent control of behavior. Yet he must remain totally or partially dependent upon someone else (his parents) for food, clothing, housing, and spending money for entertainment and other incidental expenses. Is it any wonder that many slow learners move in the direction of crime and delinquency as a solution to their difficulties? That they do is attested to by numerous studies showing that the average intelligence of inmates in state schools for delinquent boys and girls is at the slow-learner level. This does not mean that all delinquents are slow learners or that all slow learners are delinquents. It does mean, however, that a disproportionately large number of slow learners become delinquents.

The school, through the lack of a realistic program designed to provide the slow learners with meaningful experiences that have intrinsic values to them, is at present a contributory factor. Of this there can be little question.

Many modern teachers have been trained to organize and plan their instruction and content in consideration of good mental hygiene practices. The need for good emotional or mental health is much more highly emphasized today than it was in the past. One way of partially achieving this objective is to provide experiences in which each child may have success and a feeling of accomplishment or achievement. Classroom instruction has been changed so that many concepts are introduced and taught through the use of units of experience rather than by each child reading and answering questions from a graded textbook. In this way numerous resource materials at all levels of difficulty can be used. Appropriate selections can be made according to most of the children's discrete levels of ability. This has been a long forward step but does not necessarily eliminate the comparisons children will make of their levels of work and the level of work performed by the majority of the class.

Teachers have also attempted to explain to their classes that children differ in their academic abilities in much the same way that they differ in height, weight, and ability to play games. While this explanation may be understood by the normal and superior groups, it is doubtful that the slow learners achieve as good a grasp of the concepts because of their somewhat limited intellectual abilities and because they are also emotionally involved—it is their problem. Unfortunately, this explanation is sometimes supplemented by a demonstration that the slow learners can perform tasks in and around the classroom more easily and better than the average group (because they may be superior physically and/or older and more mature). The slow learners, like other children, do not attend school to adjust the shades, erase blackboards, or help clean up the room even if they can perform these tasks better than anyone else in the room. They attend school, at least initially, for the same reason as other children—to learn. Satisfactions can only be obtained by success in the achievement of their objectives. Even older slow learners who have learned to hide their desire for learning (in many instances even from themselves) with an "I don't care" attitude can only find school experiences satisfying when they are able to achieve their goals. There is no assurance that they will derive any sense of achievement from the performance of housekeeping tasks. These tasks have no relationship to their educational objectives. The probability is that these activities will not provide an adequate substitute.

The slow learners present many emotional and behavioral problems. These difficulties are not intrinsic in the make-up of the slow learners. They are rather the result of the various problems they face just because they *are* slow learners. All children face frustrating situations in and out of the school environment. The problems facing slow learners may possibly be more severe, and they have less ability to solve them than most children because of their limited intellectual development.

SUMMARY

There are many misconceptions concerning the characteristics of slow learners particularly in the physical and behavioral areas. Slow learners generally are about average in physical development and appearance. They cannot be identified by a casual look. They are tall and short, fat and thin, athletic and non-athletic in much the same proportion as the total population. If there are any characterizing features of the slow learners as a total group in the physical area, they are in the direction of slight inferiority. It is probable that their physical development is somewhat retarded, with a higher incidence of illness and disability. Their motor skills and coordination are probably also somewhat inferior.

Behaviorally, educators have not been favorably impressed with slow learners. They are considered to be discipline problems, truants, inattentive, and lazy. That these observations are accurate is born out by Gordon Liddle's study of adolescents who created problems in the school and community.[4] He found that the school failure, drop-out, discipline problem, and delinquent adolescents were often non-achievers with I.Q.'s between 75 and 89—slow learners. This behavioral pattern is not, however, an intrinsic part of the psychological make-up of the slow learner. It is, instead, a picture of the behavior of persons continuously frustrated in their attempts to succeed in areas of value and importance to them. These behaviorisms then develop as substitutes or compensations for the behavior they cannot achieve. A second cause of these kinds of behavior is the value system of a social group that places a premium upon it.

A logical solution to the problem must be two-fold. One, a program must be developed that takes into account the learning and developmental characteristics of the slow learners as well as a content that has meaning relative to their environment and experiential background. Two, a value system that places a premium on socially acceptable behavior must be taught and substituted for the one presently accepted. Unless the school with its tremendous impact upon children's attitudes and learning makes a positive approach in the indicated directions, it will continue to actually teach (indirectly) and help precipitate undesirable behavior. No one agency has a greater potential for positive change than the school.

The fundamental characteristic of the slow learners is a retarded intellectual development as reflected in an I.Q. between 75 and 90. Their developmental rate is from three-fourths to nine-tenths that of the normal learner. Since their development stops at about the same time it does for all children, their final intellectual level is somewhat below the average for the general population. They have ample intelligence as adults to manage their own affairs and earn a

4 Gordon P. Liddle, "An Experimental Program for Slow Learning Adolescents," *Educational Leadership,* 17, No. 3, December, 1959.

living, but are restricted in the types of vocational and social activities in which they can participate effectively.

The slow learners are usually accepted in adult society as normal members of the community requiring no special considerations. This is probably because society in general does not make specific demands upon them in terms of requiring a set standard of performance. There are many social groups and many vocations in any one community. It is possible for slow learners to find a job and a group to which they can adjust on equal terms. In a sense, because the demands of their environment can be dealt with in a satisfactory manner, as adults they are not slow learners in *that* environment. There are no norms established for adult behavior and work in the same sense that norms for academic achievement have been established by the schools.

The educational problems of the slow learners are acute where *equality* of educational opportunity has been equated with *identical* educational experiences for all children. Approximately 20 per cent of all children cannot, as the result of their retarded intelligence, achieve at or near enough to established achievement norms to make the traditional school offerings satisfying or meaningful. Almost nine-tenths of these children would be considered slow learners with the remainder being classified as mentally handicapped. Slow learners start first grade with an intellectual level between 6 months and 1 year-6 months below that usually considered essential for success in learning to read. These relatively small discrepancies from the average become greater as the children grow older. By the time they are 18 years of age and should be enrolled in or completing the twelfth grade they are capable of performing at somewhere between high sixth and low ninth grade levels as compared to national norms.

The slow learners' primary problem during childhood is an educational one. It is not sufficient to merely adapt the instructional level to their learning level. With slower development, lower level of learning ability, lower final potential intellectual level, and restricted psycho-social stimulation in the majority of the cases, they require a unique curriculum that takes these factors into consideration.

Evidence strongly indicates that where programs have been instituted, designed specifically to meet the needs of slow learners, most antisocial, deviate behavior is either materially reduced in intensity or vanishes altogether. Truant and delinquent behavior and attitudes of disinterest and dislike for school and learning activities are not inherent in the slow learners although they are often considered to be of an intrinsic nature. They are, instead, a reflection of their reactions toward continuous frustration, failure, and subjection to meaningless activities a perfectly normal reaction.

SELECTED RELATED READINGS

Barber, R. W., "My Slow Students Are Personality Problems," *Clearing House,* 29:203–205, December, 1954.

Cox, W. M., "Slow Learners Have a Normal Interest Span," *Clearing House,* 26:472–73, April, 1952.

Featherstone, William B., *Teaching the Slow Learner.* Bureau of Publications, Teachers College, Columbia University, 1951, pp. 1–11.

Featherstone, William B., "What Do We Know About Slow Learners?" *Clearing House,* 25:323–28, February, 1951.

Freeman, Frank S., "Individual Differences in Mental Abilities: Their Educational Implications," in *Educational Psychology,* ed. Charles E. Skinner. Englewood Cliffs, N. J.: Prentice-Hall, Inc., pp. 697–740, 1959.

Gesell, Arnold I., *The Retarded Child: How To Help Him.* Bloomington, Illinois: Public School Publishing Company, 1938, 100 pages.

Johnson, G. Orville, "The Relationship of Learning Rate and Developmental Rate," *Exceptional Children,* 26:68–69, October, 1959.

Kirk, Samuel A., *Teaching Reading to Slow Learning Children.* Boston: Houghton Mufflin Company, 1940, pp. 1–21.

Liddle, Gordon P., "An Experimental Program for Slow Learning Adolescents," *Educational Leadership,* 17:189–92, December, 1959.

Lightfoot, Georgia F., *Personality Characteristics of Bright and Dull Children.* Bureau of Publications, Teachers College, Columbia University, 1951, 136 pages.

Meade, Mary E. and Raymond A. Green, "What Program of Education for Slow Learners?" *National Association Secondary School Principals,* 35:17–32, March, 1951.

Orr, Kenneth N., "Helping the Slow Learner," *Social Education,* 19:107–108, March, 1955.

Terman, Lewis M., *Intelligence of School Children.* Boston: Houghton Mifflin Company, 1919, 317 pages.

3

Diagnosis of the
Slow Learners

The use of an adequate diagnosis is fundamental to any educational program designed to meet the needs of any specific child or group of children. General education over a period of years has developed and evolved the curriculums and the methodologies found in relatively general use in modern education. The application of accepted psychological principles discovered during the last half century has brought about marked changes in techniques. The acceptance of modern schools of educational philosophy has also added to a change in methodology as well as in content and objectives. The various modern curriculums have gradually evolved from those inherited from the Latin Grammer School and the academy. This evolution has been influenced by recent psychological knowledges, changes in educational philosophy, and a new concept of the individual and his relationships to society.

Notwithstanding the thinking and study that have gone into the evolution of education resulting in modern concepts, instruction is still organized and applied so as to be of the greatest value to the central or major group of the children. Children with learning problems are not as well cared for. The American public school is committed by philosophy and law to provide relatively universal educational opportunity for all children to a certain degree or level. The majority of the children are required to attend school for a specified period of time. As a result, the educational emphasis has been such as to primarily provide for the mass or the group rather than the individual. Despite the fact that educators and psychologists have been emphasizing the characteristics and needs of the individual during the past two or three decades, curriculums are still planned and practiced for the group. Instruction is all too often thought of solely in reference to the content, with specific methods of instruction designed or selected on the basis of the general learning characteristics of the large middle section of the class.

The information necessary for appropriate grouping and instruction is potentially available in the folders of most children. Where it isn't, it can usually be collected fairly easily. A visit to the child's home by the teacher, psychologist, social worker, or nurse can provide a great deal of information concerning the neighborhood as well as the immediate home environment. The visitor should be able to come away with a fairly good idea of the child's acceptance and the general relationship he and other members of his family have with each other. Good cumulative teacher reports can provide a picture of a child's school adjustment, his ability to establish social relationships and take responsibility, as well as how he performs academically. In addition, the folder should contain reports or results of the various tests that have been periodically administered. The information is or can be made available—information that is sufficient to do adequate school planning for most of the slow learners. It must be gathered and used intelligently, however, if it is to be of any value.

Too often the job of collecting and collating this information is seen as a routine, meaningless activity. Consider the routine administration of group intelligence and achievement tests, for example. Usually the scores of the various subtests are recorded on the covers of the test booklets; perhaps profiles are carefully drawn. Then the covers are removed, carefully filed in the children's folders, and the tests destroyed. For diagnostic purposes, the least valuable part of the test is often kept and the most valuable parts are discarded. The process of administering tests to children, scoring the tests, and recording the scores has no intrinsic value for either the children or the teacher. The process in itself does not insure the planning and organization of a curriculum or instruction designed in terms of the characteristics and learning problems of a particular child or a particular group of children.

In discussing the testing program many teachers have stated a number of objectives that adminitrators and supervisors would categorically deny almost universally. Yet, the teachers' attitudes largely determine the actions they will take and the use that will be made of the results. Many teachers seem to have a feeling that tests are used for the purpose of measuring their ability as an instructor. They are, therefore, more interested in how well a class of children scores on the standard test than in the learning that should have taken place. Nor are they apparently interested in the learning problems pointed out in some children. When renewals of contract, yearly class assignments, or raises in pay appear to coincide with test results, who can blame teachers for these attitudes? If the teachers' understanding of the purpose of administering standardized tests is at fault, if teachers do not know how to use test results, the solution is not to keep the information from them. An in-service training program is strongly indicated so that the children will receive a better education and the taxpayer will receive more on his investment.

In one not unusual but extreme situation, a principal displayed his lack of understanding of the purpose of testing. The children enrolled in a number of classes within a given school were given a group intelligence test. The mean I.Q. was in the low 90's. The school and groups of children had been selected for the experiment because it was suspected that this would be the situation. When the principal was informed of the results, he was greatly disturbed and sincerely hoped these facts would not be reported to the assistant superintendent who was also the elementary school supervisor. He felt the relatively low average score was a reflection on him, the school personnel, and the level of instruction rather than a description of the kinds of children with whom they were working. Since all children received group intelligence tests and achievement tests periodically, the administration must have been aware of the situation. If not, the results of the previous tests had probably been altered prior to being reported or the teachers had consciously taught the test items to enable the children to receive a spuriously high score.

The latter practice is followed in many instances. Because of administrative pressure or lack of understanding concerning the values and use of standard tests, many teachers consciously teach the test items and their answers to the children for some time prior to the administration of the test to insure high scores on the part of the children. This is true not only in the academic skills areas but in the aesthetics areas as well. For example, many schools including a music appreciation program within the curriculum assign a specified number of records to be played for the children at each grade level. Toward the end of the year the teachers play these records and excerpts from these records for the children day after day. To test the music appreciation developed by the children the music teacher or supervisor does not attempt to assess the enjoyment the children have derived from these musical experiences. Instead he plays brief passages from each of the assigned records and requires that each child be able to identify the composition and the composer. This is only one of the many possible examples of misapplication, misunderstanding, improper use of tests—any kind of test.

There are many other misuses indicating a lack of understanding of the values of tests and test results. It is impossible to describe them all in detail but the following are a few, brief additional examples: comparing children on the basis of a singly administered group intelligence test and stating that M is brighter than L because M has an I.Q. of 136 and L has an I.Q. of 135; telling children and/or parents that they (the children) are the brightest children in the class because they received the highest scores on a group intelligence test administered to the class; seating and grouping children for instructional purposes solely on the basis of the results obtained from a group intelligence test; and so on.

Tests, test results, and information derived from the critical examination of a test are extremely valuable when wisely and intelligently used. The need for diagnostic information is of utmost importance if educational experiences are to be provided that will be of the greatest value to each child. This, however, requires not just the information but the intelligent use of the information as well.

NEED FOR DIAGNOSIS

Within the general classroom, a number of groups of children with rather widely varied needs and distinctly different basic characteristics may show similar kinds of problems on the surface. The slow learners, the educationally handicapped, and emotionally and socially maladjusted children are usually deviate in their behavior within the classroom and recognized as discipline problems. They do not usually participate actively or make meaningful contributions to class discussions and projects. Their academic achievements are usually retarded (or appear to be retarded) in comparison to the rest of the class. In addition, their deviations often carry beyond the classroom and into the relationships they may have in the neighborhood and community.

Superficially these three distinct groups of children seem to be one, having a common problem or common problems, and are therefore treated in much the same way. Unless an adequate diagnosis is provided to determine the cause and characteristics of each child presenting these problems, the treatment tends to be a reaction to the overt, aggressive behavior of the child by punitive action of some sort. The diagnosis is essential to determine the nature of the problem and appropriate measures that must be taken to alleviate it.

The slow learners

It is not within the province of this discussion to suggest or provide the solutions to the problems of educationally handicapped or emotionally and socially maladjusted children except to point out that their basic problems are different from those of the slow learners. The basic characteristic of the slow learners (Fig. 2) is that they have some degree of intellectual retardation that prohibits them from acquiring basic academic knowledges and skills as rapidly as

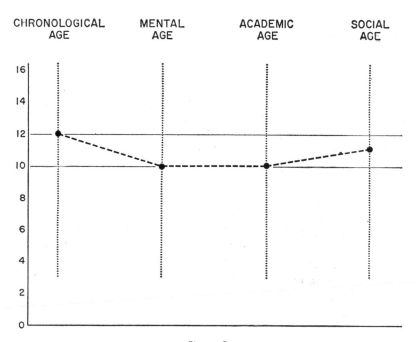

PROFILE OF A SLOW LEARNER
(I.Q. 85)

Figure 2.

or to the same extent as the average or normal child. Their chronological ages are greater than their mental ages, academic ages, and
social ages. Under an adequate instructional program, their mental
ages (verbal) and academic achievement ages should be relatively
the same. Their social ages, understanding and use of social concepts,
and level of interpersonal relationships may be somewhat superior
to their mental and academic ages but will definitely be below their
life or chronological ages. They have lived longer than the normal
or average child with the same mental age and academic achievement. They are, however, usually unable to derive the same amount
of benefit from their years of experiences as the normal or average
children of the same chronological age. Two factors tend to prohibit
slow learners from achieving the social level indicated desirable or
appropriate for their chronological age. One factor is limited intelli-

gence. The other factor is the environmental restrictions placed on most of them. Accepted or condoned behavior in their home and neighborhood environment is often not acceptable in the school or the community as a whole.

The educationally handicapped

Educational remedial problems are quite different from the special problems of the slow learners, (Fig. 3). Children of average, superior, or slow-learner intelligence may all be educationally handicapped. That is, they may not be achieving academically at or near their intellectual potential. This deficiency will be reflected not only in the academic area immediately affected but also in related areas as well. A child who is not reading adequately will score low on the various phases of a reading test. In addition he will have been unable to read health, science, social science, and other materials and will also show a deficiency in them. This deficiency will even be reflected in his ability to solve written problems designed to test arithmetic comprehension, primarily because of his inability to read and understand the problems. If, however, he is deficient in only one basic skill such as reading, which is usually the case, this deficiency should not show up in those areas not requiring reading ability, such as arithmetic mechanics.

Educationally handicapped children may also have difficulty in achieving a valid score on many group intelligence tests, particularly if the deficiency is in the area of reading. Most group intelligence tests, particularly at the older age or grade levels, require proficiency in reading. As a result, a child with relatively average intelligence may score as a slow learner on a group intelligence test. For this reason the results of a group administered intelligence test cannot be used as a single diagnostic instrument and thus interpreted except in reference to the total clinical picture. A child who scores low on a group intelligence test and low on the reading portions of an achievement test but relatively normally on the non-reading parts of the achievement test can and should be suspected as a remedial problem rather than a slow learner unless the higher non-reading scores can be explained in other ways. Under any circumstances, a child such as this should be given a non-verbal intelligence test to determine whether or not he can score within the average range on a test where the verbal factors are at a minimum.

PROFILE OF AN EDUCATIONALLY HANDICAPPED (READING) CHILD
(I.Q. 100)

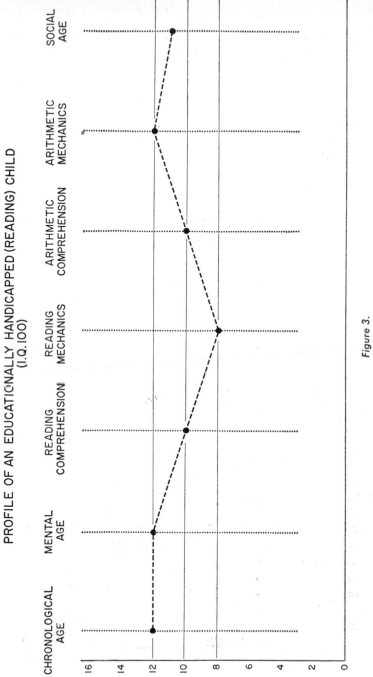

Figure 3.

The emotionally maladjusted and socially deviate

Reasons for antisocial or socially unacceptable behavior are multitudinous. The behavior of emotionally disturbed children is best defined as behavior that interferes with their emotional, social, and academic growth. In terms of scores on intelligence tests and measures of academic achievement they present no clear-cut or even relatively common pattern or profile. They may be of average, superior, or retarded intelligence. These children may be achievers, nonachievers, or educationally handicapped. But it is essential that the cause be determined before the symptoms can be treated. Retaliation by punishment of overt, aggressive behavior is a reaction to symptoms but does not necessarily have any basic effect upon the cause of the individual's misbehavior. The causes of antisocial behavior must be alleviated before socially acceptable behavior can be induced.

The emotionally maladjusted children who come to the attention of the teacher are those whose primary disability is an inability to react in socially acceptable ways to their environment. They often fail to see themselves in the proper perspective in relation to their problems and their environment. Educational handicaps and slow learning ability may contribute to and intensify the problem of the emotionally maladjusted child but are not necessarily primary factors. These are psychological problems that often must be dealt with by persons other than the classroom teacher. Ordinarily the child, the school, and the home must be included in a program designed to correct the problem.

Many socially deviate children, children whose behavior is unacceptable, are not emotionally disturbed. With these children, the behavior is planned and purposeful. It is often appropriate behavior in relation to the value system of their social group. Here the teacher and school may be able to do a great deal of good over a period of time. These children need to have their value system changed; substitutes must be accepted for the unacceptable values, and appropriate behavior must be learned.

Many slow learners are also behavior problems within the school situation. This deviate behavior may also carry over into the home and neighborhood. In most instances, however, it is the result of the community and school environments—the frustrations the children encounter as a result of their inability to perform in ways that are expected or as they desire. Many parents, particularly of those slow learners who come from better homes, have aspirations for their children beyond the children's abilities to achieve. The children, aware of these aspirations, attempt to satisfy the parents' desires and become frustrated by their inability to do so. The children, too, have aspirations to perform as do other children. They again become frustrated in their inability to learn as rapidly and to the same degree as the majority of the children. The reactions to frustrations and inabilities to perform according to accepted general standards cause the slow learners to react to their frustrations. They obtain their desired satisfactions, attention, and approbation from their peer group in socially unacceptable ways. Unless this is understood by the school and teacher, the reaction of school personnel will be to actually encourage the development of deviate behavior by mishandling the problem. A planned program is required to help the children understand and accept their limitations and strengths and develop aspirations at a level compatible with their abilities and potentialities. Curriculums should be developed that will provide the slow learners with instruction designed in reference to their slow learning abilities rather than insisting upon conformity to a prevously conceived curriculum supposedly applicable to and designed for all children.

THE ROLE OF THE SCHOOL PSYCHOLOGIST

The school psychologist is, by training, the professional person who should be responsible for the over-all testing and evaluation programs. The school psychologist is competent to organize a routine group and aptitude testing program for all the children in the school. He should also work with the elementary and secondary school supervisors in developing a coordinated, regular achievement testing program, and with school guidance personnel and counselors in solving specific problems in those areas. In addition, the school psychologist will work individually with children requiring services beyond those available in the regular classroom or for whom the diagnostic information obtained on the group tests and survey instruments is not adequate for program planning.

The school psychologist is a person with specific training and orientation. The training required is in many ways similar to that required of both a teacher and a clinical psychologist. The clinical psychology background is necessary to provide the school psychologist with information and understanding about problems affecting individuals; familiarity with testing instruments and their use and other techniques for assessing the extent of problems and their influence upon the individual's growth, development, and personal adjustment; and finally, methods of dealing with these problems to eliminate or alleviate them. The educational background is necessary in order that the school psychologist will be familiar with the kinds of services that are and can be made available through the schools. He must also know the characteristics and problems associated with classroom instruction in order that the recommendations for care and treatment are realistic in relation to the structure and limitations imposed by the school and classroom environment.

The school psychologist should be the central figure in planning and operating a school survey and diagnostic program. As a result of the various phases of the program, information concerning the characteristics and specific problems of the various children should be provided and interpreted to the classroom teacher. With the material available, the teacher is in a position to interpret the data and information. Only then can an educational program be planned for the child. The translation of the information into a meaningful educational program is the co-responsibility of the teacher and supervisor. Putting the plan into action and providing the specific experiences and the use of specific techniques is the sole responsibility of the teacher. Where personnel is available, the problem of organizing educational experiences for children who deviate is a group responsibility, with the administrator, supervisor, psychologist, and teacher participating and contributing their knowledge and experience to its ultimate solution.

In many school districts, school psychologists are not available. These districts must depend upon itinerant clinics, county or state guidance clinics, or university clinics to provide the psychological diagnoses for children the schools have been unable to help effectively without this additional aid. Many communities which have a school psychologist or a number of school psychologists find that the load of acute cases requiring the immediate, personal attention of the school psychologist is so great that anything approaching a total survey or plan for general psychological services for all the children requiring them is quite out of the realm of the psychologists' physical ability. Usually, the most that can be hoped for is a psychological diagnosis for the majority of the children referred and a brief psychological report including an evaluation and a few general recommendations. If sufficient special services are provided by the school, the load of the psychologist is considerably reduced. He can provide better diagnostic services (more time) and the children receive better programs. The psychologist cannot do everything himself. School systems that want the most for their money must plan to include special services along with the services of the psychologist or much of his effort may be wasted.

Fortunately, the selection and diagnosis of the majority of the slow learners can be accomplished through the use of a good group testing program administered intelligently by the teachers.

RECOMMENDED GROUP TESTING PROGRAM

A well conceived and executed group testing program can take much of the routine diagnostic load from the school psychologist. In communities and school districts it can provide much of the diagnostic service required, particularly for the selection of relatively large groups of children such as the slow learners, who need some kind of differentiated educational programming.

Briefly, a comprehensive testing program should start during the first year of the child's school experience and continue throughout his school life. This ensures the recognition of educational problems at an early date and provides the administration and teaching personnel with an opportunity to correct them before they become acute. Through the elementary school years the tests should include readiness tests at the kindergarten and/or the initial first grade level and regular administration of group intelligence and achievement tests from then on. These basic tests should be continued through the secondary school level for the children about whom this information is required, plus additional specialized tests depending upon the students basic interests, aptitudes, and abilities. This information is used for counseling purposes and present and future planning.

Readiness tests

The chart, story, and whole-sentence method of teaching reading in common usage today presupposes a basic readiness or background on the part of the child. The various reading readiness tests [1] are designed to provide the teacher with the necessary information as to whether or not a child has sufficient background to derive benefit from a formal reading program. In short, they attempt to determine, among other things, whether or not a child is ready to learn to read. If a child is not ready to profit from reading instruction, a careful examination of the readiness test may provide the teacher with some clues as to the areas in which he is deficient. As a result, a program can be designed to help him overcome his deficiencies. Specific kinds of readiness experiences can then be provided.

Readiness tests, in general, are designed to measure the abilities of a child in the areas of visual discrimination, auditory discrimination, identification of items, use of context clues, association of ideas with words, vocabulary development, and information. Some tests also include items designed to test motor skill and articulation ability. The hypothesis is that a certain level of competence is required in these areas before a child is ready to derive benefit from formal reading instruction. In general, this is substantiated by the administration of these tests to several thousand children in order to obtain necessary standardization norms. Through an analysis of the data thus collected, it has been found that children who are most proficient on these items have the least amount of difficulty with their initial reading experiences. Usually no absolute scores are available on a readiness test but the responses are scored on percentile ratings or rankings. Thus, children with a high total percentile ranking are more apt to be ready to learn to read than those children receiving a low ranking on the basis of their responses.

It is very important to know the readiness level of a child prior to providing him with his initial academic experiences. If a teacher is aware that a number of children in his class are not ready to profit from the initial reading instruction, he can provide them with ex-

[1] Among the most commonly used readiness tests are, in alphabetical order: *Gates Reading Readiness Tests*, Bureau of Publications, Teachers College, Columbia University; *The Harrison-Stroud Reading Readiness Tests*, Houghton Mifflin Company; *Lee-Clark Readiness Test*, 1951 Revision, California Test Bureau; *Metropolitan Readiness Tests*, World Book Company; and *Murphy-Durrel Diagnostic Reading Readiness,* World Book Company.

periences that will be of greater value to them. He will not waste his time or theirs in a premature attempt to have them learn to read. Children who demonstrate great intellectual and readiness immaturity at the close of their kindergarten experience should be carefully evaluated. This evaluation should include their social and emotional maturity as well as their readiness skills. This is to determine the most advantageous placement for their next school experience—a repetition of the readiness experiences included in the kindergarten program or an extension of these experiences to be provided in the first grade. Insisting that a child participate in the regular academic experiences provided in the first grade when he is unable to profit from them may do infinite harm. As a result of his failure he may become frustrated with and react adversely to academic learning. This in turn may effect his relations with other persons and also build up such attitudes toward school that make it impossible for him to derive maximum benefit from the instruction provided in the future.

Intelligence tests

Group intelligence tests should be administered periodically but need not be administered yearly. If there is some definite reason for suspecting that previous results are invalid because of poor administrative procedures, or if there are marked changes in an individual's environment (either physical or psychological) that would cause one to suspect that previously obtained results do not show an accurate picture of his intellectual capacities, or there are rather marked discrepancies between the level of tested intelligence and the level of academic achievement that would lead one to question previously obtained results, then an earlier readministration of an intelligence test to this individual may be appropriate.

Many group intelligence [2] tests are available. They are designed to obtain much the same kinds of information regarding the intel-

[2] *California Test of Mental Maturity and Adaptations,* Elizabeth T. Sullivan, Willis W. Clark, and Ernest W. Tiegs, California Test Bureau; *Chicago Non-Verbal Examination,* Andrew W. Brown with the assistance of Seymour P. Stein and Perry L. Rohrer, Psychological Corporation; *Detroit Intelligence Tests,* Harry J. Baker, Public School Publishing Company; *The Henmon-Nelson Tests of Mental Ability,* V. A. C. Henmon and M. J. Nelson, Houghton Mifflin Company; *The IPAT Culture Free Intelligence Tests,* R. B. Cattell and A. K. S. Cattell, Institute for Personality and Ability Testing; and *Kuhlman-Anderson Intelligence Tests,* F. Kuhlman and Rose G. Anderson, Personnel Press, Inc., are representative of the various group intelligence tests available for use in the schools.

lectual abilities of individual children, tested in a group situation, as individually administered intelligence tests. It is true that group intelligence tests have the same kinds of limitations as those ascribed to individual intelligence tests in chapter 2 plus many additional ones. It is also true that the results are apt to be less valid and open to greater question than the results of individual intelligence tests. Nevertheless, they are extremely valuable instruments when properly used, interpreted, and administered. They can provide a great quantity of information that will be of infinite value in terms of the academic potential and consequent academic needs of individuals.

Group tests, like individual intelligence tests, have specific characteristics and should be selected in regard to the kinds of information desired. The instrument that is best suited for the peculiar job it will be required to perform should be selected. The characteristics of group tests are generally somewhat similiar in content although the methods of using the content may vary widely. They commonly contain items that measure such abilities as vocabulary, visual discrimination, quantitative concepts, recall, spatial relationships and orientation, recognition and understanding of similarities, understanding of analogies, ability to make inferences, and so forth. The different tests contain items designed to measure these abilities to a greater or lesser degree depending upon the number of items included from each area. Two tests purporting to be measuring the same characteristic may be attempting to measure it in two different ways (through verbal and auditory or through visual means, for example) and as a result be actually measuring two different things.

Group intelligence tests, like the individual intelligence tests, also attempt to measure verbal and non-verbal factors of intelligence. Some of them require verbal ability on the part of the child while within others the requirement of verbal facility is at a minimum. Discrepancies are found between verbal and performance scores on individual intelligence tests; similar kinds of discrepancies can be expected to be apparent in the results derived from verbal and non-verbal group intelligence tests. Group tests also vary in the emphases placed upon speed and accuracy. Some are known as power tests where the time limits are liberal and the emphasis is placed upon content and accuracy. Speed tests emphasize the amount of work that can be accomplished (and with what degree of accuracy) within a restricted period of time. It is necessary, therefore, to become familiar with the characteristics of the various group intelligence tests. Only then can the one be selected that will do the most effective job in relation to the particular group of children with whom it is to be used or the kinds of information that are desired.

It must be kept constantly in mind that the results obtained on any standard intelligence test available at the present time cannot be used to predict perfectly any individual's potential acquisition of academic learnings and skills. Of the instruments now in use, the verbal or language scales probably predict potential academic ability better than the non-verbal, non-language, or performance scales. Thus, for predictive purposes in planning an academic educational program, the verbal or language scales should be used whenever possible. In general, it can be anticipated that an individual should be performing academically at or relatively near his mental age level as measured on a verbal intelligence test. The intelligence quotient is relatively meaningless in this respect without additional interpretation in relation to the chronological age of the individual. The I.Q. is of primary value in determining the approximate rate of development and achievement level that can be anticipated from that individual; i.e., what his mental age will be at 10, 12, or 15 years of age.

The verbal intelligence test for most academic purposes is, then, the one that is and probably should be in most general use. At times, however, it is either impossible to use a verbal intelligence test or available information has not been obtained from a verbal test. In such cases the data cannot be used to predict academic success with the same degree of confidence. Just what the specific differences are between group verbal and non-verbal intelligence tests has not been definitely determined except that it is well known that the results of the two kinds of intelligence tests are not necessarily comparable even when both tests are valid and have been properly administered. As a result, the scores on the two kinds of tests can never be legitimately compared or equated. Also, the results obtained by one person on a verbal test cannot be compared with the results obtained by another person on a non-verbal test. Beyond this warning, any further interpretations and uses of comparative results on the two kinds of tests should be made by a psychologist familiar with the child, his characteristics, and the test results, and the characteristics of the test.

Under ordinary circumstances, the non-verbal tests are used for those children who have a verbal disability or in whom an inability to achieve at or near their intellectual level on a verbal test is suspected. Children who are hard of hearing, foreign-born children, children from homes in which a foreign language is usually spoken, or children who have a speech or language disability for some other reason should probably be administered a non-verbal intelligence test. Despite the fact that some children may be unable to take a verbal test and must take a non-verbal intelligence test, their results on a non-verbal intelligence test are nevertheless not as valuable in predicting potential academic achievement as the verbal scores received by other children.

Achievement tests

Achievement tests,[3] in general, are designed to measure the level of academic achievement of a child as compared to other children. It has been found that most children in third grade can read (word recognition, comprehension of the material, and so forth) at a certain level or can answer certain questions on a test. Any child that is reading at this level or can answer these questions is said to be achieving at the third grade level, regardless of his chronological age, mental age, intelligence quotient, or grade placement. Similar comparisons are also made in the other skill areas such as spelling, arithmetic, and so forth. This is also true of more specific kinds of achievement tests dealing with a single subject or area, such as science.

Achievement tests should be administered yearly, at least throughout the elementary grades and junior high school, to determine whether or not each individual is profiting from his educational

[3] Among the most commonly used general school achievement tests are: *American School Achievement Tests,* Public School Publishing Company; *California Achievement Tests,* California Test Bureau; *Coordinated Scales of Attainment,* Educational Test Bureau, Educational Publishers, Incorporated; *The Gray-Votaw-Rogers General Achievement Tests,* Steck Company; *The Harlow Battery Achievement Tests,* Steck Company; *The Harlow Battery Achievement Tests,* Harlow Publishing Corporation; *Iowa Every-Pupil Tests of Basic Skills,* Houghton Mifflin Company; *Metropolitan Achievement Tests,* World Book Company; *Modern School Achievement Tests: Skills Edition,* Bureau of Publications, Teachers College, Columbia University; *Municipal Battery: National Achievement Tests,* Acorn Publishing Company; and *Stanford Achievement Test,* World Book Company. Numerous other tests designed to measure knowledge in specific subjects are also available.

experiences. If he has shown little or no gain over his previous test, steps should be taken immediately to determine the cause of his lack of growth. Every effort must then be made to correct the condition before the problem becomes more acute and begins to effect his behavior and personal and social adjustment.

Achievements tests are designed to evaluate growth and determine specific educational abilities and disabilities. Unfortunately it is felt by some teachers and apparently some administrators that they are a measure of the teachers' competency. They believe that competent teachers will have groups of children who score at or above grade level and poor teachers' incompetencies will be reflected in a class average achievement score below standard norms. Concepts such as these encourage teachers to obtain copies of standard achievement tests previously used and teach the content and skills measured by the test rather than the content and skills recommended by the curriculum. Much of this "learning" is not learning at all, since the instruction is for the purpose of answering questions and may or may not be at the intellectual and skill level of the children and in terms of that content and those skills that will be of greatest value to the children.

Achievement testing may be done either in the spring, shortly before the termination of school, or in the fall, shortly after school commences. Spring testing is primarily for the purpose of determining the amount of growth the child has achieved during the past year. It should not be used as a basis for determining the mark a child receives on his report card. The primary purpose of a fall testing program is diagnostic—to determine the children's achievement level and the particular areas in which they may require additional help. The fall testing program also has value in measuring the amount of growth accomplished during the previous year if the results are compared with those obtained on previous tests administered in the fall. This is essential because the results of tests administered in the spring and fall are not necessarily comparable because of the forgetting that takes place over the summer when the child is not normally engaged in any academic activities.

Spring achievement testing programs are also limiting in other ways. The teacher who administers the test is quite familiar with the children in his room by this time and the results of a standard test essentially confirm his subjective evaluation of the children.

This evaluation has been made on the basis of daily observation, instruction, and achievement on day to day assignments. Any new or diagnostic data the teacher finds as a result of the test administration and scoring are actually of little value since there is no time left to provide any remediation. The best he can do is to place the scored test booklet in the children's folders for use by the next teacher.

The fall testing program provides many advantages over the spring testing program, and suffers few, if any, of the disadvantages. As previously indicated, it can be used to determine whether or not steady academic progress is being achieved by each child. Furthermore, it provides the teacher with an excellent opportunity of becoming intimately acquainted with the academic achievement levels of the various children in the class early in the school year. It also gives the teacher the necessary information he requires for any remedial work a child may require before valuable time has passed and the need is finally discovered as the result of ordinary classroom observation of the child's daily work.

The very mechanics of administering and scoring the tests provide the teacher with much of the important information. As the separate parts and subtests are scored, the teacher will observe the vocabulary level, ability to attack new words, ability to grasp the thought of a sentence or paragraph, level of performance in arithmetic mechanics, level of comprehension and use of arithmetic mechanics, and other diagnostic information available about specific children. This information is not ordinarily available in the children's folders as the result of tests administered in the spring by another teacher. Usually, only the cover of the test booklet with a summary of the information is retained in the file folder. If the entire test book is kept, the new teacher is unable to study the material prior to the opening of school because he does not know the children nor has he the folders available. After he becomes acquainted with the children it is seldom that a careful examination of all the data contained in all the folders is made because the teacher becomes involved in the day by day class preparations and problems. Only in the case of recognized problems (usually of an adjustment or social nature) is the folder examined for pertinent data. Even then, attention is paid primarily to the numerical, summarized results of the tests available with little use being made of the potential diagnostic materials and information contained in the body of the tests.

SELECTION AND USE OF STANDARD TESTS

Standard tests, whether intelligence or achievement, need to be carefully selected to best provide the specific information required. The slow learners are not and will never become intellectual giants. They will never display outstanding intellectual or academic abilities. They are and always will be limited in their ability to grasp and put to use new ideas and concepts. As a result, they will not, in all probability, earn their livings in academic activities. Speed tests essentially penalize the slow learners and do not provide the kinds of information desired. The primary information desired in regard to the slow learners is the concepts and skills they can use given adequate time. Power tests with liberal time limits are designed to provide this kind of information and are, therefore, most valuable for testing slow learners.

Standard group tests are usually designed to be administered to a certain grade level or certain grade levels of children. They are standardized upon the average achievement of children of that age or those ages. The tables are usually quite accurate for the middle part of the range with high and low scores calculated and interpreted by statistical means rather than on the basis of actual data collected. As a result, children scoring abnormally high (possibly gifted children) or children scoring abnormally low (possibly slow learners) may not have their scores accurately interpreted as far as the age or grade level norms are concerned.

It is seldom that a specific form of a specific test is adequate for all the children in a single class or grade unless they have been grouped very homogeneously upon the basis of academic achievement and intellectual ability. Ordinarily a test will not be difficult nough for the most advanced children in the class and they may not score as high as they should. The same test may be too difficult for the slow learners. By average chance selection, they can usually get approximately one-fourth of the items correct if they understand the mechanics of recording the answers and guess at each item. Since the test is standardized for use with a specific age or achievement group, a basic assumption is always made that the children taking the test have a proficiency at least equal to the bottom of the test. Any scores attained, whether by knowledge or by guess, are then added to this base. Thus, the slow learning individual is often given a spuriously high score.

The level of test selected for any child should be one where, from his observation of the child's work in class, the examiner would judge that he will score approximately in the middle range of the test. It is seldom that a single form of a test is applicable to all the children within a single class. It is usually necessary to select at least two and sometimes three forms of a test to provide the superior, average, and slow students with a form which they all can read and comprehend and upon which they can score legitimately.

A comprehensive testing program provides for periodic intelligence testing and yearly achievement testing. Tests conceived and standardized by different persons and by different companies are not completely comparable in the derived results. Consequently, any long-range testing program should use those tests that have several forms for different grade levels or provide tests that can be used throughout most or all of the grades. Different forms of the same test are actually different tests but they have been standardized on similar populations using the same kinds of statistical analyses of the data. Comparisons of the various forms have usually been made and these data are also available. Consequently, the results of different forms of a test can be compared safely with the assumption that they are measuring relatively the same things to the same degree with the standardization done on the same or similar populations.

Intelligence tests like achievement tests can also be selected for speed or power. Speed and power intelligence tests are used with the same groups as speed and power achievement tests and for similar reasons. In addition, intelligence tests should be selected for their context or kind (verbal or non-verbal) depending upon the specific problems presented or information desired.

Other types of tests may occasionally be necessary to provide additional diagnostic material. The primary ones among these are the educational diagnostic tests that are used to determine the degree and kinds of educational problems.[4] Where a child is not perform-

4 Among the most commonly used diagnostic tests in the area of reading are: *Durrell Analysis of Reading Difficulty*, World Book Company; *Durrell-Sullivan Reading Capacity and Achievement Tests*, World Book Company; *Ingraham-Clark Diagnostic Reading Tests*; California Test Bureau; and *Gates Reading Diagnostic Tests, Revised Edition*, Bureau of Publications, Teachers College, Columbia

ing academically up to his intellectual potential he is in need of a remedial program of some type. Before any such remedial work can be instituted a diagnosis is necessary. Therefore, the various diagnostic tests are essential for children requiring them but should not be used as general tests administered routinely to all children as a part of the general testing program.

ADMINISTRATION OF GROUP TESTS

One of the major advantages of the group test is that it can be administered and scored by someone other than a school psychologist or other highly trained specialist. In addition, much of the diagnostic information can be obtained for most children without referring the materials to one of these specialists. Under ordinary circumstances, the regular classroom teacher is not only competent to administer group tests, if a number of precautions are taken by him, but should do so. In many ways, it is best if the classroom teacher administers and scores the tests because the test situation thus remains a relatively normal classroom situation in which the children feel most secure and will probably do their best. The teacher is the person most familiar with the children and can probably motivate them to a greater degree. Furthermore, the mechanics of scoring the test blanks (this is not true for answer sheets) aids in familiarizing the teacher with the specific items achieved and failed by the individual children.

The following are points all teachers should follow carefully to obtain maximum results from any test and test results.

1. The directions for administration of the tests are usually written very clearly and should be followed carefully. All directions to be given to the children should be read *verbatim*. Any deviations in directions or attempts to clarify the directions by the administrator will invalidate the results so that any scores obtained will not be

---

University. Other kinds of diagnostic tests in fairly common usage are *Gates-Russell Spelling Diagnostic Test,* Bureau of Publications, Teachers College, Columbia University; *Brueckner Diagnostic Arithmetic Tests,* Education Test Bureau, Educational Publishers, Incorporated; and *Diagnostic Chart for Fundamental Processes in Arithmetic,* Public School Publishing Company. In addition, most standard achievement tests in the various areas have diagnostic features and can be used for this purpose as well as for measuring the developmental level of the child.

able to be compared to scores reported for the group upon whom
the test was originally standardized.

2. Where time limits are specified, they should be adhered to
rigidly.

3. No supplementary help or explanations should be given any
child. Directions can usually be reread but nothing more in terms
of supplementary aid may be offered. During the test, the proctor
should move about the room to make sure each child is working,
that each child is doing his own work and working on the correct
part of the test, and to replace dull and broken pencils. *Do not* point
out incorrect responses and urge the child to look over those items
again. *Do not* read specific questions to a child so that all he has
to do is select the correct response.

4. The particular form or level of a test should be selected in
relation to the abilities and level of achievement of the individual
rather than the average of the group or class. Make an estimate of
an individual's ability and use the test form upon which he will
probably score near the middle range. In this way the individual's
scores are usually more accurate reflections of his true abilities. The
results are more valid. If a test is too easy for a child, the questions
are not difficult enough to measure his true abilities and he scores
lower than his actual ability although his scores may be considerably higher than the average for the class. If the test is too difficult,
the child tends to score higher than his abilities warrant because of
the basic assumption of a minimum of ability to which any successes
(even by chance) are added.

Most standard group intelligence tests are standardized for a
specific grade or group of grades; i.e., primary for grades 1 through
3, intermediate for grades 4 through 6, junior high school for grades
7 through 9, and high school for grades 10 through 12. Thus, there
is a test designed for each grade and ability level. In addition, the
standardization usually includes a number of items at the immediately preceding and succeeding grade levels. Scores beyond this
small deviation are usually calculated mathematically and are not
based upon actual tabulated test scores. There is less basis to put
one's confidence in widely deviating scores as a result of standardization procedures. Even more apparent to the test user is the paucity
of test items at these widely deviating distances. Where many items
may have to be passed to achieve one year or grade-level credit in the

middle range of the test, one item may account for one, one and one-half, or two years credit at the extreme high and low ranges. Consequently a happy or an unhappy guess may give or deprive a child of from 1 to 2 years credit on one part of the test.

5. The class should not ordinarily be required to complete the test in one sitting. Observe the children carefully and stop the test when they start to get tired, fidgety, or bored. Continue the test in the afternoon or the following day. Most tests suggest places where "breaks" should be taken. Everything, in terms of physical and psychological comfort, should be done to encourage maximum achievement on the test.

6. Before scoring the individual tests, the directions for scoring and the sections referring to standardization methods, interpretation of test results, and discussions regarding diagnostic features of the test should be carefully read. In this way the greatest values will be derived from the test results and much time will be saved. Information in regard to particular children or peculiar problems should be noted during the scoring operation. Little re-referral and re-examination of the tests will then be required.

7. While actually scoring the individual tests, one should be continuously aware of: (a) any pattern of responses the child makes in the way of placement or location of answers. This is particularly important for the answers to multiple choice items. Occasionally children will develop a pattern such as marking the first item correct for number 1, the second item for number 2, the third for 3 and so on, repeating the pattern over and over with or without occasional breaks. Other children will perseverate by selecting the correct response for the first question on the page and marking that same number as the correct one for the rest of the items on that page. Using such systems or methods a child may score abnormally high or low depending upon the chance factors of his system or method happening to coincide with the correct responses. Any scores thus derived are highly questionable and the test should be repeated under closer observation with definite efforts being made to eliminate any pattern or perseverative tendencies. (b) A careful analysis should be made of items successfully passed or failed to determine whether or not there is any way to account for the success or failure. This is particularly true where the successfully answered items are erratically distributed throughout a portion of the test. Often it is

possible to determine that a child's lack of a very specific skill is the cause of repeated failures. Correction of this difficulty will enable the child to score much higher. Where a child has practically every item correct up to a point with few if any successes beyond, it can usually be assumed that that is his skill or concept level. Instruction should continue from that point with little or no need to return to skills and concepts developed at earlier dates—skills with which he is already thoroughly familiar and competent. (c) During the scoring there should be a continuous awareness of any diagnostic features that may be incorporated in the test. Early recognition of remediable educational disabilities will allow for an early program designed to overcome the problems indicated. In this way the child will soon be able to derive maximum benefit from future educational experiences and instruction.

SUMMARY

An adequate description of the characteristics of the children to be included in any program is essential if the program is to be of maximum educational value to them. This descriptive material or information is obtained from diagnostic information. Programs are designed to provide for children with specific problems. Without adequate diagnostic information, children with a variety of problems may be grouped together because they happen to display the same kinds of overt behavior to the casual or untrained observer. Programs for slow learners should be for slow learners and not for children with average or superior intelligence who are remedial problems, are emotionally maladjusted, or display socially deviate behavior.

The information required for a diagnosis of slow learners must be obtained from several sources. The slow learners' cumulative records should show a consistent pattern of inability to perform at grade-placement level. Intelligence tests (particularly of the verbal type) should indicate some degree of mental retardation. Achievement test results should show a competence level below that expected for children of that age. Where these various sources and kinds of information are in agreement, the probability is that the problem is one of "slow learning" ability.

Occasionally the results of a test or tests will not agree with the other information available. When this is true, a reason for the discrepancy must be found. One of the primary reasons is that the appropriate test or test form was not used. The careful selection of tests is very important. Tests must be selected both for level as well as for the information desired. That is, they should be selected for the job they will do in relation to the job that needs to be done. Preschool children should take readiness tests to determine their degree of readiness for academic work when they are promoted to first grade. A preschool group intelligence test may have some value except that it is more unreliable at this age than at later ages and few if any of the intelligence tests designed for preschool administration have forms extending into the later grades. As a result, direct comparisons of the results of preschool intelligence tests with the results of tests taken at a later date often cannot be made.

Achievement tests should be selected for speed or power. Where efficiency of use of skills, knowledge, and concepts are desired, the speed test or a test with rather rigid time limits is most applicable. These tests are particularly valuable for students with above average intelligence who should be encouraged to continue their formal education beyond the high school years and who will be making direct, concrete use of their academic skills throughout their entire lives in relation to their selected vocations. Where quantity and basic knowledge and use of basic skills and concepts are desired, power tests or tests with liberal time limits are more desirable. Power tests are more applicable for use with slow learners where the aim is to discover what they know and what they can do rather than how fast they can do it. The slow learners require the basic academic skills as tools to aid them in their social and academic adjustments. They require an understanding and use of the basic skills rather than high efficiency in their use. The academic skills will not add materially directly to their economic well-being since they will probably earn livings through semi-skilled and skilled trades rather than "white collar" positions requiring the direct use of their academic abilities.

Of all personnel employed by the schools, the school psychologist is best qualified to help organize the testing program and select the tests that are most appropriate. Whenever a case arises that cannot be diagnosed on the basis of available information, the psychologist has the training and skills to make the diagnosis. He is also trained to work with emotional problems that cannot be dealt with satisfactorily in the classroom setting. The availability of the school psychologist or psychological services and consultation is essential to the development of a program for slow learners.

The diagnosis has more value than mere placement, however. This information must be made completely and readily available to the teachers. It is of extreme importance in determining the kinds of educational experiences that will be of greatest value to the children, and in planning curriculums and long-term objectives. A program for slow learners should be based upon a good diagnostic program.

SELECTED RELATED READINGS

Deland, Clara, "Early Discovery of the Slow Learner," *Exceptional Children,* 14:134–37, 160, February, 1948.

Featherstone, William B., *Teaching the Slow Learner.* Bureau of Publications, Teachers College, Columbia University, 1951, pp. 12–21.

"High School Methods with Slow Learners." Washington, D. C.: *NEA Research Bulletin* 21, No. 3:63, October, 1943.

U. S. Office of Education, Department Health, Education and Welfare, *Teaching Rapid and Slow Learners in High Schools,* Bulletin No. 5, 1954. 97 pages.

part II

School Organ-
ization for the
Slow Learners

4

Grouping for Instruction

The objective of education is to help the individual to take an effective place in society and to become a well-adjusted individual. This is accomplished by helping him to become better acquainted with his personal problems and develop a greater understanding of them. Furthermore, he is helped to get along with, to live, play, and work with other children so that he will be able to carry on normal activities as an adult with other adults. Finally, but not necessarily the least important, he is provided with the basic knowledges, skills, and concepts that will enable him to make the necessary social and economic adjustments easily. Thus, the development of proficiency in the academic skills, art, music, physical training and recreation, and various group activities all add to and provide him with the kinds of experiences he now requires and will require for his entire life.

The schools, in order to achieve this objective for most of the children, have provided various groupings and curriculums depending upon their philosophies and the educational needs of children. Special curriculums have been planned for educable mentally handicapped and trainable mentally deficient children. Remedial programs in reading, arithmetic, and speech have been organized in order that children with deficiencies in these areas may improve their abilities and as a result be able to derive greater benefit from the instruction normally provided. Special groups have been organized for orthopedically handicapped, blind and partially seeing, and deaf children in order that they may be provided with the special equipment and be taught the special skills they require.

Children requiring special grouping, special techniques, special skills, or special curriculums have been considered exceptional children. It has been almost universally accepted among educators that these groups of children require services beyond those that can be provided in the regular classroom. The slow learners have not been considered to be part of this group either by the special or regular educators. While they deviate from the norm or average, the deviation is not usually considered sufficient to warrant a special program. It is the thesis of this volume that the slow learners do warrant a special program. Not only do they require a curriculum to meet their needs more adequately than do the general elementary and secondary curriculums into which they are now forced, but the grouping of the slow learners to promote maximum learning must also be studied and the most effective method adopted.

COMMONLY USED METHODS OF GROUPING

The purpose of grouping is to arrange or organize children to provide the most effective instruction as economically as possible. This is both in terms of financing and teachers' energy. While many general educators profess to advocate so-called heterogeneous or non-ability grouping, they continuously work toward other ends. The most heterogeneous school groups were in the one-room, eight-grade schools. Consolidation efforts have attempted to eliminate them and all other small educational units although it will be many more years before this objective will be achieved. Urban areas are abandoning small units and their newer senior high schools are being planned to accommodate more than one thousand students.

Even as individual grades were being housed in single rooms, teachers soon discovered that there were numbers of children who presented unique instructional problems. Prominent among them were the relatively large numbers of slow learners. Teachers of beginning primary children can do very little about grouping the children entering school for the first time except to occasionally recommend to a parent that the entrance of an obviously immature child be delayed for a year. Beyond this they have so little information about each child that even if they desired to do something they cannot. Once the child has been in school for a year, future groupings can be at least partially controlled with the information available. Differential promotional policies can also be adopted. Various kinds of class placements have been practiced and are still being used with varying degrees of acceptance and success. The four that have been most commonly used are: (1) retention in a grade until academic proficiency at that grade level has been achieved; (2) placement in a special class; (3) some type of social promotion with homogeneous (achievement or ability level) grouping where two or more classes at each grade level existed; and (4) regular class placement with social promotion. Each of these methods has distinct advantages and disadvantages. None of them has received anything approaching universal acclaim or condemnation by teachers.

Homogeneous grouping

All grouping of children for instruction is homogeneous in one way or another. Three kinds of placement are based upon some type of intellectual ability or academic achievement performance. The fourth, social grouping, is considered by most educators to be significantly different from the other three.

GROUPING ACCORDING TO ACADEMIC ACHIEVEMENT

This method of grouping (according to academic achievement level) was used extensively in many areas of the nation until about three decades ago. The primary value of this kind of grouping was that it simplified the instructional problems of the teachers as long as the premise was accepted that every child should learn the same things to the same level of competency. It provided the teacher with a relatively homogeneous group of children in regard to their intellectual development and academic skill level. Theoretically, a single presentation of materials could be made to the entire class with little or no duplication of effort or time being required. Children whose developmental rate was slower than the average of the class soon fell behind. By repeating the grade they would learn the material the following year. Bright children who advanced more rapidly than the group (usually on their own) could be skipped a grade or given a double promotion. In this way they, too, were placed with a group performing more nearly at their achievement level.

This system tended to eliminate most of the eventual pressures for graduation and aspirations for advanced schooling on the part of the slow learners. Most slow learners became discouraged prior to the completion of twelfth grade and dropped out of school or were finally excluded as behavior problems or on the basis of being over-age.

The disadvantages of homogeneous groupings, based upon mental maturity and level of academic development, far outweigh its advantages in the minds of most modern educators who are interested in the total, broad development of the individual. Following the policy of homogeneous grouping, the classes became heterogeneous in terms of physical and social development and interests. It is difficult for the slow learners to become interested in the recreational and social activities of their much younger academic peers. It is even more difficult for them to participate on a relatively equal basis in these kinds of activities. Slow learners, retained in a group of younger, normally intelligent children, become frustrated and discouraged when they are unable to perform at the same academic level as their younger classmates. It is bad enough not to be able to compete in the classroom with children of the same age and stature. Being placed in a class with younger children also provides the slow learners with a situation in which they are usually physically superior. As a result, they are encouraged to demonstrate their physical strength and abilities in undesirable ways within the classroom and to become bullies outside the classroom. In this way they can receive the attention they desire from their classmates.

Grouping according to academic achievement is rarely found to-day at the elementary level. Many school administrators have de-creed that no child may be retained more than once in any grade nor more than twice while in the elementary school. The policy of promotion is not nearly as clear-cut at the junior high school level where a great deal of ambivalence exists. The teachers are often torn between the traditional secondary school attitude of maintaining standards almost at all costs and attempting to provide meaningful learning experiences for the children. Grouping according to achievement still holds out strongly, however, in the senior high school, particularly in mathematics, the sciences, and the languages. While a slow learner may enroll in Algebra I, he must successfully complete the requirements of that course before being allowed to take Algebra II, Geometry, higher Algebra, Solid Geometry, or Trigonometry. The same is true for the sciences beyond introductory General Science and the languages—Latin, Spanish, French, German, Russian and so forth.

GROUPING IN SELF-CONTAINED SPECIAL CLASSES

This method of grouping slow learners has been used least ex-tensively although a number of schools in various communities have discussed the values of special class placement. A few classes have even been organized particularly on the secondary levels. Special classes are an extension of the principle of homogeneous grouping. Instead of placement being made solely on the basis of achievement level, however, it is usually based upon developmental (mental) rate and potential. In general, special classes have many of the same advan-tages as homogeneous grouping. In addition, the teacher of a spe-cial class is more apt to be interested in the educational problems of the slow learners because he will know the group he will be work-ing with when he applies for the teaching position. As a result he has the opportunity of deciding whether or not he is interested in working with that group of children. Too often the regular teacher can hardly wait to pass a difficult problem along to another teacher.

Usually the teacher of a special class will also have greater leeway in curriculum and program planning and be less held to traditional grade requirements than the regular classroom teacher. Or the teachers and supervisors may have developed a curriculum designed to more adequately provide for the needs of the slow learners. Thus, a competent teacher of a special class who has an understanding of the characteristics and problems of the slow learners will usually be able to give them the kinds of educational experiences that will be of the greatest value to them.

The disadvantages of a highly segregated, self-contained special class placement are even greater, in many ways, than homogeneous grouping and retaining a child at a grade level until he has accomplished the defined level of academic growth. The numbers of slow learners is so large that if all of them were to be placed in special classes, between 15 and 17 per cent of the total school population would be placed in these educational programs. The slow learners are so nearly normal in their intellectual development that, except in academic situations, it is extremely difficult to distinguish them from the norm in terms of their general personal and social adjustment and understandings. Normally, they can associate with other children on a relatively equal basis in social and recreational activities. Placing them in special classes tends to deprive them of the many opportunities that arise during the normal school day for casual contacts in natural situations that are essential to their education.

Special classes must be clearly superior in regard to curriculum, instruction, and quality of teacher. If they are not, a stigma is easily attached to them and anyone enrolled in them. As a result, the placement in a special class alone may tend to set the slow learners apart from other children. Many good social contacts may be precluded and a number of unhealthy ones substituted in their stead. If the stigma becomes intense or marked, greater resentment toward the school and academic learnings may be developed than if the slow learners had remained in regular classrooms where no special provisions or curriculum adaptations were available. It is true that the special class provides the slow learners with an opportunity to make associations with their intellectual peers, but many educators feel, and probably rightly so, that their intellectual deviation from the normal is so slight that their community social contacts are ordinarily wider and more varied. They do not confine themselves to exclusively associating with other slow learners in a free-choice situation.

Finally, the physical placement of children in a self-contained special class is not necessarily in and of itself the solution to the problem. Teachers of special classes, like teachers of regular classes, must develop an understanding of the characteristics and problems of the slow learners before any realistic program can be developed. The traditional curriculum cannot be adapted, watered down, or changed around and be expected to do the job. The same task faces the teacher and supervisor of the regular class. A curriculum must be developed in reference to the characteristics, experiences, potential, and environmental background of the slow learners. Only in this way can they be provided with the kinds of educational experiences that will be of the greatest value to them.

HOMOGENEOUS GROUPING WITH SOCIAL PROMOTION

Many schools, after adopting the policy of social promotion and social grouping, discover that a number of instructional difficulties accompany their decision. In an attempt to solve some of these problems (particularly relatively wide ranges in ability and achievement), some larger schools have settled upon a scheme of homogeneous grouping. Where two or more classes of the same grade level are housed within the same building, it is possible to evaluate the children according to their intellectual and/or achievement levels. They can then be assigned to a room or teacher on this basis. In this way greater homogeneity of instructional level is achieved reducing the spread of grade-level skills each of the teachers must instruct. It is seldom if ever possible to organize an entire class that will comprise a single instructional group. If this does happen to occur in the fall, it will no longer be true in the spring due to the differential in growth rate that occurs with the many children in the various subject-matter and skill areas.

This method of grouping has distinct advantages over the older method of grouping strictly according to achievement level. The children tend to remain with children of the same chronological, physical, and social development thus providing them with peers who have the same kinds of recreational and social interests. It has an advantage over heterogeneous grouping in that each teacher is working with children who have somewhat similar abilities and educational needs. Common experiences are more apt to be appropriate for all the children. Less diversity of preparation and planning is required on the part of the teacher. Except for skill instruction, the class can often participate as a whole.

There are numerous disadvantages to homogeneous grouping as a solution for the educational problems of the slow learners. These have caused it to be used relatively little in the past and to be less and less favored by many educators. Despite this apparent disfavor, numbers of schools are examining homogeneous grouping of some type as a possible partial solution to the instructional problems they face— problems aggravated by increasing enrollments and shortages of teachers and facilities. It is also easy to rationalize homogeneous grouping for slow learners when special class programs for educable mentally handicapped children are encouraged and partially supported by most of the state departments of education.

When homogeneous programs are organized in the schools, the following invariably occurs. No matter what precautions are taken by the school and administration to hide from children and parents the fact that certain classes are being designated for children with certain abilities or disabilities, it soon becomes common knowledge. Chldren are well aware of how they are performing academically as compared to other children. They soon become aware that children enrolled in other classes of the same grade level are learning different things from the children in their class. They are also aware of a difference in assignments, textbooks, and homework requirements. Parents are informed and their attitudes are in turn reflected by the children. Many parents resent having their children placed in a "slow" group. They do not understand the learning problems of their children and the objectives of such groups. The school is placed on the defensive by having to explain and justify its actions.

Too often the purposes of education have not been specifically defined for the "slow" groups. As a result, teachers may be assigned to them on the same basis as assignments are made to any other class. Most teachers trained to work with normal children dislike being assigned to a class of slow learners for many reasons. In working with slow learners they derive fewer personal satisfactions than in working with normal children because despite their best efforts growth appears to be very slow and laborious. The rate of growth expected of normal children does not occur. Furthermore, teachers often feel insecure working with the slow learners. They feel they know very little about them. Consequently, they do not feel competent to deal with the slow learners' emotional, social, or educational problems adequately. When teachers resent the slow learners and do not have an understanding of the goals of a program for them, they may misinterpret the objectives of the program. As a result the class may be used as a threat to hang over the heads of the children in the regular groups. The threat of placement in the special class or "slow" group may be used in an attempt to control classroom behavior of normal children. When the attitudes of parents, teachers, and children develop against special groupings, the groups become set apart from the general school population. The class and children become isolated and more harm may be accomplished outside the classroom than good is accomplished within it.

Traditionally the programs for the "slow" classes have been revisions, adaptions, or watered-down versions of those found in the regular classes. The general content remains the same, offered at a somewhat slower pace and in somewhat less detail. To make matters worse, in many instances even identical books are used—texts that the slow learners can no more read in this situation than if he were a member of a regular class. The frustrations, the failures, and the lack of a constructive curriculum are factors the children still too often must face. Many teachers continue to emphasize practice in academic skill beyond the children's ability to comprehend. When the children are surrounded by adverse attitudes plus a curriculum that provides them with few satisfactions and for which they can see little value, they come to resent and dislike the situation. In addition their general behavior often deteriorates proportionately rather than showing improvement as it should.

The preceding argument against homogeneous grouping is used primarily by elementary educators. It is also probably somewhat more valid for the elementary school than for the secondary school. The program of the junior high school often reflects the many instructional problems raised when children with widely varied abilities are placed in the same class. With secondary teachers being more subject-matter oriented than elementary teachers, one or another form of homogeneous grouping soon appears. Either the slow learners are failed a number of times until they finally learn the subject and pass (ability or achievement grouping) or fast, average, and slow sections are established, particularly in the academic subjects. The sectioning according to ability is less true of the special subjects areas much to the distress of the industrial arts, homemaking, art, and music teachers.

By senior high school, a split among the students is obvious in mathematics, languages, and science. Capable students in college preparatory programs are enrolled in the courses with the less capable students being enrolled in other, non-college preparatory courses. English and the social sciences courses (requirements for all students) may have ability sections or heterogeneous grouping, depending upon the philosophy of the administration.

Social grouping

The principle of social promotion and the consequent grouping that is theoretically based upon social development has now been in practice to a greater or lesser degree in most elementary schools for many years. The practice has been much less widely accepted and practiced by teachers and administrators in the secondary schools. At the elementary level, the primary advantage of social promotion is that it provides children with placement in a group of children who are considered to have relatively similar social skills and interests. The fundamental objectives of education are to provide each child with the experiences that will enable him to become personally, socially, civically, and economically the most effective person that it is possible for him to become, and this promotional principle or theory is thought to contribute to these objectives to a greater degree than the others previously discussed. Following the theory of social promotion, the children are provided with opportunities to live and associate with their social peers. This provides them with opportunities to learn naturally and meaningfully those social skills that are essential to maintaining oneself as an independent member of the community. As the children learn to live effectively with their classmates under the watchful guidance of the teacher, they are helped to grow and mature socially. With increasing maturity they are given opportunities to make more important decisions. Finally, they will learn to achieve independent control of their behavior. They will then have reached the status required of every adult.

Whatever single method of grouping children may be used, homogeneity of a sort will result in one area but great heterogeneity will be found in other areas. Thus, when children are grouped homogeneously according to their social development and interest, they compose a heterogeneous group in terms of their intellectual development, physical development, and level of academic performance. The children at any one grade-placement level will be performing at, below, and above that particular level. Intellectually superior children will be achieving considerably beyond their grade placement although most of them will not be accomplishing at their ability level. Slow learners will be unable to perform at that grade level although they may be performing academically at or near their ability level. As a result, the teacher must plan instruction and make assignments at several different grade levels if each child is to be challenged and also provided with work in which he can succeed.

Social promotion, although still most commonly recommended today, particuarly by elementary school educators, has never quite achieved the desired ends its proponents have claimed for it. The reasons for this are numerous. Probably the most fundamental cause for its lack of complete acceptance is the lack of a clear, concise definition of social maturity. It is relatively easy to assess the grade level at which a child is performing academically. It is much more difficult to assess a child's social maturity as accurately and place him with a group of children with the same development and in need of the same socializing experiences to continue his growth in that area. Because the criteria are vague, many different interpretations have been placed upon the meaning of social promotion. There has, consequently, been a lack of consistency in policy and application.

Social promotion also requires that teachers be able and willing to teach at different levels to meet the needs of children enrolled in the same class. Due to traditional, subject-matter training of secondary school teachers, the policy has usually been poorly accepted starting with the junior high school. Lack of understanding among the elementary educators and lack of acceptance among secondary educators has caused social promotion to have relatively little meaning: The policy that is actually practiced by most schools (under the guise of social promotion) is a form of annual promotion with occasional retention of slow learners and others who have not continued to perform at their grade placement level.

Following the policy of social promotion, a number of very basic assumptions must be accepted by the educator. Great heterogeniety of development results in the other areas—physical, intellectual, and achievement. By grouping children of widely varying interests and abilities within a classroom, society is being duplicated and they are learning to live with, depend upon, and appreciate each other. Communities are founded in this fashion but not a society. A second assumption that must be made is that all the children need the same curriculum. It is necessary to change levels of instruction but not the content. If this is true, and the concept of enrichment or extension of experiences is acceptable for gifted children, why isn't the concept of watering down or narrowing acceptable for slow learners? The entire concept of social promotion appears to be predicated upon an interpretation of the "equality of man." It is not based upon giving each person an equal opportunity (educational experiences provided in terms of need and ability), but upon an equal or similar set of educational experiences with adjustments being made in instruction and method. Like other unilateral methods used to date, grouping based on the concept of social promotion does not appear to have provided the answer for the slow learners.

NEED FOR SPECIAL GROUPING

Children with varying intellectual and learning abilities and reflecting different environments have unique kinds of educational needs. Education is committed to helping each individual develop his abilities and his potentials to the utmost. Only in this way can he achieve the most valuable and satisfying position attainable as far as he is personally concerned. Only in this way will he be able to contribute effectively to the welfare of the greater society of which he is a part. This means that curriculum must be defined in terms of the individual's needs and the methods used must be appropriate for his background and characteristics. Grouping is, therefore, dependent upon how and where these educational provisions can be included most effectively.

Curriculum

The definitions and applications of the term curriculum are many and varied. The following brief statements express the orientation of this volume and the ensuing discussion. According to Buswell [1] the curriculum is the content that is used purposely by the school to stimulate learning. It may be subjects or activities; it may be intellectual or manual; it may be organized or unorganized. The school

[1] G. Buswell, *Organization and Sequence of the Curriculum*, 41st Yearbook, National Society for the Study of Education, 1942 Part II, 445-63.

must use some kind of content or curriculum in order to stimulate and give purpose to learning. The school in order to be most effective, must have carefully planned curriculums. They will vary considerably for different children and different communities and societies. Following such a definition, the curriculum includes considerably more than the bare academic skills. Along somewhat similar lines but also indicating areas for consideration, Smith, Stanley and Shores [2] perceive the curriculum as the potential experiences set up in a sequence or order by the schools. The curriculum is a reflection of the society—what people think, believe, feel, and do. Its purpose is to help children to better understand the thinking and behavior of the group and their relationship to the group or society. Thus, the curriculum is more than individual centered. It also considers the individual in relation to society. For the slow learners then, the curriculum must be concerned with their thoughts, their feelings, their beliefs, and their actions in relation to their social group as well as the broader society and community.

The curriculum for slow learners at the pre-school and early primary level should have as one of its fundamental objectives to provide the children with those individual and group experiences that will enable them to live as effective individuals in a society with other persons. The experiences provided must be of value and have meaning in relation to their present group and level of development. This objective continues throughout the child's years in school with the emphasis and content (or experiences) changing as his needs and level of development change. Children must be helped to use their own initiative and intelligence in solving problems and selecting appropriate behavior in relation to their development and the expectations dictated by the situation. Through the use of carefully selected, supervised, and directed experiences they must learn to make decisions independently. The experiences in the social areas are, therefore, not individual experiences alone; most of them must be provided in conjunction with a group. The needs of the group must also be at the same developmental level and of a similar nature to those of the individual. If this is not true, all the children are wasting their time with the exception of the one. In the group the children (not just the child) learn about the rights and privileges of

2 B. Othaneal Smith, William Stanley and Harlan J. Shores, *Fundamentals of Curriculum Development* (New York: World Book Co., 1957), p. 685.

each individual in relation to the group. The social group, the community, and the economy in which most persons live are primarily cooperative in nature. It is of fundamental importance that each person learn how to live effectively with others—his neighbors, family, fellow employees, employer or foreman, and so forth. He cannot achieve his highest level of personal development in most existing societies except as he can relate effectively to others.

A second objective is included in the elementary school curriculum for the slow learners; that is to provide children with competencies in the basic academic skills areas. These skills are considered essential tools for the acquisition of information and the carrying on of normal daily activities effectively and efficiently. Through the development of these skills, the pupils are able to acquire information in the content areas. Competence in the skills also acts as a preparation for the more highly content-centered subjects of the secondary school. Little in the way of basic skills has ordinarily been included in secondary programs for normal children beyond a study of advanced grammar. This situation appears to be gradually changing in junior high schools where reading instruction and work with spelling and arithmetic are being included more often. Some of these schools are even including reading specialists on their staffs.

A third objective of the elementary school that is reflected in the curriculum is the inclusion of knowledges and information in the health, science, and social science areas. These studies meet two needs: they provide preparatory background for more intensive study at the secondary level, and they help the children make more effective adjustments to the demands of their environment.

These basic objectives are almost universally accepted for general education. In terms of broad policy statements, they are applicable to all children including the slow learners. The factor that is too often disregarded is that the instruction and experiences provided must be appropriate or the objectives will not be achieved. Slow learners have unique problems as compared to normal children in all these areas. For some unknown reason, educators have generally assumed that normal children and slow learners of about the same age and physical development have the same social skills, social interests, and social values. If normal children are performing in the area of social adjustment and using social skills up to their ability levels, slow learners, in the same situation, will be intellectually incapable of comprehending the demands being made upon them. These social skills, like others, are highly correlated with intelligence, and the slow learners can only achieve the lower levels of competence and understanding at a later date; they may never acquire some of the more advanced and complex concepts.

The problems presented by the slow learners in acquiring the academic skills are well known. Regardless of the grade in which he may be placed, instruction must be at the child's learning level if it is to be of value. As the discrepancy between their ability and age (and consequent grade placement) increases, the problem of providing instruction at their level becomes more acute. Children's mental development continues through the junior high school years. For those children whose ultimate level of skill is limited, it becomes most essential that they reach their maximum level. Thus, skill instruction for slow learners must be continued through the junior high school. Secondary teachers must instruct at the children's respective levels rather than teaching the subject at the grade-level designation. This calls for a major reorientation to education on the part of many teachers performing at this level.

The content areas for slow learners require at least as much change as the adjustment and skill areas. Again, the instruction must be at the level of the children, but in addition the content should have meaning and purpose in relation to their daily living experiences. With the majority of the slow learners reflecting sub-cultural and low socio-economic environments, the typical selection of specific topics in the content areas are often quite inappropriate. This does not mean that all slow learners should be taught an identical content. Those who have experiences as the result of living in better homes and neighborhoods have content needs somewhat different from the rest. They are, however, still unable to comprehend fully much of the content of the regular curriculum and also require that theirs be "tailor made" for them.

The curriculum is one of the most important reasons why grouping planned to provide for the slow learners is essential. Accepting the common, broadly stated objectives of education as being applicable for the slow learners, the curriculum must still differ both in basic content and in emphasis from that provided normal children. The slow learners are intellectually incapable of achieving academically to the degree required to earn their living applying their academic skills, as is required in many "white collar" positions and in the professions. On the other hand, they are intellectually capable of acquiring many of the academic skills to a degree that they can become competent and proficient in their use for purposes of daily living. There is a vast difference between an illiterate person and a person who can read, write, spell, and make useful computations. The academic skills should, therefore, be included in the curriculum for slow learners. They should not be taught, however, merely as discrete skills having basic intrinsic values, but as tools to use for acquiring information, transmitting ideas, and performing the many tasks facing an individual in his everyday life experiences.

Normal children acquire many of their social concepts incidentally as a result of contacts with other persons in a variety of situations. Slow learners are much less able to benefit from an incidental learning situation. They are less able to benefit from a casual experience, because they often have not understood the situation and what they can do to change it. Opportunities must be provided for varying kinds of experiences under guidance to aid them in their understandings of the factors involved. They must learn how to react to new experiences in an acceptable way. This is also true in regard to the academic skills. Slow learners have similar needs for these skills, and instruction should be provided in such a way as to not only teach the skill but its use as well.

Curriculums are often organized to provide certain skills and concepts at specific ages and grade levels. This is done on the assumption that the majority of the children will develop intellectually, socially, emotionally, and academically at approximately the same rate. They are, therefore, ready for instruction in the same skills at about the same time and can acquire proficiency in them with the same kind and amount of instruction. Theoretically, curriculums are also developmental in nature, first presenting fundamental concepts and skills and steadily building upon them as the child grows older and has acquired them.

It is much more difficult to provide the same kinds of grade placement of skills and concepts for the slow learners than for normal children because the grade placement will vary in regard to factors other than intellectual readiness. Like any good curriculum, one that is designed in consideration of the characteristics, problems, and experiences of the slow learners must also be developmental.

The most simple and the easiest learned concepts and skills should be introduced first. As each slow learner develops, new experiences should be presented as rapidly as he is capable of learning them, but not until he has reached the appropriate developmental level regardless of his grade or class placement or what is recommended in the regular curriculum in regard to the offering for children of that age, grade placement, or number of years of school experience.

Grouping for the slow learners

Grouping of children for instructional purposes should be of such a nature that all children (slow, average, and bright) will benefit. It is impossible to devise a number of different groupings based upon varying needs and different principles within the same classroom and still provide continuity and purpose. It is obvious, when one examines the curriculum and instructional needs of slow learners, that the commonly used methods based upon a single factor such as age, achievement, or social development do not meet their educational needs. These principles of grouping have not met the needs of other deviate groups either—gifted, mentally handicapped, sensory and motor handicapped, and so forth. As a result, programs in "Special Education" have been developed and greatly expanded over the past five or six decades. A grouping principle needs to be practiced that applies to all children and provides adequately for each one of them. Grouping based upon a single criterion has not proved satisfactory, so it must be based upon multiple criteria.

First, grouping should be based upon the development of the children. Their physical, social, emotional, intellectual, and academic development must all be taken into consideration. These will determine the kinds of experiences that can and should be provided to promote optimum growth in each child. Each child must be considered individually to determine with what group he will derive the greatest total educational benefit.

Second, grouping for instructional purposes should be done homogeneously. Grouping based solely on a total developmental basis results in extreme heterogeneity in terms of academic level and educational need. Following the organization of the large developmental groups, smaller homogeneous class groups must be formed. Only in this way can differentiated curriculums and instruction be provided in relation to the peculiar needs of individual children—blind, deaf, mentally handicapped, gifted, slow learners, and so forth. This will, by no means, solve all the grouping problems of the teachers. Children with varying academic and skill levels will be in each and every room and class. The teacher will still find it necessary to create subgroups within the room. But the curriculum needs will be common for the group and the instructional methods most applicable can be selected largely in terms of the group.

SCHOOL ORGANIZATION

Thus far the problems involved in the provision of appropriate instruction and programs for slow learners have been discussed almost entirely in regard to the curriculum and experiences they require. Little or no attention has been given to factors concerning the organization of school programs, administration, and facilities essential to the accomplishment of these objectives.

Too often it appears to be necessary to fit new instructional programs into existing, traditional school organizations. These organizations or administrative structures may have been appropriate at one time and were undoubtedly designed in terms of the characteristics of certain kinds of educational programs and to achieve certain objectives. Because these structures have been demonstrated to be effective in helping to accomplish these specific educational aims (usually preparing students for college), it does not necessarily follow that the same organizational structures are the most effective ones that can be practiced or devised for the more diverse educational objectives of today.

The administrative structure of the school should be designed for the primary purpose of enabling instruction to be accomplished as effectively and as efficiently as possible. Consequently, the structure must be flexible and easily changed. It must be susceptible to the influence of changing philosophies and objectives as teachers are ready and capable of changing, adding, or abolishing programs. There has probably been no time in history when social, industrial, and technical changes have occurred as rapidly and dramatically as in the modern world. The schools must be ready at all times to meet the challenges inherent in a rapidly growing and changing society and economy. The schools must be ready to provide meaningful programs of a unique nature, if necessary, to provide for a need as soon as it can be defined. Only in this way will it be possible to provide sufficient numbers of trained personnel who can continue to solve the technical and social problems as they develop. School organization must be prepared to change with the development of new programs. Changing programs, addition of new programs, elimination of outdated programs and methods, actively searching for ways to improve instruction, and a willingness to organize administrative structure taking into consideration new and unique programs are all essential.

The primary school

It has been assumed by many educators that of all school levels, the primary grades have met the needs of the slow learners most adequately. In fact, they have done so well that one seldom hears any demand that "something be done" for them at this time. That the primary grades are doing the best and most effective job with the slow learners is probably true. Certainly these teachers more than any others are well oriented in regard to a child's readiness to learn. A great deal of time is devoted to "readiness" activities and children often continue in a readiness program, regardless of grade placement, until they are capable of benefiting from the more formal, academic instruction. This is appropriate for the slow learners because they require a longer readiness period. In the majority of primary classes, most slow learners probably receive fairly adequate preschool, readiness, and academic skill instruction.

Does this then mean that primary programs, as they are presently constituted, provide for slow learners better than any other method? Not necessarily! From sociometric studies there is some indication that despite the fact that instruction may be provided at the level of the slow learners they, nevertheless, react to the frustration and failure of being unable to perform at the same level as the majority of the children. Even at the kindergarten and first grade levels they are selected as friends and playmates somewhat less often than the normal children in the group. This must have some adverse effects in regard to the attitudes they develop toward school and learning.

One of the major reasons why little or no agitation for defined programs for slow learners at the primary level has developed is because acute, antisocial behavior has not become apparent as yet to any great degree. There are probably two major reasons why this is true. One, most slow learners enter school initially with either a positive attitude (all the older children are going to school and they, too, want to be engaged in the same kinds of activities—a sign of growing up) or no well developed attitude, either positive or negative. It takes time for their attitudes to change from positive to negative ones or to thoroughly "set" their attitudes of a negative nature. As a result, the overt or external behavior can be relatively easily directed and controlled throughout most of the primary school. Two, children in the primary grades are young, immature, and easily intimidated by an adult. Most of the children do not mature sufficiently during this period to become defiant toward the teacher and antagonistic toward school and learning. This will come later.

During the primary period, however, the foundation is being laid for future growth and development—for future behavior. Numerous studies [3,4,5,6,7,8] with slow learners and the mentally retarded indicate that intellectual developmental patterns, attitudes, and modes of behavior are not only established early in life but are also much more amenable to change at that time as well. These can also be changed at a later date, but with greater difficulty and probably to a somewhat lesser degree. If this were not true, many of the accepted objectives of education today would be meaningless and unattainable. The fact still remains that early programs are of extreme importance and must be included as an integral part of any program designed to meet the educational needs of slow learners.

Traditionally, children enter kindergarten between the ages of 4 years-9 months and 5 years-9 months depending upon the date of

3 Frank N. Freeman, Karl J. Holzenger, and B. C. Mitchell, "The Inuflences of Environment on the Intelligence, School Achievement, and Conduct of Foster Children," *The Twenty-Seventh Yearbook of the National Society for the Study of Education: Nature and Nurture, Part I* (Bloomington, Illinois: Public School Publishing Co., 1928).

4 Newell C. Kephart, "Influencing the Rate of Mental Growth in Retarded Children Through Environmental Stimulation," *The Thirty-Ninth Yearbook of the National Society for the Study of Education: Intelligence: Its Nature and Nurture, Part II* (Bloomington, llinois: Public School Publishing Co., 1940).

5 Harold M. Skeels and H. B. Dye, "A Study of the Effects of Differential Stimulation on Mentally Retarded Children," *American Association on Mental Deficiency*, 44, No. 1 (1939), pp. 114-136.

6 Harold M. Skeels, *et al.*, "A Study of Environmental Stimulation," *University of Iowa Studies*, Iowa City: University of Iowa, 15, No. 4 (December, 1938).

7 Harold M. Skeels, "Mental Development of Children in Foster Homes," *Journal of Consulting Psychology*, 2, No. 2 (March–April, 1938), pp. 33-34.

8 Samuel A. Kirk, *Early Education of the Mentally Retarded* (Urbana: University of Illinois Press, 1958), 216 pages.

their birth. They remain in the primary school for four years before being promoted to fourth grade in the intermediate school. Where kindergartens are not provided, entrance to the primary school is delayed one year and the time of enrollment is reduced to three years. Slow learners usually enter the primary school at the same ages as normal children but are intellectually less prepared to cope with the program. As a result, a substantial proportion of them, particularly the youngest and slowest, are kept at one level for an additional year thus lengthening their stay in the primary school. This retention does not necessarily provide for their educational needs more adequately. It merely ensures that they will be performing at a higher academic level when promoted to the intermediate school. The stigma of retention and the brand of failure are nevertheless placed upon them.

Some communities have attempted to solve the problem of making more adequate provisions for individual differences at the primary level that organizationally makes more sense than the more universally found, traditional graded school. These schools have first established a preschool survey where all prospective new enrollees are briefly observed and evaluated to determine whether or not they are ready for school experience. When there is any question, a more comprehensive examination is provided by the school psychologist. Parents of children who are too young to be routinely considered, but who think their children are ready for school and have some observational evidence to support their petition, may also have their children examined. In this way the children with experiences and maturity of a sufficient level to indicate that the initial school experiences will be of value are enrolled. Strict age limits are not adhered to; more realistic admission standards have been established.

Assuming a primary program that the normal child can and ordinarily will complete in four years, the child is not enrolled in a grade or kindergarten. He is enrolled as a new, beginning pupil. Grades and grade concepts are abolished. Groups are not re-formed annually or by the semester as is true with the graded school. Instead, the program is organized in much the same fashion as a good teacher organizes his class. Anyone who has worked with groups of children or knows anything about child development recognizes that children grow at different rates and that their growth often is not steady but moves in "fits and starts," periods of rapid growth followed by periods of little or no growth. The beautiful textbook growth curves are composites or averages made up of the growth of many children.

Regrouping must occur whenever the children in one group show such a disparity of development that they no longer derive relatively equal benefit from the instruction provided that group. In addition to regrouping within the room, regrouping under the primary program also occurs among the rooms. Initially, the instructional grouping is based almost entirely upon the level of the readiness program at which the children can effectively participate. Later, reading becomes the primary factor. Still later, grouping must also be based upon arithmetic skills as well as reading. When a child reaches this level he may find that he has been placed with one group for reading skill instruction and another for arithmetic. These may well be within the same room under the same teacher or, in the case of an extreme ability or disability in one or the other subject, he may be placed with a completely different group for that part of his instruction only. At the upper levels this may appear to be departmentalization and it is to a certain extent. The departmentalization, however, is the exception rather than the rule. Grouping is based upon an individual's characteristics and a problem area rather than upon subject-matter departmentalization.

The length of time a child remains in the primary school depends entirely upon his growth. The majority of the children will complete the program in four years. Bright, mature children may complete it in three years while dull, immature children may require five years. Applying the criteria for promotion, discussed earlier in the chapter, will determine when a specific child is ready to leave the primary school, ready to enter the intermediate school.

The primary program has many advantages for slow learners. Under it they will always be provided with instruction at their level, not for just a short period but throughout the day—during discussions, for skill instruction, and for other activities. With the slow learners somewhat slower rate of development, they never have a chance to fall too far behind the class because of the continuous regrouping. This also acts to reduce frustration because all the instruction tends to be more nearly at their level of performance than is true for the traditional graded class. While the feeling of failure is reduced under the primary program, it may not be eliminated completely. With the elimination of grades and regrouping taken out of the context of annual or semi-annual promotion, the concept of retention and failure is at least deemphasized. Both the teacher and children are working toward positive growth. The repetition commonly associated with retention does not occur. The rate of introduction of new skills, concepts, and knowledge is introduced at the rate of the children's development. Eventual grouping of slow learners together will result under this program. In this way, a unique, meaningful program can be developed.

The intermediate school

The intermediate school should be organized on the same basis as the primary program. Here, too, the concepts of grades and promotion should vanish with the emphasis being placed upon continuous, systematic instruction provided at the developmental level of each child. Some movement in this direction has already been made through the introduction of the ungraded elementary school. It is not sufficient to merely remove grade names while continuing to operate as usual, grouping and regrouping in traditional fashion. Grouping must be flexible with regrouping occurring whenever necessary. When a child is finally promoted to the junior high school after satisfactorily completing his intermediate program, the junior high school program will satisfy his educational needs more adequately. The average stay in the intermediate school should be three years, but for some children it could be two and for others four.

Instruction in the skills should continue in the intermediate school in much the same way as in the primary school with grouping being based upon the skill being taught and the children's abilities in that skill. Each child should be placed with the group for which the level of instruction in that skill is understandable to him. Content is also introduced at the intermediate level, but to a much greater degree than is true for the primary school. Thus, plans must be made for instruction in English, science, and social studies as well. Since learning in these areas is largely dependent upon reading skill, the reading groups form the foundation for grouping in these areas. Occasionally a child who is a remedial problem in reading, for example, may be placed with a more advanced group and be given some special help. With appropriate reading instruction he should soon be capable of performing independently at the higher level.

Greater departmentalization should be apparent in the intermediate school than was true for the primary school. Each child, however, should have a teacher to whom he is primarily responsible; one who provides most of the instruction and plans his school experiences. Special subjects, such as art, music, physical education, and library, may be taught by special teachers either in rooms designed for these activities or in the child's "home" room. Today it is common for these specialists to act as "supervisors." Each one of these areas has skills and techniques that are necessary for satisfactory performance. These skills should be taught, but the activities should be related to the regular classroom activities and projects insofar as possible. This requires that each special teacher be intimately familiar with each of the programs and levels. They must be aware of the particular activities at a particular time in all areas. This is not too difficult with flexible grouping where there is little necessity for carrying on a multiplicity of activities within a "class."

The junior high school

Traditionally the junior high school has been organized along departmental lines comparable to the classical high school. The students, however, are all given a similar program (particularly in 7th and 8th grade) consisting of specified subjects and go from class to class and teacher to teacher receiving instruction in them. Most of the children have little more opportunity to contact children from other classes during the school day than they had in the self-contained elementary classroom. They are organized into a home-room group which remains intact as the children attend the various classes.

A movement that may attain some impetus and may also have real potential for aiding slow learners has been developed in the junior high school. Elementary and secondary teachers are being considered for possible work in the junior high school. If this comes to pass, the teaching staff will be oriented toward education somewhat differently than is true today. More emphasis will be placed on instruction at each child's level. Subjects will be taught to a greater degree with the aim of meeting children's needs. This movement fits into another that has been gaining some momentum—that of moving away from the strict secondary departmentalized approach and setting aside blocks of time for instruction in all of the non-special subjects. One teacher should ordinarily be responsible for this block instruction. As a result, these teachers require a broader educational approach than is true for most secondary school subject-matter specialists today.

Using a block system, departmentalization is formulated on the basis of children's developmental levels, educational needs, and special subjects. The teacher works with relatively few children and consequently becomes better acquainted with each one. He becomes the child's teacher, someone who feels responsible as well as someone to whom the child is responsible. Grouping should again be placed upon a non-grade or an educational need basis. Since the junior high school years include the final intellectual growth years of the children, skill instruction at each child's appropriate level is essential if they are to be expected to eventually achieve at or near their maximum level. For slow learners the block system provides an opportunity for continued growth without the unrealistic comparison to grade-level norms. Again the prospect of failure is largely eliminated. How can a child fail when he is being continuously taught at his learning level and being regrouped when another group will provide for his instructional needs more adequately?

Generally there should be little difference between the organizational structure of the intermediate and junior high school. The specific objectives are much the same. Most of the difference occurs in the size of the schools, number of pupils, and provision of more highly specialized and better equipped art, music, industrial arts, and homemaking rooms as well as a library and a gymnasium. In short, junior high schools are equipped to provide for older, more mature children with more highly developed skills and different social needs from the children in the intermediate school.

The discussion concerning promotion in regard to the intermediate school children is also appropriate for the junior high school level.

The senior high school

Whether or not the block program that provides for greater integration of instruction is appropriate to the senior high school is a question that certainly has not been settled in the minds of many educators. It is true that greater integration of use and instruction of common skills in related subjects or subjects requiring them than is generally true today is essential. Even within a highly departmentalized senior high school it is organizationally possible to provide block instruction for slow learners. And block instruction is certainly indicated as providing most adequately for the educational needs of slow learners, if for no other reason than that their general inability to progress sufficiently far in subjects and special areas does not make the emphasis of a departmentalized program worth while.

The use for broad interest cores in the social and/or vocational areas will be the basis of an effective core program. In this program, the children can learn to apply their various skills to the solution of a problem. For the individual with abilities that can be directed toward a vocation, opportunities must be provided for additional instruction with groups performing at a high level in the industrial arts program or vocational school. The organization of the school must also provide for teacher time to contact employers, supervise students on the job, do follow-ups of "graduates," and release students for part-time, school directed work.

One additional organizational problem must be mentioned that may appear to be of a minor nature but can be of great importance to the slow learners. Provisions must be made so that slow learners can participate in all general school activities of a social, extracurricular, and athletic nature. If the problem of eligibility arises, they are eligible as students of the school who are performing satisfactorily in the program in which they are enrolled. They are not "second class citizens." [9] They are an integral part of the student body, as the teachers working with them should be considered to be an integral part of the faculty. As such, they have the same rights and the same responsibilities as the rest of the students. They belong, but they also need to feel they belong.

SCHOOLS WITH LIMITED ENROLLMENT

Schools in rural and isolated communities often have very limited enrollment. It is not unusual for them to have a single class at each grade level and at times two classes or grade levels may have to be combined to provide a sufficient number of pupils to warrant

9 G. Orville Johnson, *The Slow Learner—A Second Class Citizen?*, Richard J. Street Lecture, Syracuse University, Syracuse University Press, 1962.

the employment of a teacher. As one discusses programs for slow learners, educators working in these schools often think that these program require several classes at each grade level. Only in this way, they think, are a sufficient number of children available to plan for homogeneous groups, for without separating the slow learners into class groups separate from the rest of the children it isn't possible to provide a differentiated program for them. Therefore, discussions regarding slow learners sound good, and it would be nice if they could be provided for regardless of the characteristics of the school they attend. Unfortunately, these educators feel, the programs are designed for centers of population—urban areas where there are many children and numbers of classes at each grade level. The schools with small pupil populations can do little or nothing. This attitude, which is all too prevalent, could not be farther from the truth.

One of the first things the educator working in a small school should do is to look very carefully at the children attending school, at their parents, and at the community. What kind of children are they? Are they generally average, above average, or below average in ability? Many isolated areas have a relatively homogeneous population so that the children can be fairly well categorized in terms of their intelligence. It is seldom that one will find a normal distribution of intelligence and ability. Sometimes a school will service two discrete groups—one of average or above average intelligence and one where slow learners predominate.

After becoming familiar with the ability characteristics of the children, parents, and community, it is necessary to determine the value systems in operation. Is an education an important asset? How much education is an important asset? How much education is considered to be essential? How many of the children who are capable of continuing their education in schools of higher learning are encouraged to do so? This varies considerably from community to community. For example, in some of the "bedroom" commuter suburbs of large urban centers where the adult members of the community are professional people, executives, and so forth, the average I.Q. of the school children is 115 or 120. Not only are the children above average in intelligence, but great value is placed upon a higher education. As high as 85 per cent of the high school graduates will continue their education beyond that provided by the public school.

In other communities the intelligence of the children is much lower. Only a very small number of the children may continue with their education upon the completion of public school. The ratio may be as small as 1 out of 10 or even 20. Yet these schools may be following essentially the same curriculum—college preparatory. For one school it may be appropriate, for another it may be so inappropriate as to be disastrous. Before a program can be initiated for a defined group, such as the slow learners, a careful, critical evaluation must be made of the general curriculum now being followed. It may be that the general curriculum should be designed for slow learners since they make up the major portion of the school population. If this is the case, special planning must be done for the average and bright children who should be considering learning experiences beyond those available in that school.

Where slow learners are in the minority, the situation is far from hopeless. Some of the best examples of individualizing instruction can be found by examining the teaching done in the one-room school which various states are still attempting to do away with. Despite efforts at centralization, the one-room school can still be found in every state. Teachers interested in learning more about handling multiple ability levels in one room would do well to visit one of these schools and observe the teacher carefully. Two grade levels in one room is easily found and four grade levels in one room is far from a rarity. Children in these schools are grouped for instructional purposes according to ability regardless of age or grade designation. Content areas may be included bi-annually rather than each year in order to reduce the number of subjects and groups that must be taught. Yet, every child receives instruction in every subject although for many the original order or sequence may be reversed.

There are obviously a number of ways in which a relatively small proportion of the students may receive the differentiated instruction they need. Schools that have at least one class at each grade level can often solve the instructional problem of slow learners at the primary and intermediate school levels by instituting the ungraded primary project and the ungraded elementary school. The flexible grouping possible, following these concepts, permits placing the slow learners with instructional groups being taught at or near their developmental level, with different groupings being provided for the content areas, special subjects, and social experiences. With the elimination of grade levels and annual or semi-annual promotion it is easier to give seven or eight years of primary and intermediate instruction to those slow learners for whom a more extended period is appropriate and still reduce the feelings of frustration and failure that normally accompany retention in a grade.

The problem of providing appropriate instruction at the secondary level may be somewhat more difficult. One structure that might well be considered is to set up the program along the lines of the organization commonly used for secondary classes for mentally handicapped children. All the slow learners in the junior high school (or senior high school) who have need for a special program can be grouped together. The teacher of the class should be carefully selected. He must be a competent teacher and have a real interest in working with slow learners. Thus, there would be "seventh," "eighth" and "ninth" grade slow learners in the same room. Some of them would be just entering the program while others would have been in the program for 2 or 3 years, ready for promotion to the senior high school program (or for graduation in the case of senior high school programs). The children might be housed in appropriate grade-level homerooms but report to their own teacher for skill and content instruction. The teacher should continue with the class from year to year. In this way he becomes very familiar with each child and can better define the educational needs that exist. He is also aware of the previous secondary school experiences each child has had and can plan the program so as to continuously introduce experiences that are both new and meaningful to each one of the children. This is much the same method used by the one-room school teacher.

While a certain amount of attention is drawn to children who attend a program of this type (since other children have a number of teachers and different content and level of instruction) there need be no stigma attached to it. The stigma, when present, is usually associated with an inappropriate, infantile, or "play program" approach, inappropriate social behavior on the part of the children enrolled in the program, or the attitudes of adults (parents and teachers) toward the program. Where good programs exist, not only is there no stigma, but the program often becomes so attractive that other students express a desire to participate in it. In actual practice, slow learners enrolled in a good program that may even require a different organizational structure from that followed by the rest of the classes may be less stigmatized than had they remained in the regular classes and struggled along in the best way possible with repeated failures. Because of reduced contact with slow learners in academic situations, the body of students in general are less aware of the slow learners disabilities in these areas. They thus have an opportunity to evaluate each one upon an individual basis in activities and situations in which slow learners are more adept and consequently able to deal with fairly adequately.

Slow learners, like all children, have educational needs that lie outside the academic and content areas. The teacher assigned to the class, who is, consequently, more familiar with the children than any other person in the school, is in the best position to evaluate these needs and insofar as possible plan programs to meet them. Most of the slow learners will be able to participate in some of the special subjects areas (art, music, physical education, industrial arts, homemaking, and so forth) with normal children. It is the teacher's responsibility to determine which of these experiences are needed by each individual in the class and with which regular group or groups they can best be provided. The teacher is also the counselor. For some of the slow learners the seventh grade activities will be appropriate while for others the eighth and ninth grade activities should be selected. It should be noted that the basis of placement is recommended in reference to need and ability to participate and benefit rather than upon an arbitrary grade-level placement or designation.

The senior high school program, as indicated, should operate in much the same way as the junior high school program. Again the "special class" organization is recommended with a selected teacher being responsible for the program and guidance of the slow learners year after year. Since the teacher will have some "free" time when the children are with teachers in the special subjects areas or participating on work programs, he can also participate in other than the special classroom activities. For one thing, he may be assigned a regular class in his area of academic training thus becoming an integral part of the school faculty. He might become active in general school affairs as a club sponsor, coach of the debate team, or class

play, or as an athletic coach, a supervisor of athletic and social
events, and so forth. Any such activity increases the teacher's value
to the school. This cannot be overdone, however, since he must have
the opportunity and time to visit employers and prospective employers on behalf of his students as well as supervise the work program of the students.

The smaller schools present a somewhat more difficult problem.
Often arrangements can be worked out with state departments of
education to include the slowest of the slow learners with the children in the special class for mentally handicapped. Since the difference between the slowest of the slow learners and the brightest of
the mentally handicapped is indistinguishable, and there is very
little if any difference between their educational needs, this often
proves to be a good placement for everyone concerned. Again, if the
general school program has been carefully planned in regard to the
characteristics of both the children and the community, the higher
level slow learners may, with only a little additional help and attention, fit into the regular school program.

At the primary and elementary levels, teachers with multiple
grade levels in one room usually have enough children at any one
developmental level to have groups with whom the slow learners
may be placed for skill and content instruction. Since the slow learners have relatively the same basic skill needs as normal children at
this level, that aspect of the instruction is appropriate. The same
cannot always be said in regard to the content areas. Here the teachers may find it necessary to organize a separate group of slow learners with subject content selected to meet their needs. In order to
reduce the number of groups, it may also be feasible to place all the
slow learners in one room with one teacher who will, as a result,
work with a reduced number of normal children. It may be possible
to select the normal children so that they form a fairly homogeneous,
grade-level group. In this way the teacher will be able to divide his
time between the slow learners and the normal children.

Similar kinds of arrangements will have to be made at the secondary level. Grouping all the slow learners together with one
teacher who will also be responsible for a number of normal children in specific subject-matter areas is probably the best solution.
In this way a minimum of excess expense is entailed with the possibility of a relatively adequate program being provided. The keys

to the entire objective of providing adequate programming and instruction are (1) a willingness to teach at the child's level, (2) planning meaningful educational experiences, and (3) changing existing structure and school organization in any way necessary to achieve these aims.

SUMMARY

A great deal has been written and said, primarily by elementary educators and often with more heat than the problem warrants, concerning the grouping of children in school. The basic purpose of grouping is too often forgotten; it is to enable the teachers and administrators to achieve the objectives of education as effectively, as efficiently, and as economically as possible. As the objectives of education have changed, reflecting a changing philosophy, different methods of grouping have been and must be adopted. If one has read the preceding sections regarding school organization carefully and is aware of their implications in regard to grouping, only one conclusion is possible. Some type of homogeneous grouping is essential—it is an inevitable outgrowth of the educational principles set forth. Actually the question is not, "Shall educational organization and planning be in terms of homogeneous or heterogeneous grouping?" Rather, it is a question of the kind of homogeneous grouping that shall be used. It can be in terms of age, entrance to kindergarten, or first grade as is generally practiced today. It can be in terms of social development, theoretically most commonly practiced following the initial admission today. Or, it can be in terms of the total development and educational characteristics and needs of the various individuals attending the schools.

When one considers seriously the necessity for unique and specific kinds of educational experiences and instruction for slow learners, homogeneous grouping on this basis must be accepted. Only in this way can the purposes of education be achieved by the schools for the slow learners. The slow learners, like all children, must be provided with meaningful instruction at their own level of learning ability.

Attitudes in opposition to this type of homogeneous grouping spring from a number of sources. The grouping of all educational problems into "opportunity rooms" was, in most instances, very unsatisfactory. Theoretically these programs were supposed to provide the children who were having learning problems, regardless of cause, with greater individualization of instruction. Therefore, they provided the children with an opportunity to derive greater benefit from instruction than had been possible in the regular classroom. In actual practice they too often only provided teachers with an opportunity to get rid of the children they didn't want in their classes—learning problems, emotional problems, behavior problems, slow learners, and the mentally retarded. In addition, the classes seldom had a defined curriculum planned in reference to the needs and characteristics of the children. Teachers were not carefully selected in regard to their interest in these problems and their ability to cope with them. Rather, the opposite was too often true. Incompetent teachers who had been unable to provide satisfactory instruction in a regular classroom were too often selected to work in this much more difficult situation.

Is it any wonder that conscientious educators have rebelled against the concept of homogeneous grouping if this is what was meant by it? The very multiplicity of the problems presented by the children made it an educationally impossible situation. Actually, they were not homogeneously grouped classes; they were really more heterogeneous than classes in general when one considers the multiplicity of the problems presented.

Another type of homogeneous grouping is based upon skill or ability. An extreme example of this kind of thinking was a "teacher" of gifted children who recommended that one of the children in her class be transferred to a class for mentally handicapped children. The reason for the recommendation was that the child was a severe reading disability case and was performing in that skill at the level of a mentally handicapped child of his age. A more common practice of this concept is the use of A, B, C or X, Y, Z groups where multiple sections of a grade level exist. This grouping is based largely upon achievement or academic performance. Again, teachers are too often selected who have little or no interest in slow children and children with educational problems. Their primary objective seems to be to "serve their turn" and then have a chance to teach normal or bright children again. These are the children who can learn the subject at the level they are interested in teaching.

Appropriate homogeneous grouping will never be achieved and its values put to use as long as the concept of "getting rid of" continues to be the principle followed in organizing the "slow" groups. When the grouping of children is placed upon the basis of providing appropriate instruction for each child, better education for *all* children will result. The best instruction can only be provided all children economically when each child is carefully placed with those children who have similar educational needs. From past experience, one additional ingredient must be added before proper grouping will prove to be of value to slow learners particularly. Teachers of slow learners must be of at least equal quality to teachers of normal and superior children. They must see a challenge in working with slow learners. They must have a desire to teach them. It requires no more effort and it is no more difficult than working with normal children. It does, however, require a somewhat different orientation to education than is commonly found among teachers who tend to be primarily academic-achievement oriented. An understanding of slow learners, their abilities, limitations, potentials, and educatonal needs is essential.

Grouping according to the program and school organization described in this and other chapters is not based upon a specific I.Q. range or range of achievement. Rather, the entire development, the anticipated rate of growth, the probable potentials, the social and cultural background, and the calculated future status (socially, culturally, and economically) of the children must all be taken into consideration. The too commonly used meaning of educational integration (which has no relation to the race, creed, or color controversy) is inappropriate and inapplicable when planning educational programs. This meaning equates identity of educational experiences with equality of educational opportunity. It is practiced by placing all children of an age or grade level within a single classroom without regard to educational need. In some instances it has been carried to such extremes that in large metropolitan centers children are transported from their own school districts into others. There is little value in placing a child in a school environment where he becomes part of a small minority reflecting a cultural background alien to the background of the majority of the children. Schools tend to reflect the community (or neighborhood) in which they are located. Consequently, transporting children to schools representing cultural groups with different value systems places them in an environment that they neither understand (an environment with which they have had no personal, intimate contact) nor place any value upon.

These are important factors that are too often forgotten or ignored by many educators and most over-zealous reformers. They see little value in "special" educational programs and unique programs for minority groups of children. They feel that all children should be given essentially the same experiences even though they have been defined as educational problems and obviously require different programs from those provided the large, normal group. If one were to follow the recommended principles rather than the unrealistic biases, *all* children would have available to them well defined programs planned expressly for their needs—slow learners, normals, gifted, sensory handicapped, and social and emotional deviates.

The purpose of school organization and administrative structure is to enable programs to be developed that are designed to most effectively meet the needs of the children, including slow learners. It also enables instruction to be provided in the most efficient and effective possible manner. No program should be placed in an advantageous position administratively. Each program is of equal importance. Programs for slow learners should be able to be provided as easily as programs emphasizing training in the commercial areas or preparation for college and institutions of higher learning. Organizing educational programs according to the concepts embodied in the primary and intermediate schools on an ungraded basis provides an opportunity to achieve these objectives at the elementary level. Applying the same concepts to the organization of secondary programs for slow learners, even in highly departmentalized schools, permits a continuation of these principles, principles that can even be practiced by schools with limited enrollments in rural areas and small, isolated communities. In this way the slow learners may receive the education that is their right and for which have need.

SELECTED RELATED READINGS

Bloom, I. and W. I. Murray, "Some Basic Issues in Teaching Slow Learners," *Understanding the Child,* 26:85–91.

Buswell, G., *Organization and Sequence of the Curriculum,* 41st Yearbook, National Society for the Study of Education, 1942, Part II: 445–63.

Featherstone, William B., *Teaching the Slow Learner*. Bureau of Publications, Teachers College, Columbia University, 1951, pp. 23–29.

Havighurst, Robert J., "Dealing with Problem Youth," *Nation's Schools,* 61:43–45, May, 1958.

Herkner, M. W. and J. F. Malone, "How Shall We Provide for the Slow Learner in the Junior High School?" *National Association Secondary Principals Bulletin,* 38:95–100, April, 1954.

Hull, J. R., "Multigrade Teaching," *Nations Schools,* 62:33–37, July, 1958.

Liddle, G. and D. Long, "Experimental Room for Slow Learners," *Elementary School Journal,* 59:143–49, December, 1958.

Peller, Helen, "Adjusting an Adjustment Class," *High Points,* 29:72–78, April, 1947.

Schuker, L. A., "The Slow Learner in the High School," *High Points,* 37:11–31, April, 1955.

Seeley, R. M., "A Junior High Care Program for Slow Learners," *School Executive,* 73:64–66, October, 1953.

Smith, B. Othaneal, William Stanley and Harlan J. Shores, *Fundamentals of Curriculum Development.* New York: World Book Co., 1957, 685 pages.

Smith, Donald E., "In Behalf of the Slow Learner," *Peabody Journal Education,* 29:154–56, November, 1951.

Varner, Glenn F., "Youth with Non-Academic Abilities and/or Interests: What are Secondary Schools Doing to Provide for Youth with Non-Academic Abilities and/or Interests?" *National Association Secondary School Principals Bulletin,* 39:294–97, April, 1955.

5

The Primary and
Intermediate Schools

The schools of the not too distant past were traditionally divided into two broad levels. These were the elementary school consisting of the first eight years and the high school encompassing the last four years. During the last three decades a movement has been taking place that has changed the organizational structure as well as the instruction in many ways. Physically, the school structure is being divided into six elementary and six secondary grades. The secondary level, since incorporating six rather than four grades, has been subdivided into two three-year units, the junior and the senior high school. More recently a movement has developed separating the primary grades (kindergarten through second or third) from the upper elementary or intermediate grades. When one considers the normal development of children, as well as the differences in emphasis between the primary and intermediate grades, this separation also has much to be said for it.

The description of programs for the slow learners in this chapter and chapter 6 will follow the four-division organization of the school that appears to be attaining wider and wider acceptance. Each of these groupings (primary, intermediate, and junior and senior high school) are unique in regard to both organization and program. First, the characteristics of the children attending each level can be fairly well described. Second, relatively clear-cut objectives can be defined for each of the levels. Finally, each of the levels is of sufficient duration (an average of three years for each child) to allow for the achievement of the objectives.

THE PRIMARY SCHOOL

Characteristics of the children

Most school systems select an arbitrary date before which a child's birthday must fall if he is to enter school that year. The date selected for purposes of better defining and clarifying the following discussion is December 1. Thus, any child whose birthday is November 30 or before is eligible for admission while any child whose birthday falls on December 1 or later would not be admitted. The youngest child to enter kindergarten, except under special consideration, would be about 4 years-9 months and the oldest child would be a year older. The range of ages among normal children in any one grade would be 1 year and the complete range of ages for the primary grades would be a minimum of 4 years (from 4 years-9 months to 8 years-9 months) (Table I). This assumes, of course, that no child has "failed" or been "retained" or required to repeat a grade. Since this situation rarely occurs, the spread of ages for any grade is usually greater than the minimal one year, particularly beyond the kindergarten. The retention of the youngest and slowest among the slow learners is also shown in this table. Reading the two sides of the table, it soon becomes apparent that a group starting in kindergarten with only about a one-year span in chronological ages will, conserva-

TABLE I

Chronological Ages of Children Enrolled in the
Primary Grades—September 1 and June 30

| | Ages of Normal Children | | | | Ages of Slow Learners | | | |
| | September 1 | | June 30 | | September 1 | | June 30 | |
Grade Level	Spread	Average	Spread	Average	Spread	Average	Spread	Average
Kindergarten	4–9 to 5–9	5–3	5–7 to 6–7	6–1	4–9 to 5–9	5–3	5–7 to 6–7	6–1
First	5–9 to 6–9	6–3	6–7 to 7–7	7–1	5–9 to 6–11	6–4	6–7 to 7–9	7–2
Second	6–9 to 7–9	7–3	7–7 to 8–7	8–1	6–11 to 8–1	7–6	7–9 to 8–11	8–4
Third	7–9 to 8–9	8–3	8–7 to 9–7	9–1	8–1 to 9–3	8–8	8–11 to 10–1	9–6

TABLE II

Approximate Mental Ages and Appropriate Grade-Level Achievements for
Slow Learners Enrolled in the Primary Grades—September 1 and June 30

| | Mental Age | | | | Grade Achievement | | | |
| | September 1 | | June 30 | | September 1 | | June 30 | |
Grade Level	Spread	Average	Spread	Average	Spread	Average	Spread	Average
Kindergarten	3–7 to 5–2	4–5	4–2 to 5–11	5–1	– to –	–	– to –	–
First	4–4 to 6–1	5–3	5–0 to 6–10	5–11	– to –	–	– to 1.7	–
Second	5–2 to 7–0	6–1	5–10 to 7–9	6–10	– to 1.8	–	– to 2.6	1.6
Third	6–1 to 7–11	7–0	6–8 to 8–8	7–8	– to 2.7	1.8	1.6 to 3.4	2.5

tively, have a span of almost a year and one-half by the completion of third grade. The slow learners, as a group, become older than the rest of the group with each successive year.

Since the average I.Q. of the general population is approximately 100, the average mental ages of the normal children will also correspond to the average chronological ages indicated for that group in Table I. Their average academic achievement will also correspond to the expectation for the ages indicated under normal conditions. Actual practice shows, however, that the grade groupings even among the normal learners will be much less homogeneous than indicated when mental ages and achievement levels are the considerations. This is due to the variability of I.Q.'s even in the so-called normal range and added variability of academic achievement. Consequently, the spread of mental ages and grade-level achievement scores will be much greater than the one-year chronological age spread shown. These discrepancies in spread will become successively greater with increasing age and for each successive grade level.

Slow learners with I.Q.'s between 75 and 90 will show a somewhat greater distribution and a somewhat older average chronological age than normal children even at the primary level. This is due to occasional retentions that may start at the kindergarten level but definitely becomes operative in first grade. In order to better understand their relative positions at the various primary grade levels, the approximate spreads and averages of the slow learners' mental ages and grade achievements are summarized in Table II. This table will show what one should expect of slow learners both individually (spread) and collectively (average) during the primary years of school.

All slow learners are at the readiness or pre-readiness level during the year in kindergarten. At the beginning of the year their mental ages may range from 3 years-7 months to 5 years-2 months. Their average mental age is 10 months lower than would be expected for the general population. At the end of that year their mental ages would have increased from 7 to 9 months during the 10 month period—an average of 8 months, for a mean mental age of 5 years-1 month. Being promoted to first grade upon an annual or social promotional basis, they would start wih mental ages from 4 years-4 months to 6 years-1 month—an average of 5 years-3 months. None of them, according to test standardizations, would be ready intellectually for formal academic instruction. During first grade only the highest of the group would achieve sufficient intellectual maturity to learn academic skills and they would be expected to achieve at only 1.7 grade level where the average for all children should be 2.0. The average mental development for the slow learning group would not indicate that any achievement in academic learning should be expected in first grade. The majority of the slow learners would benefit from academic instruction in second grade. Here an average grade level achievement of 1.6 could be expected. The highest would be achieving at 2.6, 0.4 grades below the general average.

Not until third grade, their fourth year in school, would all slow learners have achieved sufficient intellectual development to benefit from academic instruction. The slowest would achieve less than one year, performing at 1.8 grade level in June. The highest would continue to develop more rapidly, achieving at 3.4 grade level. The average grade-level achievement for slow learners at the end of third grade would be 2.5.

The other characteristics of slow learners are much the same as are found among children who live in the same areas of the community, have similar cultural experiences, and are governed by the same value system. Most slow learners come from the subcultural, low socio-economic areas of the community. Their parents may be foreign born (as is often the case in New York City and other urban centers of immigration) and/or have relatively little education compared to the rest of the population. As a result, they tend to live in over-crowded conditions, often several families residing in an apartment designed for one family. Sanitary facilities are often at a minimum level. The psycho-social stimulation present in the home and neighborhood does little to promote school learnings. In many instances, the reverse is true. Pressures encouraging deviate behavior in school and early drop-out are often present. Satisfactions are gained by activities not only unrelated to school but actually discouraged by the school and the larger community.

The school attitudes of slow learners are, therefore, often of such a nature as not to be conducive to learning. Truancy is high. Where programs of a special nature, planned for children with limited learning ability residing in a subcultural, low socio-economic environment, are not provided, the school has little of a positive nature to offset the attitudes brought to school by the children. Add to this

an inability to progress through the school at a normal rate and innumerable problems arise—problems the teacher is unprepared, untrained, and consequently too often unable to solve.

By the time most slow learners have passed from the primary into
the intermediate school, they have repeated at least one grade. The
retention has usually been based upon a definition of immaturity.
The immaturity either would not have been noticed or would have
been considered of insufficient importance to seriously influence a
decision for selective placement had it not been for the low academic-
achievement level. This retention may occur any place along the
line but is most often used in first grade. Occasionally a child may
be asked to repeat kindergarten, particularly if he was one of the
youngest children in the group. Those slow learners who escape
retention in first grade (the oldest, most mature, and brightest) are
usually retained in second or third grade. Relatively few slow learners complete the primary school in the normal four years.

Another result of coming from homes where the parent is employed in a lower paying job and the educational level of the parents
is comparatively low is a higher than average incidence of disease
and physical disability among slow learners. Lack of cleanliness and
inadequate hygiene facilities precipitate and promote the spread
of communicable disease. The incidence of visual and auditory
problems among slow learners is higher than is normally found
among children. In addition, these conditions are less apt to receive
early, appropriate treatment. Too often the parents do not consider
them to be of primary importance. These conditions also contribute
to the children's learning disabilities. Other physical disabilities,
particularly of a relatively minor nature, are found more commonly.
There is a high incidence of dental problems. There is even evidence
indicating that bone ossification is delayed in slow learners.

Genetically the slow learners *may* have the same physical and motor abilities as children in general. They deviate widely in these
abilities, some being very good, many being about average, and
some being below average or poor. As a group, their average general
physical and motor development is probably slightly below normal.
Studies [1] carried out with the brightest mentally handicapped chil-

[1] James D. Beaber, *The Performance of Educable Mentally Handicapped and
Intellectually Normal Children on Selected Tasks Involving Simple Motor Performance* (Unpublished Doctoral Dissertation, Syracuse University, 1960), 146
pages.

dren (mean I.Q. about 68) who are very little below the slow learners intellectually and come from the same cultural backgrounds and socio-economic areas of the community show that their psycho-motor skills compare favorably with normal children of the same mental age. Normal children of the same chronological age are significantly superior. There is no reason to suspect that the same characteristics do not hold true for the majority of the slow learners who also reflect the same kinds of backgrounds.

Primary curriculum

The following recommendations for a primary curriculum are based fundamentally upon the slow learners' retarded intellectual developmental level and slower developmental rate and the fact that the majority of them come from homes in the low cultural and socio-economic areas of the community. The children reflect this background in their approach or attitudes toward school and the experiences they carry with them to school.

As a result of retarded intellect and a paucity of school-meaningful experiences, the slow learners require both an intensified and prolonged pre-academic program. It is essential to their future learning. Upon entrance to kindergarten they require a pre-kindergarten or nursery school program. Some of the oldest and most mature may require this program for only two, three, or four months; others will need it for as long as three years. If a child is developing intellectually close to the rate of a mentally handicapped child (I.Q. between 75 and 80) and by accident of birth is among the youngest of the group, it would be appropriate in most instances to have him repeat a year in the kindergarten room. Actually, it would have been preferable in most cases to have placed him initially in nursery school rather than kindergarten but few schools have these facilities available. Following the completion of a second year he will be better prepared to move on with the group, although he is still incapable of profiting from the instruction normally provided in the first grade. In the meantime he is only slightly older rather than somewhat younger than his classmates and consequently in a better position to participate with them on a relatively equal basis. Physically, emotionally, and socially he is better off than had he received an annual promotion following the completion of his first year in school.

The pre-academic program

The purposes of the pre-academic or readiness program are multifold. The order in which they will be discussed by no means is indicative of the order of their importance. They are all important, and a program is deficient if all are not included. In addition to preparing the children to benefit from academic instruction at a later date, the readiness program helps them develop positive attitudes toward learning, social skills essential to effective group participation, and behavior necessary for group learning and instruction. The time schedule for slow learners is relatively similar to that used with normal children at this level (Fig. 4). The fundamental difference in the programs is the result of emphasis, content, and time spent at this educational developmental level.

The aspects of readiness most commonly discussed are those related or essential to future academic learning. These include visual and auditory memory, visual and auditory discrimination, speech and language development, improvement of motor skills, and the inclusion of supplementary experiences children require to better understand their environment. These are often called reading-readiness activities. While they are essential to the acquisition of reading skills they are also important for other school learnings as well. These along with other activities compose the total readiness program for children performing at a pre-academic level. Among the other readiness activities fully as necessary as those mentioned are quantitative experiences, experiences with varied materials, learning to listen and follow directions, having carefully planned and controlled social experiences with other children, and understanding the values of these experiences as well as having success with them.

Innumerable planned activities of both a group and individual workbook nature are available commercially for the purpose of developing a readiness for reading. Visual discrimination is developed by teaching the child to select an object that is different from another, to find two or more objects that are alike, and to distinguish similarities and differences in size, shape, or color. Visual discrimination is essential if a child is later going to be able to note differences between the configurations of sentences and words on the charts, and words and letters and the order or sequence of letters in more advanced reading and spelling. Visual discrimination is also used in

CURRICULUM EMPHASES FOR NORMAL AND SLOW LEARNING CHILDREN—PRE-ACADEMIC LEVEL

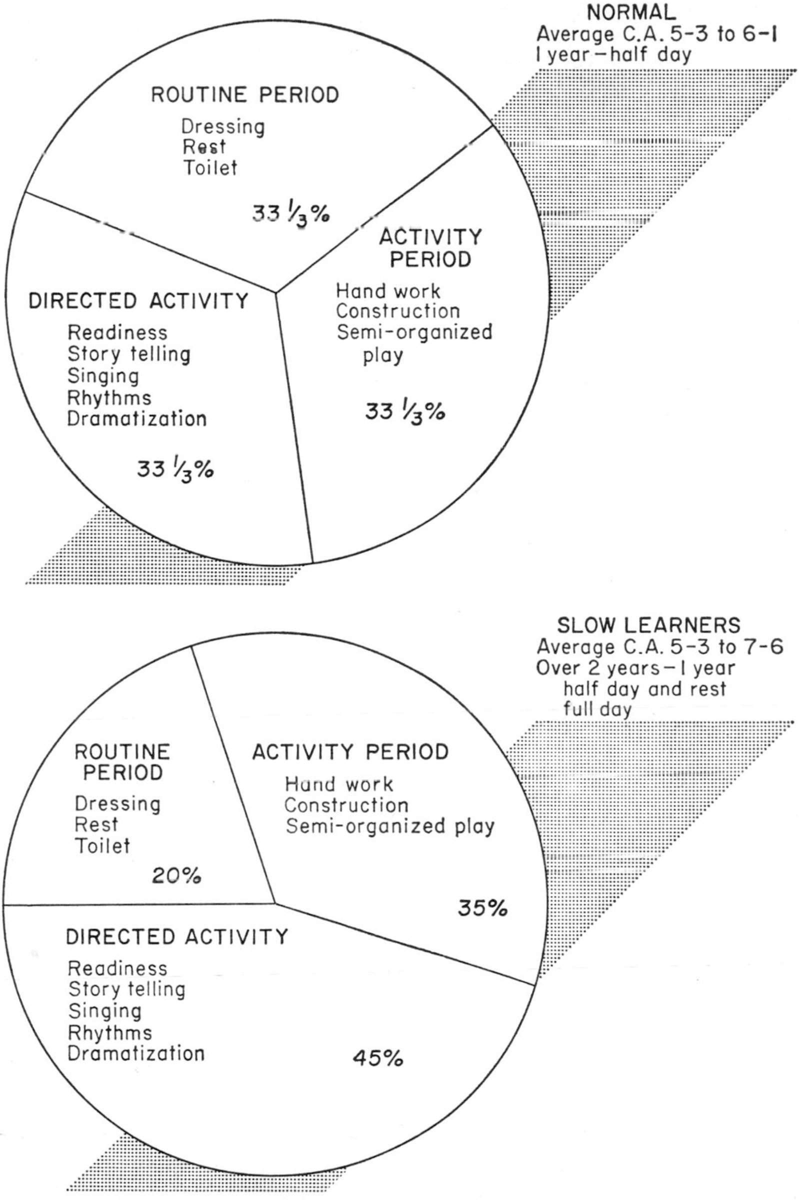

NORMAL
Average C.A. 5-3 to 6-1
1 year—half day

ROUTINE PERIOD
Dressing
Rest
Toilet

33 1/3%

ACTIVITY
PERIOD
Hand work
Construction
Semi-organized
play

33 1/3%

DIRECTED ACTIVITY
Readiness
Story telling
Singing
Rhythms
Dramatization

33 1/3%

SLOW LEARNERS
Average C.A. 5-3 to 7-6
Over 2 years—1 year
half day and rest
full day

ROUTINE
PERIOD
Dressing
Rest
Toilet
20%

ACTIVITY PERIOD
Hand work
Construction
Semi-organized play

35%

DIRECTED ACTIVITY
Readiness
Story telling
Singing
Rhythms
Dramatization

45%

Figure 4.

arithmetic for understanding relationships, differentiating between sizes and amounts, recognizing numbers, and determining signs.

Auditory discrimination is usually improved through helping the children distinguish the differences between sounds (amplitude, pitch, and quality). These activities are usually initiated with sounds that are grossly dissimilar. As the children can make the appropriate selections indicating a grasp of the principle involved as well as the ability to make differentiations at this level, sounds are presented of a successively more similar nature requiring finer and finer auditory discrimination. Rhymes and songs, and listening to records and rhythms also contribute to the improvement of performance in this area.

Reading is usually taught by the "look and say" method today. This requires good visual and auditory discrimination. Auditory discrimination is also essential at later stages in reading where the children are developing an independence of word attack. It is essential in word analysis, syllabication, use of prefixes and suffixes, and along with sound blending or synthesis in phonics. Good abilities in auditory discrimination are essential not only to the learning of reading but also in many other areas of learning. It is essential in the production of good speech, and to the understanding of all stimuli of an auditory nature. Following directions, learning any and all materials presented verbally, and better understanding of the environment are all partially or almost totally dependent upon good, accurate auditory discrimination.

Improvement of children's visual and auditory memory is usually accomplished through helping them to place a high value upon these kinds of activities and providing them with meaningful opportunities to make use of them. Sharing of experiences and relating what one has seen, heard, or experienced are all valuable activities directly related to the daily living experiences of the children. More formal kinds of activities that appear to be games to the children or which the children enjoy can be presented. The important thing is that they promote growth in abilities in these areas. Games where the children cover their eyes and a number of objects are struck require auditory memory to determine (1) how many, (2) order, and (3) which ones. For a game requiring visual memory place a number of objects on a table, have the children examine them, and then remove several. Which ones were removed?

Visual and auditory memory are important skills in the development of reading ability. It is essential to remember things seen and heard in the development of an initial sight vocabulary, associating the correct word and sound with printed symbols, and developing the use of syllables, prefixes, suffixes, and phonics essential in becoming an independent reader. While these things have been recognized for a long time and instruction is included routinely in reading readiness programs by most teachers, competence is also essential to learnings in other areas. Visual and auditory memory have purposes that carry their import well beyond reading. Instruction in almost all areas, arithmetic, science, health, social studies, and many others is dependent upon them. Instruction in general is carried on or associated with verbal instruction and visual demonstration. In order that these instructions be of value, that the individual learns as the result of them, he must remember them.

All good readiness programs include experiences designed to improve language and speech production. Common techniques used consist of providing the children with experiences preceded by an oral planning period and/or followed by a discussion. Children also are encouraged to describe and discuss classroom activities, assignments, pictures, activities—in fact, anything that is subject to description and discussion.

Most children enter school with a wide background of experience and language. In the case of the slow learners who are being raised in subcultural homes, the stimulation has usually been much less. Parents with relatively little education place much less stress upon those activities which are largely concerned with the presentation and discussion of school-centered activities than parents with more education. The entire neighborhood reflects this paucity of language stimulation so that the deprivation of the home cannot be even partially offset by the neighborhood experiences. Language experiences are essential for all children but slow learners have a much greater need for them than most children. Educators must consciously plan for the inclusion of experiences in these areas to make up for the stimuli the children have missed.

Good speech and language development will enhance the learning of reading since reading is merely putting information and ideas into language through the use of visual symbols. Its importance, however, goes far beyond reading. Verbal communication is the single most important method used to transmit ones desires, needs, ideas, explanations, descriptions, and so on. One is severely handicapped both socially and vocationally if this means of communication cannot be used effectively.

Motor skills are not usually considered to be important in the teaching of the skills thought to be the primary responsibility of the school. But even in learning to read, motor skills are of great importance. The eye must be able to focus on the appropriate word and move in the proper direction from word to word. Upon the completion of a line, the eye must be able to drop just *one* line, move to the left side of the page and repeat the process. This must be taught; children must learn this skill—witness the necessity for markers under the lines commonly used with normal children in first grade. Strauss [2] has recommended more extreme measures for brain injured children. Only one word may be presented at a time because of their inability to follow along and return to the beginning of a new line.

Other motor skills are also essential to learning. Writing requires good eye-hand coordination and the ability to copy a good example. Much instruction is provided through activities—learning through doing. One cannot do satisfactorily without good motor skills. Even turning the pages of a book requires motor skills and coordination. More highly developed skills are required in arts, crafts, industrial arts, and home-making activities—activities that are an integral part of most curriculums. In the more academic areas, experiments in science, physics, and biology require good coordination if the student is to derive the greatest possible benefit from the instruction provided him.

The broader field of health is also essential in helping ensure children's best learning performance. This is the reasoning behind the inclusion of health, physical education, and nutritional programs (milk, noon lunches, and so forth) in the school. It is true that there is little or no evidence that a child in good physical health will acquire more from instruction than one who is not. But, a child must be able to attend school regularly or he will miss much of the instruction. Slow learners, having a higher incidence of minor physical and sensory handicaps, require more attention regarding their

2 Alfred A. Strauss and Laura Lehtinen, *The Psychopathology and Education of the Brain Injured Child* (New York: Grune and Stratton, 1947), 206 pages.

physical and motor development than is true for normal children. The tendency toward unhygienic conditions in the home as well as inadequate diet means that slow learners are not taught these things incidentally in the same way as their normal peers. Finally, with restricted intellectual abilities and potential, slow learners are usually going to earn their livings through their physical activity and effort. If they have not learned the importance of good health and how to maintain and promote it, or if their motor skills have not been sufficiently developed, they will be unable to perform at their appropriate level of effectiveness. They will be unable to make their best community and economic adjustment and to contribute to the welfare of the society as they should. Many of the practices essential to good health are or can become habitual in nature. Thus, attention must be drawn to them in the pre-academic program with continuous emphasis and practice throughout the school life of the children.

The slow learners also need a more systematically presented and extended program in the other readiness areas than do normal children. The learning of quantitative and numerical relationships will enable them to derive greater benefit from arithmetic instruction at a later date. Such concepts as more, less, greater, smaller, longer, shorter, higher, lower, later, first, last, middle, and so forth are essential. These are concepts they can and should be using.

Other experiences, not as directly related to future formal learning but nevertheless fully as important must also be included. Children coming from environments where little value is placed upon academic skills and the learnings fostered by the school must learn the values and importance of these learnings. The revelation that books contain interesting stories and may be used for answering questions that arise may help the children to understand the need for reading and stimulate their desire to learn. Similar kinds of experiences must be introduced in the other skills and informational areas. In this way the desire to learn is developed, making the job of instruction easier and the learning more effective. In this way more learning takes place.

Many of the basic attitudes the children will carry with them throughout their school lives as well as the attitudes they will have toward school during their post-school, adult years can be established during the years in the pre-academic and primary programs.

If positive attitudes and meaningful experiences are emphasized and provided here, the succeeding levels need only continue in the same fashion.

Children normally enter school being essentially individualistic in nature. They are almost exclusively interested in *me* and *mine*. They have had contact with other children of the same age only on a limited basis, having had opportunities to play with only the few others who may reside in their immediate neighborhood. Entering school and learning the complexities of living with a large group of children is a great change. They must learn behavior that is appropriate for that environment. They must also learn what behavior is appropriate for the activity being carried on. They learn to follow directions, to listen, to explain and describe, to live with a large group without interfering with the rights of others, to cooperate, to share, and many more things essential to school success.

While there is no reason to suspect that slow learners deviate from normal children in their learning characteristics and their ability to acquire these skills, certain factors must be kept in mind. Because their intellectual development is somewhat slower than normal and the ability to acquire these skills follows a developmental sequence, it may be necessary for the teacher to delay their instruction. This doesn't mean that the slow learner merely waits. Essential pre-readiness activities of a nursery school nature should be introduced until the child is capable of benefiting from kindergarten-type activities. Kindergarten activities are continued until the child is ready for first grade activities, and so on. A second important consideration is the attitudes fostered by the home and neighborhood. A subcultural home in a subcultural area will not provide the child with many of the experiences and attitudes considered of importance by the school whether the child is a slow learner or of normal intelligence. It is, therefore, the responsibility of the school to make additional provisions for the development of these attitudes and to offer contacts with those experiences considered essential to enable the child to learn.

The academic program

The academic aspects of the primary grades for slow learners is very similar to the program for children in general. The emphasis is initially placed on reading instruction with provision for the

CURRICULUM EMPHASES FOR NORMAL AND SLOW
LEARNING CHILDREN—PRIMARY SCHOOL

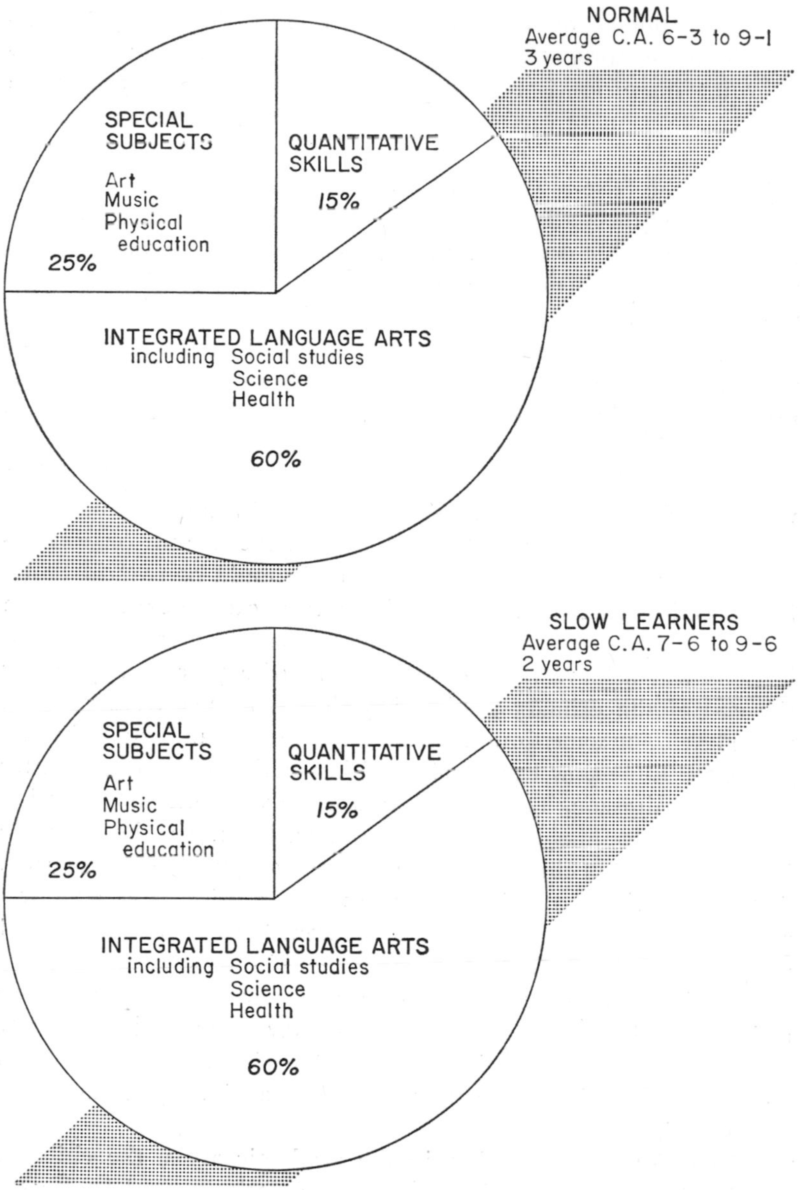

NORMAL
Average C.A. 6-3 to 9-1
3 years

SPECIAL
SUBJECTS

Art
Music
Physical
education

25%

QUANTITATIVE
SKILLS

15%

INTEGRATED LANGUAGE ARTS
including Social studies
Science
Health

60%

SLOW LEARNERS
Average C.A. 7-6 to 9-6
2 years

SPECIAL
SUBJECTS

Art
Music
Physical
education

25%

QUANTITATIVE
SKILLS

15%

INTEGRATED LANGUAGE ARTS
including Social studies
Science
Health

60%

Figure 5.

development of writing, spelling, and arithmetic skills. The times allotted to the various activities for slow learners should also be about the same as for normal children (Fig. 5). The primary difference is in the content and instructional level. While most of the following discussion is related to instruction in the language arts and development of quantitative concepts and abilities, it will be noted that time should also be assigned to the special subjects.

One of the false assumptions often made by teachers is that the slow learners form a homogeneous group. They do to a certain extent, insofar as the curriculum is concerned within a specific school setting; they do not for curriculum in general or for instructional purposes. Table II indicates the spread of achievement that can be expected under an annual promotion policy. Even with the use of selective, restricted retention practiced under a philosophy of "social promotion," only the most retarded will not be present in the indicated groups after kindergarten or first grade.

Instruction, to be of the greatest value, must be provided just when the child is ready for it. The oldest and brightest among the slow learners are ready (intellectually) to benefit from reading instruction by the middle or first grade and should be reading at 1.7 by the end of that year. This is higher than can be expected from some of the youngest, most immature normal children. These slow learners will achieve eight or nine-tenths of a year each year. By the end of the primary grades they should be performing at 3.4 grade level. For some slow learners, formal instruction starts in first grade. For some slow learners formal instruction starts in the latter part of third grade. The last group are the youngest and most immature, who could only be expected to be achieving at the 1.2 grade level at the end of third grade if promoted annually. Kindergarten, first, second, and most of third grade would consist of pre-readiness and readiness programs for these children. On an average, formal academic instruction for slow learners should start about the middle of second grade. By the end of that grade they should be achieving at least at 1.6 grade level. Their rate of development academically should be about eight-tenths of a year for each year spent in school. At the end of third grade they should be achieving at 2.3 or 2.4 grade level.

In addition to instruction in the academic areas, the children should have art, music, physical education, science, and health experiences appropriate to their level and psycho-social and physical background. Basic curriculum materials prepared for use with normal children are appropriate if introduced at the correct developmental time, and if they take into consideration the physical, social, and emotional needs of the children, thus helping them to better understand their environment and participate more effectively in it.

THE INTERMEDIATE SCHOOL

Characteristics of the children

The characteristics of slow learning children in the fourth, fifth, and sixth grade levels in regard to physical development, socioeconomic status, and attitudes are essentially the same as was true for those in the primary grades. They tend to reside in culturally depressed environments and are somewhat below the norm in physical and motor development. If their initial school experiences have been frustrating ones where they have continuously faced situations in which they cannot help but fail, their initial attitudes of dislike for school have been re-enforced. Every year they learn to dislike school and all that it stands for more acutely.

This is unfortunately true more often than not as school programs presently exist. These attitudes are now, at the intermediate level, more apt to be "acted out" by the slow learners in forms of aggressive, antisocial behavior than was true at the primary level. The children are becoming older, somewhat more independent, and with attitudes that are stronger and better defined. Behavior problems in the classroom can be expected to become more common and more acute where no special program is available. Deviate, antisocial behavior may also appear in the home and community because appropriate behavior has not been taught in the home or learned in school due to the negative attitudes that have been developed. This deviate behavior may also be appropriate if children belong to "gangs" where according to the value system of the group such behavior is approved. Thus, antisocial behavior may become desirable behavior according to the values of their social group.

Tables III and IV summarize the characteristics of normal children in regard to chronological age for grades four, five, and six, and of slow learners in regard to chronological age, mental age, and the

TABLE III

Chronological Ages of Children Enrolled in the
Intermediate Grades—September 1 and June 30

Grade Level	Ages of Normal Children				Ages of Slow Learners			
	September 1		June 30		September 1		June 30	
	Spread	Average	Spread	Average	Spread	Average	Spread	Average
Fourth	8-9 to 9-9	9-3	9-7 to 10-7	10-1	9-3 to 10-5	9-10	10-1 to 11-3	10-8
Fifth	9-9 to 10-9	10-3	10-7 to 11-7	11-1	10-5 to 11-7	11-0	11-3 to 12-5	11-10
Sixth	10-9 to 11-9	11-3	11-7 to 12-7	12-1	11-7 to 12-9	12-2	12-5 to 13-7	13-0

TABLE IV

Approximate Mental Ages and Appropriate Grade-Level Achievements for
Slow Learners Enrolled in the Primary Grades—September 1 and June 30

Grade Level	Mental Age				Grade Achievement			
	September 1		June 30		September 1		June 30	
	Spread	Average	Spread	Average	Spread	Average	Spread	Average
Fourth	6-11 to 8-9	7-10	7-7 to 9-6	8-7	1.6 to 3.5	2.6	2.3 to 4.2	3.3
Fifth	7-10 to 9-8	8-9	8-5 to 10-5	9-5	2.6 to 4.4	3.5	3.2 to 5.2	4.2
Sixth	8-8 to 10-7	9-8	9-4 to 11-4	10-4	3.4 to 5.3	4.4	4.2 to 6.0	5.1

academic achievement that can be anticipated. Normal children attending the intermediate grades (four, five and six) are between 8 years-9 months and 11 years-9 months of age at the start of the school year in September. By June, 10 months have been added to the age of each child so that the spread would be from 9 years-7 months for the youngest child in the fourth grade to 12 years-7 months for the oldest normal child completing sixth grade. The average ages of normal children in fourth, fifth, and sixth grades would be 9-3, 10-3 and 11-3 for September and 10-1, 11-1, and 12-1 for June.

The chronological ages for slow learners would be somewhat greater than for normal children because of the occasional retention practiced throughout the grades. The chronological age difference between the slow learners and normal children would also become greater with each succeeding grade level. By the completion of sixth grade, the slow learners would tend to be almost one year older than their normal peers. At the fourth grade level the difference in ages would be expected to be only about 7 months.

Table IV shows the approximate mental age distributions at the appropriate grade levels for slow learners. The mental ages of the slow learners in September at the start of fourth grade would range from about 6 years-11 months to 8 years-9 months. The average would be 7 years-8 months or 1 year-7 months lower than the average for their normal classmates. During that school year, the slowest could be expected to grow about seven and one-half months and the fastest to grow about 9 months. These mental ages could be expected to be reflected in an academic achievement grade-level performance ranging from 1.6 to 3.5 in September and 2.3 to 4.2 in June. The average grade-achievement level for slow learners in September and June of fourth grade would thus be 2.6 and 3.3 respectively. After 5 or 6 years of school attendance, one in kindergarten and 4 or 5 in the grades where formal academic instruction in the skills had been the primary focus of the program, the average slow learner would be retarded over one and one-half years in academic achievement.

Similar information in regard to grades 5 and 6 can also be obtained from Table IV. The average grade-achievement level for slow learners in grade 5 will be 3.5 in September and 4.2 in June. For sixth grade, the average achievement will be 4.4 and 5.1 in

September and June respectively. Despite the policy of selective retention of young, immature, non-achieving children practiced by most schools, causing the slow learners to become older and older than their classmates, the discrepancies between their average achievement and the average achievement of normal children becomes greater and greater. At the beginning of fourth grade, the slow learners are only 0.6 or 0.7 grades below grade level in their achievement. By the end of sixth grade, they are averaging 1.3 grades behind their grade placement.

A closer examination of Tables III and IV makes it quite obvious that much heterogeneity exists even among the slow learners. This is particularly true for their intellectual development and academic achievement. These variations are caused by differences in ages and differences in rates of development among the children. The discrepancies in mental ages range from 1 year-10 months at the beginning of fourth grade to 2 years at the end of sixth grade. The discrepancies in academic achievement range from 1.8 to 2.0 grades. The selective retention policy has tended to keep the distribution or spread of ability and achievement relatively constant. But where they are placed with normal children it has been at the expense of making the slow learners the oldest children in the group, in spite of the fact that they still fall farther and farther behind the class. Considering just the slow learners, however, with about a 2-year distribution of abilities and achievement within one grade, a great deal of sub-grouping and individualizng of instruction will be required. Only in this way would it be possible to provide equal opportunty to learn. There is a great deal of difference between 2.0 (completion of first grade) and 4.0 (completion of third grade) achievement.

Aside from variations in age and mental development, other factors may cause variations in achievement levels. Because a child is a slow learner does not mean that he is immune from also becoming a remedial problem. Numerous factors are present that may cause a higher incidence of remedial problems among slow learners than among normal children. The higher incidence of sensory disabilities, particularly in the visual and auditory areas can be causitive factors. More absence due to truancy or disease causing the child to miss instruction may also be influential. Within the regular classroom setting, these factors are often offset by conscientious teachers who devote a disproportionate amount of time and effort to the slow learners. The teachers' efforts are not always realistic in that their purpose is to bring the slow learners up to grade level and may result in frustrations for all concerned. Their problem is not remediable. A more appropriate objective is to stimulate the slow learners to generally achieve at or near their intellectual potential.

The intermediate program

The academic program of the upper elementary or intermediate grades is a continuation and extension of the program initiated at the primary level. Between 50 and 60 per cent of the day should be devoted to formal instruction in the academic skills areas (including reading, writing, spelling, and arithmetic). The other 40 to 50 per cent is devoted to science, social studies, and special subjects including art, music, physical education, and so forth (Fig. 6).

At the beginning of fourth grade, the slowest child should be performing at least at the beginning first grade level and probably somewhat higher due to selective retention practices. The most advanced slow learner should be performing at the middle third grade level (Table IV). It can be expected that with instruction being provided at the children's levels, the slowest ones will achieve approximately three-fourths of one year during each of the three years they are in the intermediate grades, for a total academic achievement of two and one-fourth years. The fastest or brightest of the slow learners may achieve as much as nine-tenths of a year for each year attended, or almost two and three-fourths years during the three year period. These achievement rates should be generally true for all skill areas.

The unit of experience has been found to be a very effective teaching method to use with slow learning children. Ingram [3] lists seven essential criteria for the selection of a unit.

1) Units should be evolved from life experiences of the children. When an area with which all the children have not had direct contact is in need of study, a preparatory discussion and trip are essential. The

[3] Christine P. Ingram, *Education of the Slow-Learning Child,* 3rd ed. New York: The Ronald Press Company, 1960, 390 pages.

CURRICULUM EMPHASES FOR NORMAL AND SLOW
LEARNING CHILDREN—INTERMEDIATE SCHOOL

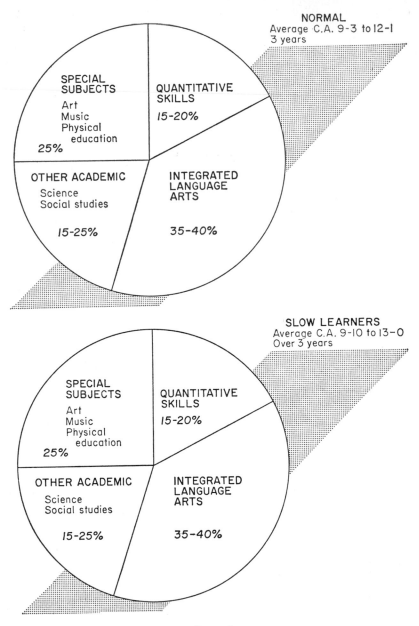

Figure 6.

unit thus develops directly from the interests of the children, but with the guidance of the teachers.

2) The children's mental, social, and physical development are determinants in the choice of the unit. In other words, the unit selected is appropriate for each child's developmental level.

3) Both individual and group participation should be fostered by the unit. Relating this determinant to 2), each child has activities related to *his* developmental level but in addition, the unit also provides experiences in cooperation and learning to work together toward a group goal.

4) Opportunities for growth in basic skills, knowledges, and attitudes are provided in the unit. Thus, it includes not only academic experiences but planned experiences to promote the development of healthy attitudes and social skills through the selection of activities.

5) The unit is not solely school centered. It helps develop an awareness of and interest in out-of-school activities in order that the child may be able to participate in them more effectively.

6) In addition to 4), opportunities should be provided for the utilization of the tool subjects and skills in the unit. The child not only learns the skill or acquires the knowledge but also understands why he should learn it and how to use it.

7) Since the purpose of the unit is to reduce the restrictiveness of subject-matter-centered instruction, it should include a variety of experiences. The inclusion of a variety of experiences aids in ensuring comprehension of knowledge as well as application. In addition, varieties of experiences may be essential to make the learnings meaningful to the children of various developmental levels normally found within the classroom.

It is thought by many teachers that the primary purpose of the unit is to provide the children with real- or near-life situations in the classroom. In this way the children can be taught the application of learning to the specific situation in which they will be used. This is far from the truth and has inherent in it the same restrictions as a strict subject-matter approach. *The purpose of experience-unit instruction is not to provide the child with the life situations in which to apply skills learned in order that he will be able to use them in these situations.* If this were true, then within an educational program it would be necessary to include units concerned with any and every activity in which the individual might ever participate. In addition, since the society and economy are changing rapidly, and these changes cannot be completely predicted at least in their detail, it would be essential that school programs be designed for life. As soon as new situations arose the individual would have to return to school to learn how to cope with them.

The purpose of an experience unit is to provide meaning and value or purpose to learning. The unit is a vehicle, an experience within the understanding of the student to which learnings can be associated. In this way he can better understand the learnings. Skills and knowledge are given meaning, are given value. The student has a purpose in learning. He consequently obtains a better grasp of materials taught, understands them instead of using rote memorization, and with understanding can better apply or use them. The unit thus forms two of the three sides of a triangle of learning or instruction. First, the teacher through the use of an experience familiar to the children (the unit) can demonstrate the need. At this stage, the unit is also used to develop the basic concepts involved. Second, the student is instructed in the concepts and skills in the most efficient manner possible. In the case of skills (reading, arithmetic, spelling, and so forth) this instruction may be completely unrelated to the unit. Third, the unit provides an opporitunty to re-enforce the learning by application and also to learn the principles appropriate to the general application of the skills and knowledges learned.

When unit instruction is used correctly, the specific topic selected is not too important as long as it meets the seven established criteria. It is unnecessary to attempt to use units that will include *all* life experiences. At times, one unit may be repeated for the same children using different activities and experiences to meet different objectives. When units are used correctly, the children learn the concepts involved, become efficient through practice of the mechanics, and learn how to use the concepts in *any* and *all* situations that are appropriate. They are taught with an objective of generalization, application, and transfer of principles rather than with the restrictive approach of transfer of identical elements. Unit instruction is *not* for the purpose of learning the skill in the situation in which it will be used and for use in that situation alone.

The experiences units are built around the science, social studies, and health needs and experiences of the children. One of the more difficult tasks of the teacher is locating reading materials of an appropriate interest level, with content that provides for the children's needs that are written at the reading levels of slow learning children. This is particularly true for the slowest members of the group as it has been true for the educable mentally handicapped ever since programs for them were instituted. No one text can provide for all their needs. Rather, resource materials (or numerous texts written at different grade levels of difficulty and used as reference books) will prove to be far more satisfactory. Discussions and activities are then related to topics rather than to assigned pages or chapters. For most topics selected, materials at several graded levels are available for use, thus providing for all the children. Each child will usually have available to him resources he has need for, written at a level he is capable of using. Upon occasion it may be necessary for the teacher to prepare materials if commercial books or pamphlets are not available. Standard, graded vocabulary should be used by the teacher in preparing these materials but the materials should not be confused with or substituted for the carefully graded materials used for developmental reading instruction.

The center of the program, aside from skill instruction, at the primary level was largely related to the development of social skills and helping the children to become more familiar with their local or immediate environment. It was primarily concerned with where the children live (their homes) and where their homes, the school, and other buildings, housing agencies, or businesses of importance to them are located (their neighborhood). They learned about the function of these facilities and their appropriate participation in them. When the slow learners were promoted to the intermediate grades, it did not necessarily mean that they had learned all there was for them to know about their immediate environment. Neither did it mean that specific reference and study of the home and neighborhood was finished and that all future study would be exclusively devoted to a broader, more all-encompassing approach to their environment.

The physical, social, and health aspects of the homes and neighborhood should be re-examined at the intermediate grades level. This time the approach should be from the point of view and the experiences of ten-, eleven-, twelve-, and thirteen-year-old children. They are still residing in the same environments as they were while enrolled in the primary grades. But their position in the home and

neighborhood and their functions in relation to the home and neighborhood have changed. They are older, more mature, and more
knowledgeable citizens of the community. They have changed from
a status of almost complete dependence to one of lesser dependence
and have a potential for some contribution. Within the home they
can begin to assume some responsibility for their own belongings.
They can begin to contribute to the welfare of the home by assuming the responsibility for carrying out simple family tasks related to
family eating and general living. While the home may be of such a
nature that such activities are either not required of the children
or not taught in terms of appropriate performance of them, the
school can do a great deal in this direction. By performing these
helpful activities, the children may in time actually improve the
psycho-social, physical, and hygienic conditions of their environment
within the home.

What is true for the home is also true of the neighborhood environment, their understanding of it, and their learning to make
the most of it. The existence of the police and fire department, association and neighborhood houses, and other social agencies was
introduced to the slow learners in the primary program. At the
intermediate level they are capable of more than just recognizing
the fireman and policeman as friends, regardless of their community's attitudes. They are becoming capable of understanding their
functions and more specifically how they can help them or call upon
them in times of need. The same development of more mature
understanding, use, and participation is true in regard to other
social agencies within their area and available for their use. Despite
the fine work performed by many of these agencies, they can have
little or no influence if the persons for whom they are organized
do not take advantage of their facilities.

Thus, the social sciences continue to be centered around the individual's relationships to other persons within the context of his
environment as well as promoting a broadened understanding of
his community. By the time the slow learners have completed the
intermediate grades they are moving freely about the community.
A planned sequence of experiences will help them understand the
community better. With improved understanding will come improved participation.

The regular social studies program of the intermediate grades is usually an introduction to world geography. At this time most children learn the names of the oceans, continents, nations, and their most important features. A far more realistic approach for slow learners is to devote this time to learning more about their community as it presently exists with visits to places of interest and importance. This study should also include the relationship of the community to the state and nation geographically, economically, historically, and politically insofar as the slow learners are capable of understanding it. These kinds of knowledges help the student to understand the characteristics of the community and the people residing in that community. In this relationship, visits to historical markers and buildings, city and county buildings, museums, centers of transportaton, and so forth are not only appropriate, they are essential. Finally, wherever possible find and develop situations where the children actually become involved in the life of the community. This involvement should be an integral part of the junior and senior high school programs but is valuable even at the intermediate level.

The physical science program should be much like that recommended for the regular intermediate grades. Like the social science program, the focus should be the physical environment of the children. The purpose of the program (including natural science) is to help the children better understand their physical environment and its natural phenomena in order that they may be better able to cope with it. Numerous commercial texts and materials have been prepared for use in the upper elementary grades. A careful selection of activities from these materials, with ample use of demonstration and experimentation, should provide a stimulating and valuable program.

Health and hygiene continue to be important problems at the intermediate level as they were at the primary level. If a good start was made toward the development of good health habits in the primary grades, the teachers of the intermediate grades should only find it necessary to provide appropriate facilities and occasionally re-enforce the things taught earlier—washing, showering, teeth brushing, general grooming, and so forth. In addition, the teacher should now emphasize the reasons for doing these things so that the children understand the need for them. At this level the children may also be introduced to simple hand washing of clothes. It is important, however, that the activities be realistic in reference to the children's needs and abilities to perform them under the kinds of home conditions in which they are so often living. Only through realistic programs that the children see a need for and that can be carried out can one expect they will improve the hygienic conditions in their homes. They cannot be taught in terms of a middle-class, suburban, split-level environment when their knowledges, experiences, and probable future is centered around a lower-class tenement environment.

The slow learners should never be permitted to miss any aspect of the total school health program. When they are absent for any examination or treatment, arrangements should be made for them to receive the service upon their return. Visual and hearing examinations, general pediatric examinations, dental examinations, and periodic communicable disease inoculations often provided through the schools are of great importance to slow learners. In the previous chapters the higher incidence of disease and physical disability was mentioned. The factors causing or aggravating these conditions are still present at the intermediate level and must be dealt with continuously. This also includes improved nutrition through noon lunch programs, mid-morning food supplement programs, and so forth.

The intermediate program for slow learners differs the least from that provided normal children in the special subjects areas—art, music, and physical education. While the great artist and great musician must have superior intelligence, slow learners are sufficiently intelligent and close enough to average to be able to both enjoy and perform creditably in these areas. Much of the art activity should be related to the unit activities in which the children and class are engaged. Other art activities are for fun, related to holidays, and for the purpose of learning techniques to improve communication or expression. These should also be included. Many of the same things can be said in regard to the music program.

Physical education is important for slow learners. It should include formal exercise as well as games or recreational activities. With generally poorer physical and motor abilities, they need to develop these skills at least to the point where they will be able to perform adequately. Formal exercise is good for correction and physical development as well as for improvement of motor skills.

However, this must be accompanied by games and recreational activities, for only in this way will these abilities be put to use not only in school but also in the children's out-of-school activities. The recreational program is dependent upon two things, physical and motor skills and intellectual development. Slow learners will tend to be interested and capable of effective participation in those activities at their intellectual developmental level. They will not grasp the complexities of advanced team play. They will do well in individual activities and will enjoy team activities if played at a somewhat lower organizational level than for normal children of the same age.

The academic skills aspect of the curriculum at the intermediate level requires little discussion. It is essentially the same as that proposed by sound texts in the reading and arithmetic areas. Instruction must be at each child's level of development and planned to help him grow and improve as rapidly as possible. All the slow learners should be capable of some academic performance at the start of the intermediate grades and progress from two and one-fourth to two and three-fourth years during that three year period is to be expected. By the completion of sixth grade, the achievement spread in reading and arithmetic should be between 3.4 and 6.0 grades. The average achievement should be at the 4.7 grade level at the least. The kinds of skills and concepts developed in the elementary schools generally at these levels are basic and appropriate for slow learners.

Spelling and writing skills should also be included in the program. Spelling should not be taught with reading. First, it isn't necessary to be able to spell every word that is read. Second, phonics used for development of independence of word attack in reading is not particularly appropriate for accurate spelling. There are separate and discrete rules of spelling the children need to learn. In addition, spelling should be associated with the written work of the children since it is the words they use in written communication that must be spelled correctly.

Along the same line of reasoning, every written lesson is a writing lesson. Where manuscript writing is taught at the primary level during the initial reading development stages, as the children become more efficient in their reading they may desire or it may be appropriate to teach cursive writing. Whichever form of writing is selected and used by the children, they should have a good, correct form or example to imitate. Only through correct practice and improvement of eye-hand coordination as it relates to writing will a clear, legible hand be developed—the objective of the writing program.

SUMMARY

Slow learners in the primary and intermediate schools are about the same ages as normal children attending programs at the same levels. It may be advantageous to occasionally retain a young, immature slow learner at one level for an extra year in order that he will be able to derive greater benefit from his education. He would complete the primary program in five rather than the normal four years or the intermediate program in four rather than three years. Thus, by the completion of the total elementary program, the group of slow learners may be, on an average, almost one year older than their normal peers.

This slight age difference would in itself make little difference in the instructional program. The basic factors influencing the program at the primary and intermediate levels for slow learners are (1) their intellectual and academic retardation, (2) their restricted psycho-social stimulation and cultural experiences, and (3) their somewhat defective physical and motor development and health.

Whenever the teacher is preparing the child for the learning of a new skill or concept (developing a readiness for learning) the slow learners' environmental restrictions must be taken into consideration. The realistic selection of appropriate kinds of educational experiences, particularly in the physical and natural sciences, social sciences, and hygiene areas, must be determined by both the needs of the children and an appraisal of their environment. Slow learners generally come from the low socio-economic, subcultural homes of the community. They and their families generally belong to the lower class. Many times the value systems of persons residing in these areas are at variance with the laws and behavioral expectations of the total community. The preparation of an individual for effective participation in a total society is a primary objective of education. The program, however, must be planned within the context of the learners' environment—what they bring with them to school.

The physical science, natural science, social science, and hygiene programs for slow learners (in reflecting their needs, their characteristics, and their environment) should differ considerably from programs planned for children with normal intelligence and reflecting a background of quite a different nature.

The skills (reading, arithmetic, spelling, and writing) should be thought of as tools rather than subjects or ends in themselves. As tools they are important to all persons, including the slow learners. Much of the primary program for slow learners should place a stress on instruction of readiness for learning these skills and the initial instruction in them. At the intermediate level, approximately 50 or 60 per cent of the time should be devoted to development and improved use of these tools.

One of the most effective methods of developing a need for and competence in the application of the skills or tools is through the use of experience units. The three steps of instruction consist of (1) developing the need and basic concept (unit instruction), (2) developing efficient, accurate use of the skill (formal instruction and practice), and (3) emphasis on learning principles involved in general application or use of the skill (unit instruction). Used in this fashion, the unit of experience is placed in its proper context. The purpose of the unit is to help the learners to better understand the basic skills and concepts being taught by relating the instruction to experiences familiar to the children. By obtaining a grasp of the concepts involved, the learner will then be able to use them in any and all applicable situations. Instruction thus approaches its maximum level of effectiveness. For slow learners this is probably more important than for normal children. When normal children "learn" a skill or concept, they usually achieve sufficient intellectual development eventually to understand the implications in relation to application. Educators cannot depend upon slow learners ever achieving this level of intelligence.

SELECTED RELATED READINGS

Beaber, James D., *The Performance of Educable Mentally Handicapped and Intellectually Normal Children on Selected Tasks Involving Simple Motor Performance* (Unpublished Doctoral Dissertation, Syracuse University, 1960), 146 pages.

Featherstone, William B., "Grouping in Relation to the Education of Slow Learners," *Exceptional Children,* 14:172–75, March, 1948.

Hull, J. H., "Multigrade Teaching," *The Nations Schools,* 62:33–37, July, 1958.

Ingram, Christine P., *Education of the Slow-Learning Child,* 3rd ed. New York: The Ronald Press Company, 1960, 390 pages.

Kirk, Samuel A., "The Slow Learner—Remedial Work in the Elementary School," *N. E. A. Journal,* 48:24–25, October, 1959.

Liddle, Gordon and D. Long, "Experimental Room for Slow Learners," *Elementary School Journal,* 59:143–49, December, 1958.

Mahoney, Agnes, "The Slow Learner," *N. E. A. Journal,* 47:618–21, December, 1958.

Neel, F. G., "Work of the Junior 1B.," *National Elementary Principal,* 21:42–47, October, 1941.

Strauss, Alfred A. and Laura Lehtinen, *The Psychopathology and Education of the Brain Injured Child.* New York: Grune and Stratton, 1947, 206 pages.

Sullivan, Helen B., "Skills Instruction for the Slow-Learning Child in the Regular Classroom," *National Elementary Principal,* 29:41–46, December, 1949.

6

The Junior and Senior
High Schools

The junior high school incorporates the last two years of the traditional elementary school and the first year of the traditional senior high school. It is theoretically designed to specifically meet the needs of the pre-adolescent who has out-grown the elementary school but has not matured sufficiently to benefit from the social activities and program of the senior high school. In some ways it acts as a bridge between the elementary school and the secondary school although many persons conceive of it as a part of the latter category.

As the junior high school developed, teachers with academic majors and secondary education minors, trained for high school instruction, were selected as instructors. Some small trend is now becoming apparent whereby elementary teachers may also be certified as teachers in the junior high school. The problems presented by children enrolled in the junior high school indicate that a dual need is present. These children are still developing intellectually, physically, socially, and emotionally so that they require a continuation of developmental skill instruction to attain their maximum achievement in these areas. The development, however, is gradually slowing down and approaching a plateau that will be achieved by most children in the early years of senior high school. Consequently, they also require an introductory program that will acquaint them with the kinds of specialized instruction that will be available in the senior high school, instruction that is designed to help them makes the greatest use of the intellectual development they have achieved.

The senior high school, then, must be ready to provide the various kinds of terminal education programs required by students with varying potentials and objectives. College preparatory programs must be available for some. Technical training preparatory programs must be available to others. Courses introducing the students to business, trade, and commerce also must be provided. For a fairly substantial group the high school is going to be the terminal education program. From high school they are going directly into the work of the community. How good and conscientious citizens they become and how effectively they maintain themselves may depend rather directly upon the experiences provided them during their senior high school years. The training for this group must be completed here because no other educational institution will have a chance. A substantial proportion of this group are slow learners.

Senior high schools in different communities and in different areas of large urban centers should emphasize somewhat different programs, depending upon the characteristics of the students attending that school. Few public high schools are fortunate enough, however, to be able to eliminate any one of the programs entirely; there is never lack of demand or a lack of need. Among the few exceptions may be the technical high schools designed to provide for a specific need and servicing a number of general high school districts, and the predominantly college preparatory high schools catering to the children of executives and professional personnel residing in a preferred suburb of a large urban center. Usually, senior high schools must provide a variety of programs, including one for slow learners. The fact that about two out of every five children who start first grade never complete the secondary school program as it is presently constituted indicates that most senior high schools have failed to institute an adequate program for the slow learners. There is little question that one of the primary reasons students leave school at 16 years of age is because the program provided them has not been a satisfying one. They have not seen that it has value for them, and unless it has been designed with their needs and characteristics in mind, it certainly does not have the values that it could and should have.

THE JUNIOR HIGH SCHOOL

Characteristics of the children

There is probably more variability found among the children enrolled in the junior high school than during any other comparable three-year period of life. Following a general promotional scheme of "passing" most of the children annually, the majority of the children enrolled in junior high school will be between 11 years-9 months and 14 years-9 months of age at the start of the school year in September (Table V). At the close of the school year in June, the average seventh grader will be 13 years-1 month, the average eighth grader 14 years-1 month, and the average ninth grader 15 years-1 month of age. Slow learners will be from 13 to 15 months older, on an average, than normal children with the difference continuing to become greater for most of them with each succeeding year.

The majority of the children, including the slow learners, enter junior high school as pre-adolescents, appearing and behaving no differently from the older children attending the intermediate school. During the normal three and occasional four years they are in attendance in the junior high school, dramatic changes take place. Most of the children achieve adolescence during this period of time. They graduate looking, and in some ways behaving, like young men and women.

The approximate mental ages and appropriate corresponding expected achievement levels for slow learners enrolled in the junior

TABLE V

Chronological Ages of Children Enrolled in the
Junior High School—September 1 and June 30

| | Ages of Normal Children | | | | Ages of Slow Learners | | | |
| | September 1 | | June 30 | | September 1 | | June 30 | |
Grade Level	Spread	Average	Spread	Average	Spread	Average	Spread	Average
Seventh	11–9 to 12–9	12–3	12–7 to 13–7	13–1	12–9 to 13–11	13–4	13–7 to 14–9	14–2
Eighth	12–9 to 13–9	13–3	13–7 to 14–7	14–1	13–9 to 15–1	14–5	14–7 to 15–11	15–3
Ninth	13–9 to 14–9	14–3	14–7 to 15–7	15–1	14–9 to 16–3	15–6	15–7 to 17–1	16–4

TABLE VI

Approximate Mental Ages and Appropriate Grade-Level Achievements for
Slow Learners Enrolled in the Junior High School—September 1 and June 30

| | Mental Age | | | | Grade Achievement | | | |
| | September 1 | | June 30 | | September 1 | | June 30 | |
Grade Level	Spread	Average	Spread	Average	Spread	Average	Spread	Average
Seventh	9–6 to 11–4	10–5	10–1 to 12–0	11–1	3.5 to 5.3	4.4	4.0 to 6.0	5.0
Eighth	10–1 to 12–1	11–1	10–6 to 12–6	11–6	4.0 to 6.0	5.0	4.5 to 6.5	5.5
Ninth	10–7 to 12–7	11–7	11–0 to 13–0	12–0	4.6 to 6.6	5.6	5.0 to 7.0	6.0

high school are contained in Table VI. The slow learners in seventh, eighth, and ninth grades are continuing to develop intellectually, approaching their ultimate capacity while in ninth grade. The spread of mental ages that might be expected in September of seventh grade is between 9 years-6 months and 11 years-4 months, with an average of 10 years-5 months. These mental ages should be accompanied by a grade-achievement level between 3.5 and 5.3, with an average of 4.4. By June of that year, the average mental age of the slow learners should be 11 years-1 month, with an average grade achievement level of 5.0. The mental ages would continue to increase approximately 6 months for each of the 2 succeeding years (eighth and ninth grades) with the expected grade-achievement levels also showing about one-half year growth each year. At the completion of ninth grade, the mental ages of the slow learners should range from 11 years-0 months to 13 years-0 months with an achievement grade level range from 5.0 to 7.0. The average mental age of slow learners completing ninth grade would be 12.0, with a grade expectancy of 6.0. Thus, at the completion of ninth grade one would expect that the slow learners would be, on an average, over a year older than normal ninth graders and achieving approximately 4 years below grade level, since the average grade achievement upon the completion of ninth grade should be 10.0.

According to available studies, a substantial proportion of the slow learners in the junior high school will be designated as discipline problems, with many of them becoming delinquents. The relationship between antisocial behavior and intellectual retardation is shown clearly in a study reported by Bowman.[1] He found that most of the delinquents found in a rather complete survey of eighth graders were slow learners, with about one-fourth of the delinquents being mentally handicapped.

There are a number of very interesting and important facets to this study from the point of view of the community and the educator. A number of approaches were made to the problem with the objective of prevention. The first method used was foster home placement which was found unsatisfactory for a number of reasons; parents did not want to give up their children, good homes were scarce, and even "good" placements did not work out well. Aggres-

[1] Paul H. Bowman, "Effects of a Revised School Program on Potential Delinquents," *Annals of American Academy of Political Sciences,* March, 1959.

sive case work with small case loads proved unsatisfactory because
it was time consuming, families were difficult to work with (unco-
operative), the children were growing away from their families, and
no community agency was willing or able to assume the costs. Recreational clubs proved to be of value insofar as defining the problem
was concerned. They could not, however, solve the problems and
once again no agencies could be found to take them over. Organized
groups, such as Boy Scouts, expressed an interest but did nothing.
The conclusion was that recreational agencies could not be relied
upon to change the people. The schools were finally selected for an
experimental program with good success. This program will be discussed in greater detail later in this volume.

Most slow learners today upon entering the junior high school
have not had a program specifically designed for them, in reference
to their needs and characteristics, during their previous school experience. Much of the discussion that follows will no longer be true
when this condition has changed. The environment of the slow
learners is an atmosphere reflecting feelings of hopelessness and defeat. The slum dwellings, the inability to improve their physical
environment, homes where landlords are only interested in collecting
rent and do nothing in the way of upkeep or improvement, parents
who work sporadically, long periods of relief aid, and continuous
contact with corruption, drunkenness, and vice give the slow learners
little to bring to the school that would cause them to place much
value on traditional learning activities. This lack of initial interest
is not improved when the school also has become a place of frustration and another failure situation because educators have refused
to make adequate and appropriate educational provisions. The majority of the slow learners soon learn to hate school. They are absent
whenever the opportunity presents itself. Attendance officers spend
most of their time with this segment of the school population. The
drop-out rate is very high. The majority of them leave school as
soon as they are legally permitted to do so. In states where the compulsory education age is higher than the common 16 years of age
and "continuation" schools are provided whereby a pupil may attend school part-time and work part-time after the age of 16, the
continuation schools are filled largely with slow learners. They want
to get out of school by any means possible. School has been just one
more failure, a failure that they have been forced to face several

hours each day for many years. At least in the community they can sleep late, gang up with their friends, talk, or take some other means to evade facing up to the reality of their failure and defeat.

Is it surprising, then, that the teacher observes an attitude of disinterest among the slow learners in the classroom? Realistic, meaningful programs for the children and a change of attitude on the part of both the educators and the children must be planned for and worked on simultaneously if the educator expects to achieve any positive results with these slow learners.

The health, physical development, and motor-development characteristics of the slow learners at the junior high school level are essentially the same as was described for them at the primary and intermediate levels. As a group they will tend to be in the lower part of the normal range but a great deal of individual variation will also exist. On an average, their physical and motor skills will not be quite as good as one would expect in the population of normal children. There will continue to be a slightly higher incidence of physical and sensory disabilities, particularly of a minor nature, as well as a higher incidence of illness and disease. Consequent lack of regular school attendance may have some effect upon academic achievement.

The junior high school program

Slow learners in the junior high school are entering into their final or terminal period of intellectual development. It is, therefore, essential that instruction be planned to encourage and, insofar as possible, ensure continued growth in the skill areas. During this three- or four-year period sufficient improvement in reading, arithmetic, and other skills should continue to occur to make systematic instruction worthwhile. Thus, approximately 50 per cent of the day should continue to be devoted to these areas, as was true at the intermediate school level (Fig. 7).

The other major emphases of the junior high school program should be in the way of generalized programs in the physical and natural sciences, social sciences, fine arts, homemaking, and industrial arts. Work in the special subjects areas should be largely exploratory rather than specific in nature at this stage. Following the broad outline of such a program, the slow learners should, upon the completion of junior high school, be achieving academically at or near their ability level. In addition, they should have the generalized

CURRICULUM EMPHASES FOR NORMAL AND SLOW
LEARNING CHILDREN — JUNIOR HIGH SCHOOL

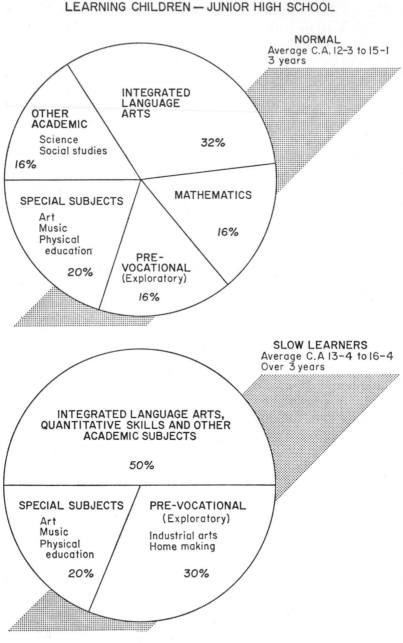

Figure 7.

kinds of background experiences that will enable them to derive the greatest amount of benefit from the more specific programs in the social and vocational areas provided in the senior high school.

These suggestions are based upon the assumption that the slow learners entering the junior high school have had the benefit of a program designed specifically for them during their years in the intermediate school. Unfortunately, this will not be true for some time to come. In many instances the junior high school personnel will recognize the acuteness of the problem and prepare to do something about it before a program has been instituted in the intermediate school. This will place an additional burden on the junior high school in at least two ways. First, although not necessarily of greatest importance, many of the entering slow learners will not be achieving at a level even approaching their academic potential. This will require that remedial provisions be included in the program. While academic skills have relatively little intrinsic value for the slow learners (they will not be able to earn a living through their competency in these areas), they are extremely important tools that are necessary to daily living and continued acquisition of information and knowledge. Second, unhealthy attitudes have developed to date; the program must be planned to change them. Only with positive attitudes toward school and toward learning can the slow learners be expected to benefit from the instruction and remain in school for a sufficient period of time beyond the compulsory age limit to be ready to take their appropriate places in the community when they do complete their education. Attitudinal changes and improvement of academic skills are both of crucial importance to those slow learners who have not had the benefit of a program until this level.

Liddle [2] found the following practices were apparently realistic for a group of slow learners in ninth grade who had never previously had the opportunity to participate in a program designed for them. (1) Provide one or two teachers genuinely interested in slow learners with whom the children would have major contact. While most of the day would be spent with these teachers, opportunities would also be provided whereby the students could participate in such activities as physical education, industrial arts, and chorus. (2) Materials used in reading and arithmetic and communications instruction were

2 Gordon P. Liddle, "An Experimental Program for Slow Learning Adolescents," *Educational Leadership,* 17:189-92, December, 1959.

carefully selected so as to appeal to the students. The purpose of
the instruction was directed toward use in jobs, in the home, and in
other community activities. (3) Many experiences that appeared to
be unrelated to academic learnings were introduced (e.g. role playing, part-time work, dramatics, ordering from mail-order houses, field
trips, and reading directions). (4) The atmosphere of the classroom
was relaxed and informal. Little threat of failure existed and much
in the way of time pressure was reduced. (5) Opportunities were
provided whereby students could discuss personal and social problems. Where necessary, agency referrals were made.

Where the program for slow learners has been of a developmental
nature—with classes provided at the primary and intermediate levels,
skill instruction usually presents no major problems. The children
should be achieving at the third, fourth, and fifth grade levels while
enrolled in seventh grade; the fourth, fifth, and sixth grade levels
while in eighth and ninth grades. Ample interesting and meaningful
reading, oral, and written communication materials and opportunities for their use are available for children with that amount of skill.
This aspect of the program need not differ markedly from the instruction that is carried on in regular fourth, fifth and sixth grades
except that the materials and topics must be carefully selected. The
slow learners are older and reflect an atypical background. This
must be taken into consideration if the reading and discussions are
to be made interesting to them. The very success the children are
having will also aid materially in the maintenance of interest. Nothing contributes as much to interest as successful performance in a
worthwhile, meaningful activity.

The study and development of skills in arithmetic (comprehension, understanding of relationships, efficiency in computational
skills, and so forth) presents a somewhat different problem. While
the slow learners' abilities will generally be at the levels indicated,
much of the formal materials and texts available are not particularly appropriate, although some of the newer texts are overcoming
this objection to some extent. The arithmetic program should develop concepts and introduce use or application through meaningful
activities. Many of these can be taken either from the practical arts
areas in school or from experiences the children bring with them
from the community. This, then, provides meaning and purpose to
the learning of skills and efficiency in their application. Some of

the newer methods also help the children to understand the basic relationships involved, which is essential if they are expected to apply them intelligently to appropriate situations where they are required.

Some schools have felt that the commercial arithmetic programs offered in many secondary schools are appropriate for their slow learners. This is far from being true. Most commercial arithmetic courses require a higher level of understanding and competency than has been achieved by most of the slow learners. In addition, the purpose of these courses, and consequently their content, is inappropriate for the kinds of arithmetic needed by most slow learners. The kind of arithmetic program that will be of value to slow learners is best described as practical, daily-living arithmetic.

Instruction of this type requires teachers who are trained and oriented somewhat differently than most junior high school mathematics or commercial-course teachers. Teachers working in the academic instruction areas with slow learners should be doing the kinds of things that are expected of good intermediate school teachers. These teachers have little use or need for an academic major except possibily for one in the social sciences. They do, however, need ability to teach in the skill areas at the elementary grade levels and the ability to group and adjust instruction to several different levels within the same class. Teachers with an elementary education background will generally find work with slow learners in the junior high school less difficult, more satisfying, and will be able to achieve better results than most junior high school teachers of today with their typical secondary school orientation and training.

In addition to the use of carefully graded materials in skill instruction, the teachers have numerous opportunities to use meaningful materials to continuously demonstrate the needs for the skills and the application of them. The other areas of work, practical and fine arts and so forth, regularly call upon skills in reading directions, methods of construction, measuring, giving descriptions, and explaining results. These give meaning to the skill instruction, but they also do more. If the teacher is aware of these activities and incorporates them into the academic phases of the program, the slow learners will be able to derive more meaning and benefit from the special areas as well.

It is obvious that a teacher must be given the primary responsibility for the education of only one or, at the most, two groups of slow learners. The accomplishment of a program such as the one described cannot be achieved by the commonly practiced, complete departmentalization. Under complete departmentalization no one teacher has sufficient time or responsibility for the kind of programming and instructional integration that is essential. The teacher responsible for all academic skill instruction can become familiar with the total program of each child, contact other teachers in the special areas, and plan for integration of experiences. This teacher should also be responsible for the social science and vocational survey aspects of the program because they are of fundamental importance in helping the child achieve the status in the community of which he is capable and deserving. They also, to a certain degree, help define the curriculum.

Many of the academic and correlational activities of the "home room," in which the child and the teacher are together for about one-half of the time, may be built around central cores or units. Units used in the Quincy Youth Development Project [3] and found to be of value were developed around the individual, the home, the school, work, the community, and the nation. Following a study of broad, content units, such as those described, provides the over-all skeleton of a basic social studies program, helping the individual to develop a better understanding of himself and to see himself in relation to the society about him—in the home, the school, the community, the nation, and working in industry. How effectively the objectives are achieved depends largely upon the skill and ingenuity of the teacher and the degree to which the school and administration is committed to a program for slow learners. This commitment is reflected in how well they provide the teacher with supplies, resources, and consultant services. The acceptance of the program as an integral part of the total program of the school is essential.

The program outside the "home room" is of equal importance to that within it. The prime consideration throughout must be a careful analysis of whether or not each and every activity has value and purpose for the slow learners. These experiences should not be just a lowering of standards or a watering down of the regular program. Classes in industrial arts and home economics have multiple

[3] Maurine Pellmann and Gordon P. Liddle, "A Program for the Problem Child," *Phi Delta Kappan*, January 1959.

purposes. One, they should be used to teach the use of tools, equipment, and materials. Two, the skills should be applicable for use by the child in his present and potential environment. Three, the knowledge acquired may form the foundation upon which future, specific vocational skills may be built. It will often be necessary to have separate classes—classes apart from the regular seventh, eighth and ninth grades to provide these experiences and achieve these objectives. For selected children, however, it may be appropriate to include them in the regular class groups. Guidance and careful planning for each individual becomes a must if each child is to hav the program or group of experiences that will be of greatest value t him.

The same principles are involved in the selection of arts, crafts, music, and physical education experiences. Whenever a child is placed inappropriately it is more than just a waste of his time and the teachers' time (unless the teachers are very adept at individualizing instruction). It may cause the child to reject school and be unavailable for future experiences that would be of value.

The unrealistic view that all children are growing up in a total society and, therefore, should be placed indiscriminately with all other children does not benefit either education or society. No teacher can be everything to all children. It is the responsibility of the school to provide each child with those learning experiences that will be of most value to him. Integration of children with different cultural backgrounds and different abilities may sound good to the naive observer. In integration, however, there is a basic principle that must be adhered to if it is to accomplish its purpose. This principle is that a child should be placed in that educational setting where the experiences have value to him and in which he can learn. The underlying assumption is that his level of ability or intellectual sophistication is about equal to that of the rest of the class. He must not be so significantly different that it is obvious to everyone he does not belong. This must be remembered when planning experiences for the slow learners in the special areas.

The programs at the various grade levels should not differ markedly in content or emphasis except for vocational preparation. With the instruction carefully graded in regard to each child's development, each child will observe his own growth as he progresses through the junior high school. As at all instructional levels, the instruction must have meaning and purpose for the child as he is and where he is. Only in this way will it help him cope with his problems more effectively, thus improving himself and helping him to make those changes in his environment which are appropriate and of which he is capable.

One of the greatest mistakes that can be made at the junior high school level is to attempt to include terminal educational experiences that properly belong in the senior high school because of the assumption that the children will leave school as soon as the law allows. While their leaving school at this time has tended to be the rule, it doesn't mean that this condition must continue. Planned, meaningful senior high school programs will encourage many to continue until they are ready to leave. Educational experiences taught for specific future, adult use will be soon forgotten, and in fact not truly learned. Consequently, the slow learners will not be able to use them when they need them. The social and vocational skills required for adult living are not appropriate areas of study for pre-sixteen-year-old junior high school pupils.

It has been previously stated that the junior high school program is a preparatory, survey or investigational, transition program. These terms and concepts particularly apply to the social and vocational areas. In the social areas the pupils become acquainted with how the community operates but the emphasis is not yet upon their role as adult citizens. If they have a good grasp of the concepts involved they will be able to put them into practice at the appropriate time. It must be remembered that what the individual is at seventeen is largely dependent upon what he was at sixteen. What he is as an adult, 21-year-old depends upon what he was as a twenty-year-old. Training should not be for an unpredictable, somewhat "foggy" future but for the development of an individual who understands himself and his relationship to his physical and social environment. He must learn the necessary basic concepts to be able to change as his environment changes, always helping that change to be for the better.

Vocationally, the same principles hold but can be somewhat better defined in terms of sequence and grade level. The seventh grade should include no experiences expressly defined as being of a vocational nature. The children should be provided with introductory experiences in manual and industrial arts. A broad study of jobs and industries of the community is indicated at this time. This study should be initiated through the use of printed and audio-visual materials accompanied by discussions. Trips should then be taken to industries with follow-up study in the classroom. Numerous activities of this type throughout the school year will familiarize the pupils with local industry and the types of jobs generally available without placing the emphasis upon a specific job for a specific child.

The manual and industrial arts experiences should be continued through the eighth grade. At this age the children are becoming more interested in jobs for themselves (although the specific vocational approach or interest has not necessarily been reached), and a more intensive study of the industries in the community should now be made. The purpose of the study in this grade is to investigate jobs and rather specific characteristics of jobs being performed within the community. Some of the children will also be working at part-time jobs; newspaper routes, packers and stock boys in grocery stores or supermarkets, baby sitting, and so forth. These jobs can seldom be used for the purpose of vocational guidance since they are not of a full-time nature, although some of them may occasionally lead to full-time employment in the future. Consequently, their primary educational value both at this time (eighth grade) and at the ninth grade level is to help with the development of concepts of money, purchasing, budgeting, and "how to work" into a life context.

The ninth grade level for most of the slow learners should be the start of job selection. Most school guidance and counseling personnel do not consider work in the vocational guidance area to be within their realm of activities. This may be true and appropriate for normal children. For slow learners it is essential everything be done to ensure, insofar as possible, that they will be competent to make the required community and vocational adjustments upon the termination of their formal schooling. This is not just the function of guidance personnel; it is an integral part of the curriculum. In ninth grade the pupils should carefully observe specific jobs, evaluate the skills required on these jobs, and evaluate their abilities in relation to job requirements. The manual and industrial arts programs should be continued. By this time the boys and girls should have had many experiences with tools, materials, and methods, giving them the background essential in learning the specific skills required

on selected jobs as well as in putting these skills to use in performing chores and repairs around the home. The children should be
helped and encouraged to perform on part-time jobs as a method
of teaching them to become effective employees.

Little needs to be said about the physical education program
since the program and its objectives, in general, are similar to those
provided normal children. Most of the slow learners can participate
in the program with the rest of the children of the school, however,
it may be necessary to place them with slightly younger children.
Their primary disability will be in the areas of organized games and
the comprehension of rules although, as a group, they will also be
somewhat more poorly coordinated. They, therefore, have somewhat
greater need for the program than do their normal schoolmates. The
same also applies to hygiene programs, which have been discussed
extensively under the topic of health in the primary and intermediate schools.

THE SENIOR HIGH SCHOOL

Characteristics of the children

The senior high school in most communities is the one school in
the public school system that has had contact with relatively few
slow learners. Most slow learners drop out of school either prior to
admission or during the first year of senior high school. A few, primarily those from better homes and with sufficient drive, eventually
"graduate" from high school by remaining enrolled year after year,
selecting as many non-academic courses as possible, and expending
maximum effort.

(The following description of the senior high school slow learners
is based upon an extension and projection of information available
concerning the younger junior high school group. The average,
normal senior high school student enters tenth grade at 15 years-3
months of age (Table VII) and graduates from twelfth grade at 18
years-1 month of age, spending one year in each of the three senior
high school grades. During the years in senior high school, the normal youngster reaches the age at which the law permits him to leave
school, even though he may not have completed his program. Many
of them take advantage of this although the majority remain in
school until graduation. The same is not true for the slow learners.

TABLE VII

Chronological Ages of Children Enrolled in the
Senior High School—September 1 and June 30

Grade Level	Ages of Normal Children				Ages of Slow Learners			
	September 1		June 30		September 1		June 30	
	Spread	Average	Spread	Average	Spread	Average	Spread	Average
Tenth	14–9 to 15–9	15–3	15–7 to 16–7	16–1	16–3 to 17–3	16–9	17–1 to 18–1	17–7
Eleventh	15–9 to 16–9	16–3	16–7 to 17–7	17–1	17–3 to 18–3	17–9	18–1 to 19–1	18–7
Twelfth	16–9 to 17–9	17–3	17–7 to 18–7	18–1	18–3 to 19–3	18–9	19–1 to 20–1	19–7

TABLE VIII

Approximate Mental Ages and Appropriate Grade Level Achievements for
Slow Learners Enrolled in the Senior High School—September 1 and June 30

Grade Level	Mental Age				Grade Achievement			
	September 1		June 30		September 1		June 30	
	Spread	Average	Spread	Average	Spread	Average	Spread	Average
10th, 11th, & 12th	11–0 to 13–6	12–3	11–0 to 13–6	12–3	5.0 to 7.5	6.3	5.0 to 7.5	6.3

Most of them are over 16 years of age before entering tenth grade (Table VII) and have, consequently, left school prior to entrance to the senior high school. Only rarely have programs been provided specifically for them at this level. If they continue, they should complete their schooling at about 19 or 20 years of age. This is approximately a year and one-half later than the normal student.

As a result of the slow learners late admission to tenth grade, due primarily to retention policies practiced in the earlier grades, they have generally achieved their highest intellectual development. If they have had proper instruction, they should also have achieved or nearly achieved their maximum growth in the academic skill areas (Table VIII). It will be noted upon examining this table that only one set of mental age and achievement grade-level figures are given for the three senior high school years and that the figures for September 1 and June 30 are the same. This is due to the previously explained mental and achievement development.

The mental ages of slow learners in the senior high school can ordinarily be expected to range between 11 years and 13 years-6 months. The average mental age will be about 12 years-3 months. The grade-achevement level will range between 5.0 and 7.5. The average grade achievement should be about 6.3. These achievement estimates are based upon the grade expectancy for the indicated mental ages. These are the grade levels slow learners should be operating at if instruction has been consistent and appropriate throughout the children's earlier school life. Unfortunately, if the senior high schools were to enroll the majority of the slow learners today, the range and average achievements would undoubtedly be considerably lower since extensive programs at the earlier levels are extremely rare. Thus, the incidence of severe educational handicaps is high and remediation provisions will be required in the majority of the programs.

On the following pages, the data referred to are taken from a "dittoed" report, *Slow Learners in the Secondary Schools* [4] by Gordon P. Liddle. This report is based upon the procedures and findings of a two-year study of children with low ability placed in an experimental high school program. This study is a part of a larger effort—*The Quincy Youth Development Project*. Facets of this proj-

[4] Gordon P. Liddle, *Slow Learners in the Secondary Schools,* Duplicated report, May, 1959, 41 pages.

ect have been referred to previously and will be referred to again (more extensively than any other articles or studies) because the work performed, the extent of the problems studied, and the controls used provide educators with not only the most recent but also the most accurate information available concerning the slow learners.

It has been stated previously that the slow learners come predominantly from the subcultural, low socio-economic areas of the community. This statement was based largely upon observation, but Liddle, in ranking the social status of the elementary schools from which the slow learners in the high school came, varifies it. He found that the elementary schools with the highest or best social status rank in the community furnished only about one-third the number of slow learners one would expect from their populations. The incidence or percentage of slow learners in the school population increased steadily as the social status of the school went down. The elementary schools with the lowest social status provided two and one-half times as many slow learners as would be expected by chance. Another very interesting and important fact concerning slow learners was brought out in this part of the report. About 50 per cent of the slow learners from the schools rated high in social status were performing fairly satisfactorily in a regular school program. Only about one-sixth of the slow learners from schools rated low in social status were performing fairly well in the regular grades. It is apparent that the major emphasis of any program for slow learners must emphasize the problems of the child living in a subcultural environment. Not only do the majority of slow learners come from homes providing relatively little psycho-social stiumulation but, comparatively few of them are able to adjust to the demands of the regular classroom.

A number of additional characteristics of slow learners were also verified by Liddle. In terms of sex distribution, it can be expected that there will be a somewhat larger number of boys than girls requiring a special program more than would be expected following the normal distribution of the sexes. Slow learners in a regular class situation are less often selected as friends and playmates by their classmates (using a sociometric technique) than are normal children. When the choice is placed in a negative statement, "Who are the children you do not like to play with (or work with)?", the slow

learners are mentioned more often.[5] Many of them have been identified, in earlier grades, as maladjusted or emotionally disturbed
children.

The same characteristics carry over into the community. Of the
slow learners who were also non-achievers, Liddle found that almost
one out of five had been in trouble with the law, and this at an age
younger than the peak delinquency period. In school, the majority
of the severe behavior problems come from this group of less than
20 per cent of the school population. Many factors, such as a
broken home, lack of religious affiliation or failure to place importance upon religious teachings, and a general feeling of inadequacy
and frustration generated by their meager general environmental
conditions undoubtedly contribute to the characteristics of slow
learners. Added to this are their health and hygiene problems and
the problems faced by all adolescents in the attempt to establish
their independence. It becomes apparent that special programs are
essential if these youngsters are ever going to approach their potential and become an asset rather than a liability to both themselves
and to society. Education cannot change their environmental conditions directly. Education can, however, help them learn necessary
skills and appropriate attitudes, provide them with tools to solve
their problems, and help them change their value systems so that
they, in turn, will help change their environment—to some degree
now, but to a much greater degree when they establish their own
homes in the future.

Actually, these improvements have been going on for a long time.
If one considers the phenomena of immigration waves into an entrance port such as New York City, the new immigrants are seen
to take over the cheapest, most deprived, slum areas of the community. Their children do poorly in school, provide a disproportionate percentage of the children enrolled in the classes for the
mentally handicapped, and comprise the largest group of delinquents. Over two or three generations they move out of those areas,
the children acquire more education, test higher on intelligence tests,
achieve more in the academic areas, and get into less trouble with
the authorities. By this time another group is ready to take their

5 G. Orville Johnson, "A Study of the Social Position of Mentally Handicapped
Children in the Regular Grades," *American Journal of Mental Deficiency*,
55:60-89, July, 1950.

place in the slums. These new immigrants may be either from a foreign country or another part of this country. In a city such as New York, this pattern has been repeated several times.

The school can short-cut this process. Instead of providing all children with the same education, provide each child with the education that is and will be of most value to him. Working in a 5 hour day, 5 days a week, for 10 to 12 years, the schools with appropriate programs should be able to shorten the period of transition to a single generation for most of these people. Much of the reduction of time must come in the way of programs for children who are behaving (learning) as slow learners.

The senior high school program

The academic skill instruction that has such an important position in the primary, intermediate, and junior high school programs may largely vanish in the senior high school program. As can be seen from Table VIII, by the time most slow learners have entered tenth grade they have either achieved or so nearly achieved their mental maturity that any additional skill development will be so small as to not be worth the effort. This is assuming good skill instruction and a satisfactory response to this instruction. However, because skill instruction should not be needed by the majority of the slow learners does not mean it has vanished completely, or that academic instruction even in the skill areas should not be included. The character of the instruction changes.

Under the best conceivable programs, remedial problems will still exist for some of these high school students. No program yet devised for any group of children is so perfect that it provides all that every child needs and can benefit from. Children who, for some reason or other, learn differently and children who have not been regular in their school attendance may be in need of remedial help. Also, there is a great deal of movement among the entire American population. Children entering the senior high school program have often attended schools in other communities where programs for slow learners were not available. An excellent example of slow learners often in need of remediation are the children of migrant workers. They have been enrolled in many different schools and their attendance is usually extremely sporadic.

The remedial program should not be confused with or even be

considered an integral part of the program for slow learners. The purpose of the remedial program is to provide the learner with those skills and abilities he should have learned at an earlier date as rapidly as possible in order that he will be able to participate as effectively as possible in the program designed for him. As such, remedial programs should be short term in nature. They are skill rather than content oriented. They do not define what the child should learn but accept this objective from the program in which he would be enrolled had he the essential skills required to participate effectively in it. Furthermore, need for remediation is not confined to any one intellectual group. Remedial problems are found among the average, the gifted, and the slow learners. The level of instruction is entirely dependent upon the level at which the child is presently performing. Remedial problems are found predominantly in the reading skills, although sub-level performance in arithmetic and spelling is not rare. Usually, deficiencies in the health, physical sciences, natural sciences, and social sciences are caused by deficiencies in one or more of the primary skill areas indicated. Thus, remedial programs in these other content areas are seldom found and seldom necessary.

The emphasis in communications and mathematics in the program for slow learners at the senior high school level becomes one of use or practice in application (Fig. 8). Through the use of descriptions and discussions the pupil is helped to listen better, to select the important and meaningful parts of the discussion, and to apply them toward the solution of personal problems. He also learns how to express himself more clearly so that others will better understand what he is attempting to communicate. This involves organizing his presentation so as to include pertinent facts or data in a clear, systematic fashion. He must learn to exclude meaningless, extraneous material that will only tend to confuse the listener. It also requires the selection of an appropriate vocabulary—words and phrases that have the same meaning for the listener as they have for the speaker. Thus, technical vocabularies related to specific jobs and situations and colloquialism familiar to the group or area must be known and used.

Communications skills are also used in other ways. The ability to use ones reading skills in the selection of materials (books, magazines, pamphlets, and so forth) and in comprehending the content is

CURRICULUM EMPHASES FOR NORMAL AND SLOW LEARNING CHILDREN—SENIOR HIGH SCHOOL

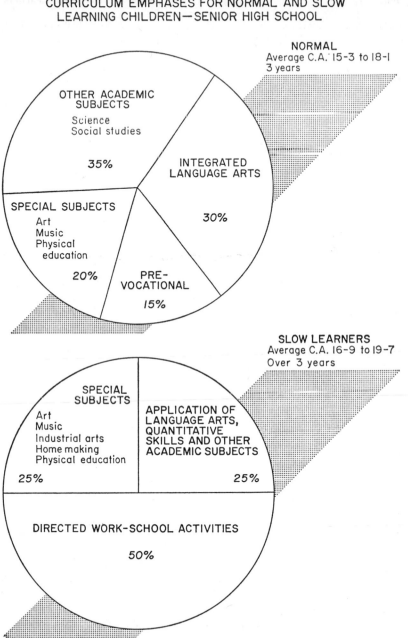

NORMAL
Average C.A. 15-3 to 18-1
3 years

OTHER ACADEMIC SUBJECTS

Science
Social studies

35%

INTEGRATED LANGUAGE ARTS

30%

SPECIAL SUBJECTS

Art
Music
Physical education

20%

PRE-VOCATIONAL

15%

SLOW LEARNERS
Average C.A. 16-9 to 19-7
Over 3 years

SPECIAL SUBJECTS

Art
Music
Industrial arts
Home making
Physical education

25%

APPLICATION OF LANGUAGE ARTS, QUANTITATIVE SKILLS AND OTHER ACADEMIC SUBJECTS

25%

DIRECTED WORK-SCHOOL ACTIVITIES

50%

Figure 8.

of utmost importance. Much of the reading done by adults is of this nature—how to make something (recipes), how to put things together ("do it yourself" activities), and what and when to do something. Without adequate reading skills and comprehension the individual is very limited in the potential adjustments he can make.

Reading is a primary means of continuing ones education after the period of formal schooling has been completed. The individual must know more than the mechanics involved in reading. He must know how to use it through a knowledge of what to read, where and how to find information, and the use of common references such as the classified ads, city directory, and telephone directory. Reading enables the person to "keep up with the times" through newspapers and current periodicals. This is an aid in both locating jobs and in being knowledgeable in regard to local, national, and world events. It is not sufficient for a person just to comprehend the things he is told and be capable of carrying out verbal instructions. Even in as highly a directive organization as the armed forces, during World War II it was found necessary to provide reading instruction to thousands of illiterates before they could be useful soldiers. Since that period of emergency and extremely high demand for manpower, the illiterate has again been turned down for armed service.

Instruction for slow learners in the high school is probably best carried on by using some type of block system. This is also true for the junior high school. Thus, one teacher has the responsibility for planning programs and providing the major portion of the instruction in those areas drawing most heavily upon the academic skills. Not only has the block system of instruction been found to be most satisfactory, but real value has been derived in programs such as the one conducted in Quincy, from having the same teacher follow or accompany the children for the entire time they are enrolled in the high school. The teacher has an opportunity to become better acquainted with each child under the block program. Furthermore, he can plan for long-term objectives and provide much greater continuity by continuing with one group from one year to the next.

One of the greatest objections to providing a special program for slow learners at the secondary level is that it will set them apart from the rest of the student body. Everyone will know that they are the "dummies" of the school, that these are "dummy" classes, and that they are in a program that is different from that provided most children. The only answer to this latter comment is that it is true; the other children as well as the slow learners do know the program is different. But, when there are a few slow learners in a regular class unable to perform at a satisfactory level in that class, everyone knows that as well.

Where the secondary program is the first special provision that has been made by the schools for the slow learners, the immediate reaction of the children involved is one of interest and anticipation. For the first time they feel that school is going to have some meaning and some purpose. The slow learners are fully aware that the program is different from that provided the rest of the school. Comments concerning their placement will be made, but if the program has value these comments will, after a short time, have little effect on most of the children in the program. As the reactions to the gibes are reduced, the derogatory remarks become fewer and fewer. There will, unfortunately, always be an occasional slow learner who is particularly vulnerable and will continue to resent the differential placement. This may be due to his never having learned to evaluate himself realistically in terms of his abilities. Or, he may be reflecting the attitudes and aspirations of his parents. This is particularly true for those who come from better homes in the middle and upper-middle class groups.

As the program for slow learners is expanded to include the entire secondary school program, the awareness of its existence is reduced. Children coming from elementary schools enter the program immediately upon starting seventh grade. The same is true for those moving from the junior into the senior high school. Since a number of elementary schools act as feeders to each junior high school and two or more junior high schools act as feeders to each senior high school, there are many strangers to each child in every class. Consequently, with large enrollments both the slow learners and normal children are often unaware of program differences and the comments and gibes common to an initial program decrease in number. The slow learners also become more accepting of school because they are securely enrolled in a meaningful program that provides the necessary continuity from year to year and from school to school.

The one other characteristic that tends to set a program for slow learners apart from the regular programs is the block-type instruction. Most secondary schools today are planned on a departmental basis. Block instruction, where a student has a single teacher and may remain in a single room for as much as half the school day, makes the program different. This problem, of course, is not faced where block-type programming has been introduced into the regular classes. More junior high schools are adopting block or modified block instruction each year. If and when this is more widely accepted by the senior high schools, the task of making the slow learners an integral part of the high school programs will be much easier.

The task then becomes one of planning a senior high school program that will have meaning and value to a group of children with limited intellectual ability, who come predominantly from subcultural homes and areas of the community where, historically, relatively little value has been placed on higher education, and who can leave school at any time because they are beyond the age of compulsory school attendance. The following program assumes three pre-conditions: (1) slow learners in the program have largely achieved as much in the academic skill areas as it is realistically possible for them to learn; (2) the program will last for an average of three years for each child; and (3) it has been preceded by the experience survey program of a junior high school.

The senior high school program should be developed around broad unit-type experiences designed to achieve two primary objectives—good citizenship and adequate vocational adjustment. In a sense, these objectives are interdependent and can be achieved to a large extent simultaneously, although at times the emphasis will be upon one goal and then upon the other. Since the broad educational objectives for boys and girls are the same and they are living together in the same society, the program should be planned within a coeducational school setting. Where necessary, experiences should be provided the boys and girls separately, for study of vocations, homemaking skills, child care, and hygiene. The social and cultural experiences, however, should be undergone together. The basic principle of instruction remains the same as was true for the primary and intermediate schools. School is a part of, not apart from, the daily living experiences of the children. The experiences the children have outside the school give meaning to the school instruction. Similarly, the school instruction has value and application outside the school. In addition, the numerous athletic and social activities of the typical secondary school provide additional valuable experiences for the slow learners.

In broad outline the program consists of approximately 50 per cent of the time being devoted to in-school adjustment, social, citizenship, and vocational activities and 50 per cent to out-of-school systematically planned vocational experiences. The in-school units might be similar to those of the junior high school, with emphasis first upon "self" and then upon learning the relationship of "self" to society. In a study of "self," such topics as grooming, cleanliness, clothing, personal hygiene, sex education, and self-criticism are of utmost importance. The teacher must always be aware that he is dealing with young adults and that his relationship must be *with* them—he must not be *above* them. The activities must be of an adult nature. For girls much can be accomplished in conjunction with a good homemaking program. This, in addition to the homemaking activities ordinarily included, might consist of washing and setting hair, use of make-up, nail care, care and cleanliness of clothes, and so forth. These same objectives can also be achieved in conjunction with the physical education and hygiene programs for both the boys and girls. General appearance and cleanliness contribute materially to an individual's feeling of personal value. This is a fact that has been observed in institutional programs for the retarded and mentally ill. Patients are no longer dressed in shapeless, sack-like "uniforms" but are encouraged to select their clothing, provided with beauty parlors, and generally helped to improve their physical appearance. This seems to change their entire outlook on life. They take pride in themselves. It has definite therapeutic value reflected in changed behavior and reduction of time in the hospital.

Regular homemaking activities of a useful nature should be included for all girls and to a lesser extent for the boys as well. These activities should be realistic. The limitations of the present and potential environments of the children must be taken into consideration. Housekeeping, serving, cooking, repairing, meal planning, family etiquette, washing, laundering, ironing, and pressing are all essential daily activities. Boys, too, should learn some of the fundamentals because situations often arise where such knowledge is invaluable. The girls, and to a somewhat lesser extent the boys, should also learn about child and infant care. This can and should also be closely tied in with sex education. Such activity will have real, personal meaning and immediate application for most of the children in that there are often young brothers, sisters, nieces, or nephews within the family. In addition, the girls can often obtain work as baby sitters for neighborhood children.

For the boys the counterpart of the homemaking program is industrial arts. From the junior high school program they have learned the basic use and care of tools and characteristics of materials. In the senior high school program the emphasis should be upon improvement of skills and their application. The general shop where simple electrical, metal, and woodworking activities can and are carried on is ideal. Home repairs and selection of materials and methods to perform a job aid materially in preparing the boy to work in industry, keep himself engaged in worthwhile avocational activities, and maintain and improve his home environment. These programs also provide the school with excellent opportunities to observe academic skills deficiencies and the application and use of academic skills. Students are given the opportunity to learn how to plan and work together in a more informal life situation than is usually possible in the regular classroom.

There is little necessity for discussing the values of the physical education program. It should be definitely included. Except where specific corrective exercise is indicated, little emphasis should be placed upon the more formal aspects of the program. Neither should a great deal of time be devoted to highly organized games and activities that require equipment and facilities rarely readily available in the community. Rather, major emphasis should be placed upon the kinds of activities that persons in the community can and do participate in. Examples of such activities are swimming, golf, tennis, bowling, and baseball (or softball) depending upon the community. In this way the physical education program will carry outside the school and into adult activities, adding also to the slow learners' potential avocational outlets.

Within the special class, approximately two periods of the day should be devoted to learning more about the community, the state, and to a lesser extent the nation and world. "How are they run?" "What is my relationship to them?" "What are my responsibilities?" "What and where are jobs?" "How do I get a job?" "What kind of job should I look for?" "What are taxes?" "Who pays them?" "What is social security?" "What is insurance—life insurance, accident insurance, unemployment insurance and compensation, health insurance, and so on?" These are representative of the kinds of problems that form the foundation of the classroom program. Each teacher must formulate the ones which are appropriate for his group in relation to their community, their state, their environment.

The other half of the day should be devoted to trips around the community to learn first hand about the things being discussed in the class. This time may also be used for work experiences. During the first two senior high school years, short-term work experiences and trips about the community should both be used. The purpose of the work experience is to answer such teacher and pupil questions as the following. "What additional experiences should be included in the school program to enhance this boy's (girl's) chances of becoming an effective employee?" "How does he get along with his fellow workers?" "Are there personal or social qualities and skills that require improvement?" "Are there manual skills that could be improved by additional experiences in selected shops or laboratories?" "Is this a good training situation?" "How does this level job fit this individual; is it too easy or too difficult?"

The work-school or work-experience aspects of the program have been purposely relegated to the senior high school. No program is complete without them, but they cannot be introduced at the junior high school, pre-sixteen-year age level. First, educational experiences to be of value must be provided at the time the individual is ready to learn from them, when he has sufficient background experiences to understand that there is a need or that the need can be developed. Children at the pre-sixteen-year age are interested in part-time jobs and in having spending money, but are seldom ready for consideration of full-time employment. These desires are in the process of development and help is required if they are to become crystallized in appropriate directions. These same experiences provided at an earlier date would be a waste of time for both the teacher and pupil. Second, child labor laws markedly limit the kinds of work experiences a pre-sixteen-year-old may have. Third, employees are restricted in the hours, working conditions, and jobs that can be given sixteen- and seventeen-year-olds. Thus, most companies will not employ persons under 18 years of age for a regular job.

The work-school program of the senior high school, whereby the pupil is placed in a number of work situations, enables the slow learners to learn to become employees, not just on one job but under a variety of working conditions on a number of different kinds of jobs. As a result they become widely employable. In observing the students on the job and evaluating their total performance, both manual and social, the teacher can plan for additional necessary experiences and also help them to evaluate their abilities and performances in terms of the social and manual requirements of the position. As the students achieve greater social and broader vocational competence, which should occur by their final year of senior high school, each of the work experiences should become longer. Only one or two should be used this year rather than the four to six per year used previously. On many occasions, this last job placement may become full-time employment upon the completion of school, although this should not be the primary objective.

The work-school program described has precedence in secondary school programs which have been used in Distributive Education and Commercial Education for many years. It is also being used with success with the educable mentally handicapped in those communities that have tried it. In order to achieve the greatest effectiveness, the teacher must be responsible for this aspect of the program as well as those parts of the program centered within the school. He must be given sufficient time to contact potential employers and make arrangements for job placements; when students have been placed he must supervise them on the job with some degree of regularity. This cannot be done as effectively by a school counselor or vocational placement officer because it is a part of the boys' and girls' education. Only if the teacher is intimately familar with problems as they arise can the necessary corrective measures be instituted within the school or classroom aspects of the program.

Employers are often very hesitant to accept the slow learners as employee trainees. This may be due to basic employment policies, promotional policies insisted upon by a union, societies' attitude toward mental retardation, or unhappy experiences they may have had in the past. Upon initiating the program the teacher should emphasize the strengths of the students he wishes to place and completely forget the terms "slow learner" or "mentally retarded." Initially, in a new program or with a new employer, those students who have the best skills and greatest potential should be placed first, although they probably require this experience the least. The purpose of this policy is to "sell" the program and employment potential of the group and to demonstrate their potential value to the employer. With regular observation and evaluation it should not be necessary for an employer to contact the school regarding an unsatisfactory worker. This conversation should usually be initiated by the school. In certain cases a student who is not performing satisfactorily should be removed from a job and placed in another before the employer has had a chance to complain. In this way industry will recognize it will not be "stuck" with a student whose performance is unsatisfactory. Experience in working with the educable mentally handicapped has indicated that following these principles, after many initially difficult placement problems, the number of training situations increases markedly and employers are glad to cooperate. It must be remembered that industry usually does not see itself in a teaching or educational role. It must produce and make money for the owners and stockholders. Only after the values of a work-school program have been demonstrated and educators have convinced employers that they are not trying to take advantage of them will numbers of training opportunities open up and the program be able to more nearly achieve its objectives for each child.

The work and school experiences available to the slow learners must be varied in nature to give each individual a variety of experiences as well as to help each individual find the kind of work he can do the best. Slow learners, as others, vary considerably in their abilities. It is ordinarily thought that the majority of them will be working in semi-skilled jobs. Some cannot achieve this level of skill while others can and do go into skilled trades and business. Careful guidance in regard to the selection of the school program becomes essential at the secondary level. Many, varied experiences are available in the secondary schools that should be used for individuals although not necessarily for the group. If a student shows a particular aptitude or skill, it may be appropriate to give him additional experiences in this area with the regular students. The areas most commonly used are manual and industrial arts, home economics, crafts, and vocational agriculture. It may even be appropriate to enroll selected students in trade courses in the vocational school if such an opportunity is available. With varied training of this type, it is obvious that the job placement and work experience must also be varied.

The one aspect of secondary education that has not been mentioned and has great potential educational value for slow learners is the extracurricular program—clubs, athletics, social events, and so forth. Because slow learners' attitudes often reflect the hopelessness of their environment and the limited opportunity they have had to participate in community affairs, it is necessary for the teacher to encourage and help them become involved in those activities in which they can participate. The teacher must also make sure they derive the values possible from them. Athletics, both intramural and interschool, help in the areas of physical development, learning and abiding by rules, establishing effective relationships with others, and pride in accomplishment. Clubs help them develop conversational and social skills. Various social events, such as attending games, participating in and attending school plays, and attending school dances and parties, all have educational value. They are important experiences that cannot be included in the classroom program but must not be excluded from the total program.

SUMMARY

The secondary program for slow learners (both at the junior and senior high school levels) varies most widely from the programs provided normal children. The junior high school is, in a sense, a transition, and offers a survey program. The children are in their last developmental years. It is, therefore, essential that the instructional program in the skills be continued so that they will achieve the highest level possible in these areas. These skills act as basic tools for continued learning and adjustment for the rest of the children's lives. At the same time, the pupils are slowing down and approaching their ultimate intellectual development and adulthood. They are becoming interested in what is to happen to them when they leave school. Thus, the other focus of the junior high school program is the individual and his relationship to his environment, both social and vocational. He is studied. His community is studied. Various skills and manual activities are surveyed and experienced by short-term assignments to the various shops and laboratories available.

The senior high school program is predicated upon the assumption that the students have achieved their ultimate mental development and near their maximum proficiency in academic achievement skills. Instruction in these areas, except where remediation is indicated, consists of use and application of these skills in meaningful situations. Once again the program is centered around the individual and his comprehension of, relationship to, and participation in the society, the community, and the economy. More general shop and laboratory experiences are provided but in addition, as the result of careful observation and guidance, some specific, intensive vocational and prevocational experiences should be incorporated into specific programs for specific individuals.

A work-school program to teach the potential employee vocational and social skills essential to becoming economically independent is an integral part of the senior high school program. These experiences also determine much of the content of the classroom instruction. Other valuable experiences used are various trips taken into the community and the extra-curricular activities available within the school itself. Upon the completion of this program the slow learners should be ready to step from school into community life, able to maintain themselves with only the help and controls normally provided all individuals. This is in contradistinction to slow learners now leavng school at 16 years of age who, having had no program to meet their needs, will sit around the community for two or three years before employers will seriously consider them for full-time employment.

SELECTED RELATED READINGS

Abele, L. W., "Administrative and Curricular Provisions for the Slow Learner," *School Review,* 59:420–26, October, 1951.

Allingham, R. B. and G. W. Connelly, "What are Secondary Schools Doing to Develop a Program for the Slow Learner?" *National Association Secondary School Principals Bulletin,* 40:261–63, April, 1956.

"Assistance for the Slow Learner," *National Association Secondary School Principals Bulletin,* 40:128–36, February, 1956.

Birch, Jack W. and Robert L. Erdman, "The Slow Learner—In the Secondary School," *N. E. A. Journal,* 48:26–28, October, 1959.

Buss, Otto E., "Educating the Submerged 25 Per Cent," *California Journal of Secondary Education,* 20:158–59, March, 1945.

Denver Board of Education, *The Development of a Program of Secondary Education for Slow-Learning Pupils, Junior and Senior High Schools,* Denver: Board of Education, 1936, 143 pages.

Carlin, J., "Five Years of Curriculum Planning in the Vocational High Schools," *High Points,* 31:5–21, April, 1949.

Dodds, B. L. and Ruel E. Tucker, "What is a Good Program for the Slow Learner?" *National Association Secondary School Principals Bulletin,* 36:329–37, March, 1952.

Edwards, Rosaline M., "A Slow Learner Program," *National Association Secondary School Principals Bulletin,* 42:130–32, February, 1958.

Featherstone, William B., "What Do We Know About Slow Learners?" *Clearing House,* 25:323–28, February, 1951.

———, *Teaching the Slow Learner,* Bureau of Publications, Teachers College, Columbia University, 1951, pp. 98–118.

Gibbs, Elsie F., "The Slow Learner in the Secondary Schools," *California Journal of Secondary Education,* 24:199–202, April, 1949.

Goldberg, M., "My Slow Learners' New I.Q.: Imagination Quotient," *Clearing House,* 28:337–40, February, 1954.

Goldin, Myron R., "An Experiment with Adjustment Pupils," *High Points,* 28:66–72, May, 1946.

Havighurst, Robert J., "Dealing With Problem Youth," *Nation's Schools,* 61:43–45, May, 1958.

Herkner, M. W. and J. F. Malone, "How Shall We Provide for the Slow Learner in Junior High School?" *National Association Secondary School Principals Bulletin,* 38:95–100, April, 1954.

Hill, Arthur S., "What Curriculum for the Slow Learner?" *National Association Secondary School Principals Bulletin,* 34:8–16, April, 1950.

Hoffman, George J., "Human-Relations Techniques and the Slow Learner," *High Points,* 37:62–68, January, 1955.

Holton, Samuel M., editor, "Providing for the Underachiever," *High School Journal,* 42:66–95, December, 1958.

Levisohn, Hortense H., "What Program for the Slow Learner?" *National Association Secondary School Principals Bulletin,* 33:58–64, May, 1949.

Liddle, Gordon, "An Experimental Program for Slow Learning Adolescents," *Educational Leadership,* 17:189–92, December, 1959.

Moskowitz, Myron, "Teaching the Slow Learner," *School Review,* 56:476–83, October, 1948.

Peller, Helen, "Adjusting in Adjustment Class," *High Points,* 29:72–78, April, 1947.

Schuker, L. A., "The Slow Learner in the High Schools," *High Points,* 37:11–31, April, 1955.

Seeley, R. M., "A Junior High Care Program for Slow Learners," *School Executive,* 73:64–66, October, 1953.

Sheehan, Mary A. and Arthur S. Hill, "What Curriculum for the Slow Learning Child?" *National Association Secondary School Principals Bulletin,* 34:4–16, April, 1950.

Yardumian, L., "Correlated Studies: A Custom-Built Curriculum," *California Journal Secondary Education,* 25:271–73, May, 1950.

part III

Instruction for the
Slow Learners

7

The Language Arts
and Communications Skills

The language arts and communications skills, including reading, spelling, and speech are among the most essential academic skills taught in school. No other skill is as important to the individual in the development of concepts, acquisition of knowledge and information, and for future vocational, avocational, and social adjustment. The language arts help the individual to perform a job, to read directions, to express to others his thoughts and needs verbally and in writing; they provide him with the skills that enable him to enjoy additional recreational activities.

The task of the school is to develop each child into an effective individual personally, socially, economically, and civically. The language arts are important in this development. They consequently have an important place in the curriculum. They should be used in relation to experience areas and other academic skill areas. They must also be taught specifically as skills to provide the slow learners with the organized, step-by-step instruction they require.

READING

The speech and much of the initial language developed by young children occurs incidentally outside the school. In most instances it occurs prior to the children's initial school experience. Reading and spelling are seldom learned outside the school situation, particularly for the slow learners. Organized reading programs are required almost universally if general competence in this area is to be achieved. It is also the area that provides the largest number of instructional problems for most primary teachers.

The majority of the slow learners achieve some reading competency by the time they leave school. Studies [1] indicate, however, that slow learners present the greatest number of reading problems found in the secondary schools. Not only are they retarded in reference to their chronological ages and grade placements, but large numbers of them are not reading at the level of which they are potentially capable. This means that the curriculum and/or the methods used are not designed to promote the maximum acquisition of this skill by the slow learners during their stay in the primary and intermediate grades and the junior high school.

Defining the slow learners on the basis of intelligence as measured by a standard test, they have I.Q.'s between approximately 75 and 90. Assuming that normal children are 6 years-3 months of age (on an average) when they enter first grade and are about ready to learn to read (i.e., are mentally mature enough to profit from initial reading instruction), the slow learners will not achieve this same degree of mental maturity until they are between 6 years-11 months and 8 years-4 months of age. Again, assuming mental growth ceases at approximately 16 years of age, at that age a normal child has a mental age of 15 or 16 years (depending upon the test) and is doing

[1] Stella S. Center and Gladys L. Persons, *Teaching High-School Students to Read*. New York: Appleton-Century-Crofts, 1937, 167 pages.

good high-school level reading. The slow learners, by the age of 16 years, have achieved a mental age between 12 years and 14 years-5 months, with potential reading ability from grade 6.4 to grade 9.0.[2]

This means that the slow learners will be ready to profit from their initial reading experiences at an older age than normal children. They will also learn and acquire reading skills at a slower rate and their final achievement will be at a lower level. Continued emphasis upon the reading skills will not enable the slow learners to "catch up" to the normal children any more than they will ever "catch up" in their mental maturity. Their reading abilities are limited and instruction must be planned within these limitations and restrictions.

Readiness

Slow learners acquire the necessary mental maturity to profit from organized reading instruction at an older age than normal children. As a result, the teaching of reading should be delayed and the readiness period extended. The extent of the delay will depend upon the individual. It may be as little as six or eight months or as much as two years.

The various activities provided for normal children enrolled in kindergarten are designed to prepare them for the more formal school activities of the future. There is more to reading readiness than merely acquiring sufficient mental maturity. Kindergarten is not just a period of waiting. Kindergarten activities are designed to promote growth in those other areas (such as ability to live effectively with a group of children, gross motor skills, ocular motor skills, speech and language, visual and auditory discrimination and memory, motivation or desire to learn to read, and so forth) that are essential to learning to read. When a normal child has acquired a certain degree of mental maturity as well as a degree of proficiency in these other areas, he is usually *ready* to learn to read or to profit from formal reading instruction. The same is true for slow learners.

There are certain of the readiness functions in which the slow learners can probably become superior. This is particularly true for those skills that are subject to training and in which they can be helped to improve while they are waiting to develop the mental

[2] From profile of *Metropolitan Achievement Tests,* Revised (New York: World Book Company).

maturity of the average first grader. There are other skills in which
they are apt to be definitely inferior and which will require a great
deal of training and emphasis in the pre-academic program. Since
slow learners are, under optimum conditions, ready to benefit from
instruction in reading between eight months to two years later than
normal children, many of them will be more physically mature than
the normal children. Thus, there should be little or no question regarding their visual maturity and their general motor skills, including the very important ocular-motor coordination. They should,
therefore, also be equal or superior to normal children in these areas
when they have achieved the same degree of readiness. Speech and
language development, visual and auditory discrimination, and
visual and auditory memory are areas in which slow learners may
be deficient. Since they are all amenable to training to a greater
or lesser degree it should be possible to overcome this deficiency.
The readiness program should include specific activities designed
to provide experiences and improve skills in these areas.

SPEECH AND LANGUAGE

Speech and language are usually developed initially in relation
to the speech and language patterns heard and as a result of the
stimulation received in the home. Slow learners come predominantly from low socio-economic and sub-cultural homes. Their parents, as a general group, are less highly educated, probably had
difficulties with school and learning when they attended, and are
not highly interested in academic activities. Their speech is often
restricted in respect to both scope and content. It is composed to a
large extent of colloquialisms, with a relatively restricted vocabulary, poor expression, and incorrect grammatical construction. Living and growing up in such an environment provides little in the
way of stimulation for good speech and language development. As
a result, when slow learners appear in school for the first time it is
usual to find a disproportionately large number of speech defects
(particularly of the articulatory, omission and substitution type),
poor grammatical ability, and poor ability to express themselves
clearly.

A great deal can be accomplished within the classroom to promote the development of speech and language. Primarily, the children must be provided with a good model; that is, the teacher must

speak the language well. Then, the children must be stimulated to use good speech and to express themselves clearly. Experiences of various kinds are made use of in order that they will have something to talk about. These should be of such a nature that they desire to share them with the teacher and the other children. Speech can be improved by aiding the children in their development of auditory discrimination so that they can hear the sounds correctly and become aware of their errors. They may also require some help in producing the sounds correctly. An available speech correctionist can give valuable help to the teacher in planning speech and language experiences and suggesting methods for improvement and for providing correction. He can work intensively with the more difficult cases and guide the program for the rest. Even without a speech correctionist, however, much can be accomplished with many of the children if the teacher is alert to their needs.

The development of vocabulary, language, and expression is primarily a total classroom activity rather than an individual activity. Vocabulary needs to be increased, language usage needs to be relatively accurate, sentence length should be increased and become more complex, and expression needs to become more organized and accurate. Some activities that will promote such growth are (1) answering questions relating to familiar activities, (2) describing pictures—first while looking at the picture and later from memory, (3) retellng stories read or told by the teacher, (4) sharing personal experiences with the class, (5) describing an organized classroom or school activity, and (6) telling how to do or make something.

These language and expression activities should encourage free, natural expression, not just the parrotting of a phrase or sentence. The objective of this aspect of the program is the development of spontaneous speech and language through their use in purposeful situations dealing with meaningful materials. Vocabulary can be increased through continuous stimulation by new words used in the context of stories and activities. Language, sentence length, and general expression should be improved through the use of meaningful, interesting situations and judicious questioning regarding details, sequence, and organization of replies. The development of language normally follows a sequence from words, to phrases, to simple sentences, and finally to more complex sentences. The mere memorization and repetition of nursery rhymes and statements has relatively little value. "Games" where the children are taught to parrot the teacher ("You have a clown," "I need a clown," "May I have the clown, please?," and so forth) achieve little in regard to language development or increased ability in expression. A far more satisfactory program is one where through discussion and questioning the children are stimulated to express their ideas and desires effectively in their own words.

VISUAL AND AUDITORY DISCRIMINATION

Visual and auditory discrimination can also be improved markedly. Since they are necessary for the development of good speech and in learning to read, time should be devoted to these skills whenever it is necessary. Discrimination involves the ability to recognize when two or more things are alike and when they are different. Thus, an individual must be able to discriminate between sounds and words in order to recognize them, give them the proper meaning, and reproduce them accurately. Since most early reading experiences are oral ones, auditory discrimination becomes a very important aspect of the development of that skill. It can be developed through the employment of numerous activities not directly related to or dependent upon the reading process. Examples of these types of activities are the use of (1) rhythms, (2) rhymes, (3) discerning the direction of a sound, and (4) recognition and identification of the origin of a sound.

Visual discrimination is also essential to reading. In reading, a person is continuously required to discriminate between the configurations of letters and words. Without accurate visual discrimination, recognition would be impossible. Pre-academic activities commonly used to improve this ability and develop the concept involved are those that require the child to note similarities and differences in regard to form, shape, color, configuration, and so forth.

VISUAL AND AUDITORY MEMORY

Visual and auditory memory are similarly important in the initial reading process. The first "reading" done by children is largely the result of memorization, first of stories, then sentences, and finally of words. These words then form a part of the child's sight vocabulary. Thus, a child sees a configuration of letters and associates them with a certain sound that is the pronunciation of a word with which he is already familiar. At a later date children learn to associate a sound with a specific letter and to make the other visual-auditory associations necessary for the development of independence in reading.

The various readiness skills do not develop in and of themselves or come about simply with age or maturation. Their development is dependent upon learning experiences provided the children. This is particularly true for the slow learner, in whom each of these skills must be developed in a step-by-step sequence to ensure their complete learning and mastery.

MOTOR SKILLS

Learning to read also involves the development of certain motor skills. The initial skills that are required in this area are predominantly ocular. The child needs to learn to move his eyes from left to right; this should be established to some degree prior to the introduction of reading. If he can do this he will have little or no difficulty in transferring the use of this motor activity to following a line of words during his initial reading experiences. Numerous readiness activities are used for the purpose of developing this skill, such as (1) following a line of dots with a pencil or crayon to draw or complete a picture, (2) following a sequence of pictures that tell a story (cartoon-like material), (3) finding the first, second, third, and fourth objects (where number concepts have been sufficiently developed), (4) setting up a series of objects from left to right, and (5) drawing lines or arrows from left to right.

The activity requiring children to follow a story through a sequence of pictures has further value. The children's comprehension of reading materials is improved through a knowledge and an understanding of sequence. They learn what came before and what happened next. Consequently, this activity serves a dual purpose. Teachers also use other activities to achieve their objective of increasing this ability. For example, they may tell or read most of a story to the children and ask them to complete it or to tell the ending. If the story is a familiar one, they are also giving the children another experience related to auditory memory. In actual practice many activities serve to accomplish two or more objectives.

Other motor skills are also important to reading. These require relatively fine coordination that will be used after the initial reading stage. When reading from a book (and charts) it is necessary to move the eyes, accurately, from the end of one line to the beginning of the next. Upon the completion of a page, the page must be turned, but just one page and not two or more at a time. Using references, indexes, and tables of contents efficiently requires the ability to turn pages rapidly and to find the correct page. Books are also valuable and should be handled carefully. Pages should not be turned so as to tear or crease or crumple them, and the backs of the books must not be broken by careless and inept handling. A number of important motor skills must be developed by each individual who wants to become an efficient reader.

ATTITUDES AND CONCEPTS

Finally, but by no means of least importance, it is essential that children develop positive attitudes toward reading (a desire to learn to read). They must also develop basic concepts concerning the nature and importance or value of reading. Primary teachers, during the readiness program, often use pictures of animals, flowers, or objects to designate a child's ownership of something. Thus, a specified picture over a certain hook indicates that this is where a certain child is to hang his clothes. This same picture may be placed on pictures he draws or paints, things he constructs, and the chair he sits in. They are all his. Later, the teacher couples the child's name with the picture; finally, the picture is removed. The child now recognizes that a certain configuration of letters indicates his name. Other meaningful words are also gradually introduced through the labeling of objects in the room (chair, desk, easel, door, window, and so forth). In this way, the children learn that all objects have verbal names and that a specific group of printed symbols (letters) designates what the object is. Thus, the children develop a very real concept concerning the nature of reading.

The slow learners who come from homes containing very limited cultural stimulation tend to place a relatively low value on reading, although they may verbalize, like other children, the desire to learn to read. Why should they? Little or no reading is done in the home by other members of the family, with the possible exception of homework assignments by older siblings. And these are often accompanied by much groaning and grumbling. No interesting-looking books or reading materials are contained in the home for them to look at. A child may have all the skills necessary for learning to read. He may have sufficient mental maturity. But unless he also has a desire, his progress will be slow, and he will never develop the ability to read as he should. Good primary teachers recognize this and provide in their readiness programs materials and experiences that will develop the desire. One method is to read short, interesting stories to the children, encouraging them to want to learn to read so that they can read these and other stories themselves. Another method is to place numerous simple books around the room. These books should contain many attractive pictures that the children will enjoy looking at. The books should be changed regularly (at short intervals) so that there is always something new available. In this way the children return to the book corner or library table over and over again. They are getting acquainted with books and developing a desire to learn more about the stories and materials they see illustrated. They are developing a real desire to learn to read. When they are ready, and instruction is provided, they will learn.

BEGINNING READING

The questions most often asked concerning beginning reading are, "When should reading instruction begin?" "When is a child ready to learn to read?" The answer to the first question is easy. Reading instruction should be provided when a child is ready. The answer to the second is more difficult to provide and also of greater importance for planning instruction. Readiness to read does not mean merely that a child has arrived at a specific chronological age or even a pre-determined mental age. A child is ready to benefit from formal and specific reading instruction when he (1) achieves a mental age of 6-plus years, (2) has acquired the language and verbal facility of the level found in most children between 6 and 7 years of age, (3) is capable of telling stories and events in the sequence of their happening, (4) demonstrates good visual and auditory discrimination and memory, and (5) being surrounded by stimulating reading materials, expresses and displays a desire to read. This readiness stage should be attained by the slow learners between the chronological ages of 7 years-3 months and 8 years-8 months provided they have also acquired the necessary skills.

Most experienced first grade teachers should be able to determine by careful observation when the children in the class are ready to benefit from beginning reading instruction. This decision is based upon the level of performance of each child on the pre-reading or readiness activities. When a child can perform all these activities fairly easily and accurately, follows directions, has good verbal expression abilities, and expresses a strong desire to read, the probability is that he *is* ready. Reading readiness tests are also valuable aids in determining the readiness level of a child and the probability of his having success in reading activities. Readiness tests also serve another purpose. They help to point out clearly those readiness areas in which a child has a deficiency. In this way a specific program can be planned for him to strengthen these skills without wasting effort and time on the areas in which he has already achieved a competency.

Modern reading methods are based upon generally accepted, sound psychological principles. The primary objective of reading is to develop understanding and comprehension. The initial stage is to develop the general concept of what reading is; i.e., that reading is the understanding of written material that tells the reader something. This, and other basic concepts and skills are taught through the use of charts.

Good chart stories have specific characteristics. First, the chart story is a complete description of an experience common to the children. The children have had an experience together and tell their version of it. This becomes the chart story. Second, the sentences of the chart story are short, usually contained in a single line. This encourages the development of normal left to right eye movements used in reading and avoids the problem of retracing from right to left to start another line to complete the thought. Third, each sentence is grammatically correct. This teaches and emphasizes correct sentence construction through normal usage. Fourth, except for nouns, the words used are predominantly those found in the pre-primers and primers. Thus, when a child moves from the charts to the first books, a basic sight vocabulary has been established that will largely ensure initial success and make succeeding reading material easier. Fifth, the most commonly used words should be repeated within the chart and from chart to chart.

Charts used for beginning reading are not haphazard reading

materials, hastily developed through unselected contributions of the children and written on the chalkboard by the teacher. They must be carefully planned to include the aforementioned characteristics and executed so that the children actively contribute to their content and writing. This is accomplished through initial conversation and discussion. Then a mutual decision is made to write a story. Careful questioning of the children will elicit the important points and careful selection of responses results in a story composed as the teacher desires. The chart is initially planned and written by the teacher. It is developed, however, in such a way that it becomes a teacher-class cooperative effort with the teacher actively engaged in leading and guiding its construction. The children accept it as their story.

Most normal children are ready to move from charts into books after 6 to 10 weeks. It can be anticipated that slow learners will not be ready to make this move in less than 10 to 15 weeks. This same slower development will be noted in all succeeding reading activities.

A number of specific skills and concepts are developed during the chart stage, each of which requires additional time for the slow learners. Initially, chart stories are memorized in total by the children. Three, four, or five line stories are written on the board, read aloud by the teacher, and then read by the children collectively and individually. These charts are then copied on large sheets of tagboard or chart paper, illustrated, and become part of the class's collection of their stories. The children first recognize each story by the illustration and general configuration of large blocks of sentences, words, and blank areas. Stories are memorized by the repetition of listening to other children "read" them and by "reading" them themselves. Actually, children are not reading in the true sense of the word at this stage. They are developing a concept of reading and a feeling of success related to a reading activity.

After the children have become proficient in recognizing a number of different stories, they begin to note some differences within the stories, such as the varying lengths and configurations of the sentences. The teacher should then break the stories down into sentence reading, helping and encouraging the children to recognize the individual sentences in the new charts as well as in their old ones. Here, too, the concept of left to right movement in reading should continue to be incidentally developed through the organization or format of the chart. Finally, discriminations of similar and different words within the sentences are made. When the children can discriminate between words and begin to recognize them individually, they are beginning to read. After sufficient chart experiences to learn a basic sight vocabulary, they are ready to read the pre-primers and later the primers.

Additional stimuli and unique experiences may be required for slow learners in order to maintain their interest in the charts and in reading. This is partly due, as far as interest is concerned, to the longer time they remain at the chart stage, partly due to seeing other children being given books, and partly due to previous experiences of failure with these activities. It is not just because of their slower development that slow learners often require longer chart periods. It is also due to the general inappropriateness of most pre-primers for older children residing in a sub-cultural, low socio-economic environment. As a result, it may be difficult, if not impossible, to transfer these children to the initial book experiences in the pre-primer although they have developed sufficient reading skills to cope with them. Because they are somewhat older and may be more mature than normal children at the same developmental reading stage, the content, method of presentation, and illustrations contained in most pre-primers and primers may be considered to be "baby stuff." Most pre-primers emphasize activities in which normal 6-year-olds living in a middle or upper-middle class neighborhood participate. The only solution is to use class-developed books and reading materials until sufficient vocabulary is achieved for these slow learners to read books with a higher interest level. Such methods as mimeographing stories and stapling them together into individual books to be read and illustrated, and using long rolls of paper on which their stories and illustrations are pasted in order to make a "movie," have been demonstrated to be of value in prolonging the chart period and as substitutes for pre-primers.

Some children have difficulty in developing an initial sight vocabulary by the "look and say" method. This is particularly true for those who have visual and auditory perceptual difficulties. As a result of these disabilities, they find it difficult to attend sufficiently to the immediate reading stimuli and to derive sufficient benefit from them. It is then essential to either emphasize the word or words sufficiently to ensure active attention, or to reduce extraneous stimuli to a point where the word or words become the dominant focus and maintain the child's active attention.

Strauss and Lehtinen,[3] working with brain-injured children, advocate the latter method. When it is found that a child cannot maintain his attention to the task at hand and that his mind tends to wander to other things, the other things should be removed. The following are some of the methods used. If the child is apparently distracted by normal room noise and activity, change his seat so that he is more removed from the center of general activity. In more severe cases Strauss and Lehtinen even recommend that the child turn his back to the group, that a clinical screen be placed between him and the group, or even that he be removed entirely from the group to an adjoining room or cubicle. Since the reading materials themselves may contribute to such a child's lack of controlled attention, it may be necessary to remove the pictures, prolong the use of guides under the specific line being read, or even present the reading material one word at a time. These procedures are all designed to intensify the reading stimulus (word, sentence, or story) as compared to the reduced environmental stimuli. Thus, the child is more actively attracted by the reading than by other extraneous things.

Fernald [4] has recommended the use of another method to increase the comparative intensity of the stimuli of the word to be learned. She advocates supplementing the visual and auditory stimuli with a kinaesthetic stimulus. This is done by first having the teacher write (cursive) the word on the board, telling the child what it is. Second, the child traces the word with his finger and pronounces it at the same time. After this has been done a number of times, the child copies the word and pronounces it. Finally, the word is pronounced by the teacher, erased, visualized, pronounced, and written by the child from memory. When this stage has been reached, the child knows the word. The task then becomes one of putting the word to use in conjunction with meaningful material.

The Fernald method and the method advocated by Strauss and

[3] Alfred A. Strauss and Laura Lehtinen, *The Psychopathology and Education of the Brain-Injured Child* (New York: Grune and Stratton, 1947), 270 pages.
[4] Grace M. Fernald, *Remedial Techniques in Basic School Subjects* (New York: McGraw-Hill Book Co., Inc.), 1943.

Lehtinen make use of the principle of emphasizing the task at hand as compared to the surrounding stimuli. The Fernald method also applies the psychological principle of re-enforcement. Other methods that accomplish the same objective will undoubtedly achieve comparable results. It is primarily a task of ensuring active attention, presenting the material in an orderly, sequential manner, and finally re-enforcing, re-teaching, and reviewing until the concept or skill has been thoroughly established. These methods are primarily applicable to the development of the initial sight vocabulary. Once the child knows how to learn to read they are no longer necessary.

Independent reading

After children have learned to discriminate between different words and recognize familiar words when they see them, they are ready to begin to put their reading to use. They can recognize the words in various combinations and grasp the context of the material. As they encounter new words, however, they must be told what they are in order to incorporate them into their reading vocabulary. Eventually some independent method of word attack must be developed. Only in this way can children advance through reading material without depending upon some other person to pronounce each new word for them. Word attack should begin to be developed at the upper first grade reading level; development continues through the second and third grade reading levels or until the child has achieved reading independence.

The development of an independent method of word attack involves finer discriminations (both visual and auditory) than are required in the development of a sight vocabulary; additional concepts must also be learned. The child must become aware of the parts of words and learn to use them in attacking new words. He must learn to analyze a word, use syllables, suffixes, prefixes, decomposition (compound words, for example), plural endings, changes due to tense, context clues, and sounds of individual letters for phonics. Slow learners, to a greater degree than normal children, should be provided with an organized and systematic method of word attack. Phonics probably lends itself to this approach most readily.

Much of the instruction concerned with the development of independence in word attack for normal children is incidental. As the need arises, the teacher presents the method appropriate to that situation. Instruction provided in this fashion has immediate value and meaning because it is directly related to need. It is, however, most difficult to ensure that all phases of the instruction will be adequately dealt with in this fashion. In addition, there is little provision for showing the relationship between the instruction provided at one time and that provided at some unspecified time in the future. Most normal children eventually grasp the relationships and, consequently, understand the principles involved. Teachers cannot depend upon slow learners ever arriving at a high enough level of intellectual maturity to be able to arrive at these principles independently. These skills, like others, must be specifically taught. Principles must be evolved and instruction provided to ensure an understanding of the principles and the ability to apply them.

It is, therefore, not sufficient to teach phonics in conjunction with reading, or solely as it is related to that skill. It should be taught in a way that gives meaning to the phonic skills. It should also be taught with specific practice included to develop complete grasp and understanding of each sound and its relationship to the letter and its use in words. To ensure systematic presentation of phonics material, an organized method of phonics instruction should be used. One of the best methods is that designed by Hegge, Kirk and Kirk.[5] It is highly organized and incorporates the use of other phonics methods—individual sounds and initial and final families of sounds.

Phonics is based upon the letters and families of letters and their sounds rather than their names. While it can and does aid in the development of spelling ability, it does not require the spelling out of the word by the child. In fact, the mere naming of the letters of a word will not and cannot aid in the pronunciation or reading of the word.

Phonics, like other skills, also is dependent upon a readiness. A child is not necessarily ready for phonics when he is capable of visually recognizing and pronouncing the words contained in the first year reading materials. To be ready for phonics instruction, children must be able to blend sounds and thus pronounce the complete word. They must be able to blend *c-a-t* into *cat* and *r-u-n*

[5]Thorleif G. Hegge, Samuel A. Kirk and Winifred D. Kirk, *Remedial Reading Drills* (Ann Arbor, Michigan: George Wahr, Publisher, 1936), 58 pages.

into *run*. Whether or not a child has this necessary ability is easily checked by asking him, "What are these words?" "Sh-i-p." "Sh-oe." If he demonstrates blending ability on these and a number of similar words, it is obvious that he is ready to benefit from instruction in phonics. If he cannot recognize and pronounce these words, he must be provided with instruction in blending, first with words having two sounds pronounced with only a brief pause between them. As he improves his ability, words containing three or four sounds and longer spaces between the pronunciation of each sound should be used.

Formal phonics instruction should be supplemented with instruction in its use during all normal reading activities. Whenever a child finds a word he does not know, but which he can attack using the phonics instruction he has had, he should be helped and required to "figure it out." He is thus learning phonics and how to use it. This is integrative instruction, although not necessarily simultaneous instruction.

Efficient reading

The initial phonic method of word attack is not an efficient method of reading because it involves a careful analysis of each word. As children become proficient in its use, they should be helped to extend it to the use of families of sounds, syllables, and entire small words contained within larger ones rather than individual letter sounds. Quantities of highly interesting, easy reading material containing only an occasional new word should be provided to encourage independent reading. The more a child reads the better reader he will become. He will recognize and pronounce news words more easily and rapidly, he will greatly increase the number of words he can visually recognize, and his speed of reading will increase proportionately—with no decline in comprehension. Greater interest in, and concentration on, reading material leads to better comprehension. Other skills related to reading must also be consciously taught to the slow learners. These include the use of the dictionary and other reference materials, indexes, tables of content, and how to read and interpret maps, graphs, and charts of various kinds.

Slow learners are potentially capable of achieving from sixth to ninth grade reading ability and comprehension. Reading ability of this level can and should be an efficient tool. Continuous use should be made of reading skills in the acquisition of information and to find the answers to questions and solutions to problems. Slow learners require the basic skills, but they also require the knowledge and practice of how to put the skills to work. Finally, reading for the slow learners can and should become a valuable recreational activity. This can only be accomplished by making the reading activities interesting and pleasurable experiences. It is, therefore, necessary to provide the slow learners with recreational reading materials that are of value and interest to them, even with their somewhat limited abilities, as soon as they are able to enjoy them. Do not expect them, as a group, to show great interest in the accepted classics or even in the classics that have been rewritten with a simplified vocabulary. These rewritten classics often lose much of their descriptive beauty as the result of rewriting. In addition, such books tend to be concerned with concepts and events that are out of the realm of interest of most slow learners. Instead, slow learners should be provided with more common, everyday types of materials—books with recognizable, understandable, and realistic characters, plots, and wording.

Slow learners continue to develop intellectually during the time they are enrolled in the junior high school. As a result, formal reading instruction, specifically for the purpose of improving the skill, should be continued through that level. Once the child has learned to read in the primary school, he should be using the skill for the purpose of acquiring information and knowledge. The better he learns to read and the more efficient and effective the skill becomes, the more it can be put to work. It is used more at the elementary school level than at the primary level and continuously applied to a greater and greater degree throughout the junior and senior high school. By the time slow learners have moved into the senior high school program, most of them should be able to use reading exclusively as a tool. Only those who are remedial problems should then be provided with reading skill instruction.

Remedial reading

During recent years different terms have been used to denote those children who are not performing at or near their potential reading-ability level, depending upon the cause of the deficiency. For purposes of this discussion, anyone (regardless of cause) who is reading significantly below his ability level will be considered to be in need of special instructional help or remediation.

Slow learners, like normal and intellectually superior children, may be in need of reading remediation. These are children who are not only failing to work up to their grade-placement level, which is to be expected with slow learners, but who are also failing to perform up to their reading-potential level as well. Various formulae have been developd to determine whether or not a normal child is a remedial reading problem. These formulae usually take two factors into consideration, the child's age, grade level, or number of years he has spent in school, and the child's mental developmental level. The assumption underlying this type of formula is that a child's reading ability or level is dependent upon the number of years of instruction he has received as well as upon his mental ability. A child who has had very little instruction, regardless of his mentality, cannot be expected to be reading as well as a child who has had adequate instruction. These formulae work well with normal children and, theoretically, take into account the higher grade placement of slow learners and the lower grade placement of bright children whose intellectual level would appear to warrant higher placement. In actual practice, however, they tend to indicate a disproportionately large number of slow learners as being remedial problems whereas many of them are not. Because a child is placed in the fourth or fifth grade under a scheme of social promotion does not mean that he should be reading at or even near that grade level, despite the fact that he may have been exposed to the instruction. For slow learners the use of the single criterion of mental age is usually more accurate and appropriate than most of the formulae devised. Generally, children should be expected to be reading at or near their tested mental age. When they are not, a reason should be sought to explain the situation and a program should be planned to correct it.

Under normal circumstances, the slow learners, as a group, perform quite adequately in reading if they are evaluated against their mental development rather than against the level at which most children their ages are performing. Considering the meager environmental stimulation the majority of them bring with them to school, they read surprisingly well. Those who are remedial cases have had their problem caused by the same factors that cause the same problem for normal children. Among the causes for reading disabilities are (1) lack of instruction (children of migrant workers who have had only sporadic experience in school, prolonged or recurring illness, truancy, or residence in an area where school facilities were short-lived or inadequate), (2) negative rather than positive attitudes toward learning (unsatisfactory early school experiences or a reflection of parental and environmental negative feelings), and (3) inappropriate instruction. Such instruction may have been inappropriate due to lack of readiness, because it was at too high a level, because it was meaningless in terms of the children's experiences, or because of unique learning problems that may have precluded the deriving of maximum benefit from the commonly used instructional methods. Whatever the cause, treatment should be instituted as soon as possible. Only in this way can the condition be corrected and the children have a chance of achieving at or near their potential. The longer the condition is allowed to exist the more difficult it will be to effect the necessary change.

Under normal circumstances, little or no remediation for slow learners needs to be considered at the primary level. On an average they will have achieved only middle second grade reading ability at the completion of the primary program. This is not sufficiently high to warrant a definitive diagnosis and plan for a remedial or corrective program. In the primary program the emphasis should be upon reading development. However, remedial reading should be considered during the children's attendance in the elementary, junior high, and senior high school programs.

Several discrete steps are essential in planning a program of this nature. First, it must be determined in each individual case that a remedial reading problem actually exists. A knowledge of the child's potential and his current level of performance is essential in making this evaluation. Second, probable causes for the situation must be examined. Wherever possible, theses causes should be eliminated or at least their impact reduced. Children with a history of irregular attendance should be encouraged and helped to attend with greater regularity. Negative attitudes toward school-centered learnings should be changed by the introduction of more appropriate programs and instruction. Third, a careful evaluation of the child's present reading level should be made. This should include information, obtainable from good diagnostic instruments, that will indicate specific areas of reading strengths and weaknesses. Fourth, a careful psychological examination should be obtained that will include the child's intellectual developmental level, his intellectual "peaks" and "lows," and any particuar psychological or intellectual traits that may interfere with his learning the various skills essential to becoming a good reader. Finally, a remedial program should be planned and put into effect that will provide the child with the specific kind of instruction he has need for. This instruction, in addition to being clinically planned in reference to his specific and peculiar needs, must also be organized so that he will be provided instruction regularly, and in a systematic fashion, with no steps omitted under the assumption that "he will pick them up." This "picking up" may never happen.

The methodologies used for slow learners are not unique. They are the same ones that are appropriate for and used with normal children. For a specific child it may mean simply using the method commonly used in teaching reading initially, with a few minor adaptations that take into consideration the slow learner's older age, apparently negative attitudes, previous lack of success, and restricted experiential background. Other children may require a combination of those remedial methods in standard use. It should always be remembered that the slow learners are not unique or different organisms, requiring special methods and special techniques. They are an integral part of the total population. Those techniques and methods that are appropriate for children in general are also appropriate for them. And, the percentage of success, when these methods are used correctly, will be about the same as is generally true for the total population.

SPEECH AND LANGUAGE

The development of speech and language starts long before the development of reading and is one of the skills upon which reading depends. This does not mean that it is fully developed when a child is ready for formal reading instruction or that no more emphasis needs to be placed upon it once the child begins to learn to read. Adequate speech and language are invaluable skills; they are of even greater importance than reading.

The development of speech and language, in most children, occurs at relatively the same time or concurrently, and the two skills are quite interdependent. Speech has little or no value in itself without language. Their original acquisition usually takes place prior to the time the child first enters school. Children learn speech and language imitatively from their parents, siblings, and other adults and children with whom they come in contact. If a good early speech and language pattern is provided, the children will tend to develop good, acceptable speech and language patterns. If poor speech and language patterns are provided, these will be imitated and poor speech and language will result.

Children are bombarded with speech and language from the time they are born. The mother talks to the baby when she feeds him, changes him, and dresses him. Other adults and children talk to the baby when they see him and play with him. In addition, there is continuous speech stimulation from conversation, play, radio, and television. In a relatively short period of time the infant associates speech with pleasurable and pleasure-giving situations (food, dry clothes, attention, and so on) and he attempts to respond to them in kind.

Children's initial speech attempts consist of sounds such as cooing. They become aware that they can make sounds and enjoy the sounds and the sensation of making them. This gradually changes into babbling, in which the young child repeats the same sounds over and over (ma, ma, ma; da, da, da, da; pa, pa, pa, pa; and so forth). These sounds still are not speech, are not language, and have no particular meaning to the child, although the fond mother or father may believe he is saying "mama" or "dada." Since the parents react to these babblings positively, the child soon learns to associate certain sounds with these persons. This is the beginning of meaningful speech and language for the child.

Language begins when the child starts to use this speech to express himself—his wants and his desires. Initially he may call "mama" when he is hungry, uncomfortable, or desires attention, knowing that a response will be made by some adult, usually his mother. Speech and language are still quite undifferentiated at this stage. Gradually he will acquire more sounds and organize these sounds through imitation and repetition to be associated with various objects. Soon single words will be used to express whole ideas, e.g. "baba" may mean "I am hungry" or "I want my bottle" or "I lost my bottle." Language development from this point is a development toward greater clarification and specificity through the additional use of groups of words, inclusion of verbs, adjectives and adverbs, development of phrases, and finally, complete simple sentences.

Slow learners follow the same speech and language developmental pattern as other children except that their development is ordinarily somewhat delayed as compared to their physical development and chronological age. They can also be expected to remain at each developmental stage for a somewhat longer period of time. The speech and language development of the slow learners is slightly inferior to that of the majority of the children when they first enter school, but only partly because of the foregoing reasons. In addition, slow learners, as a group, because they tend to come from lower socio-economic and lower cultural homes, receive less speech and language stimulation at home than do normal children. Less conversation takes place and the speech and language patterns tend to be poorer. During the past two or three decades this factor has not been as important as it was formerly. The introduction of the radio into the home gave young children a great deal of good speech stimulation that their parents and older siblings had missed. More recently, television has added even greater amounts of speech stimulation to their environment.

It is recognized by most authorities that there are a larger number of speech problems among the slow learners than are found in the general population. During their initial school experience this may be due to their intellectual immaturity and the fact that they have not developed beyond the infantile omissions and substitutions stages. To some extent at this age, and particularly at later ages, it is more probably due to poor and inaccurate speech patterns in their environment and poor auditory discrimination. As a result of hearing their own inaccurate production of the sounds for so long a period of time during each developmental stage, infantile speech patterns that normal children maintain for only short periods of time may become habitual in slow learners. They may become so accustomed to their own speech that they are not aware it is different from the speech of others.

The speech correctionist should make an early diagnosis of each articulatory, or other speech difficulty. Then a cooperative, correction and speech improvement program should be evolved with the teacher so as to alleviate the difficulty as quickly as possible. The early development of correctly produced speech will also aid materially in the reading-readiness growth of the child. The teacher must not stop here, however. This program must be extended to include the ability to express thoughts and ideas clearly and concisely.

Verbal communication is the most commonly used and most important form of communication. It is continuously necessary to communicate with others in all kinds of social and economic relationships. It is essential that the slow learners be taught to communicate as effectively as possible so as to learn to make good social and vocational adjustments as easily as possible. The early speech correction and speech improvement program will aid in this program but it must also be extended beyond the pre- and beginning reading stages. At the primary level a great deal of stress should be placed upon discussions of various kinds regarding individual and common experiences, how to do things, telling and retelling stories, and so forth. All of these activities are for the purpose of improving speech and language (communications) abilities.

As time goes along the children should be given continued practice in oral communication. Every opportunity that presents itself should be taken full advantage of toward the improvement of these skills. The children should be helped to observe and report accurately, to report events in proper serial order and in relation to other events, and to report clearly and completely in language another can follow and comprehend. When reporting, a child is apt to assume, unjustifiably, background and knowledge on the part of the listener. It is essential that the teacher and other children elicit the complete story through selective questioning. Questioning is far superior to prompting because it requires judgment and selection of words and phrases on the part of the child. Promptings are more apt to bring forth merely a parrotting of the phrase or sentence, with little or no thought or organization.

Verbal communication should be supplemented with written language and communication skills as the child becomes capable of using them. Written communication should not replace oral communication in emphasis, but it should also be stressed. Throughout the children's everyday lives continued opportunities for oral communication in natural situations should be provided. Planned social and vocational situations should be organized so that they will have numerous opportunities to practice these skills in life or near-life situations. This will enhance their chances of making effective use of them in those life situations where they are essential.

WRITING

Writing is primarily a motor skill requiring visual-motor coordination. It has no intrinsic values but is of value only insofar as it enables the writer to communicate with some person with whom he cannot communicate verbally, or for the keeping of records. It entails not only the mechanical motor skill required in the formation of letters and words but also requires spelling, language, and grammatical abilities as well. Language and grammatical abilities have been developing since the children have learned to talk and have been and are being improved through the oral communication program. The function of writing, then, is to legibly record the thoughts, ideas, questions, and information of the individual for transmission or safekeeping. Consequently, the primary emphasis of any writing program should be in terms of legibility, with speed and specific method of writing being of secondary importance.

Writing should, in many ways, present fewer difficulties to the slow learners than it does to normal children. It is primarily a motor skill and slow learners are usually somewhat more mature physically when they are ready to use writing than are normal children. This assumes that they are provided with writing instruction when they are ready for it, rather than at any specific chronological age or when the majority of the normal children are beginning to use it.

The first writing experience children usually have is learning to write their names. This enables them to label pictures and objects on which they have been working so as to establish ownership. This is followed by simple writing activities, such as answering questions, filling in blanks, and so forth, after the child has developed some proficiency in reading. It is thought by most authorities in reading and in early childhood education that these initial writing experiences should be with manuscript rather than the cursive writing that is more commonly used by adults. Manuscript is probably a somewhat easier method for most young children in that it is made up of a number of discrete movements, whereas cursive writing re-

quires a continuity of movement. Manuscript writing is more difficult to mutilate to the point of non-legibility than is cursive writing;
it is also more similar to print. The reading and writing of manuscript materials contributes to reading growth as well.

The initial teaching of writing should consist of instruction and
practice in the proper formation of the letters so that they will be
produced correctly and most easily. The continued emphasis should
then be on legibility and correct letter formation, with many opportunities to write being provided. *All written assignments and
materials should be writing lessons.* Since writing is a functional
communication skill it should be taught in functional situations,
in those situations in which writing is being used and has value.

Many schools make a practice of teaching the children cursive
writing during the latter part of second grade or the early part of
third grade. Since legibility is the primary emphasis in teaching
writing to slow learners, there is no specific reason for ever changing
from manuscript to cursive for these children. The majority of
them, however, will request the change in order to be carrying on
the same activities as the other children. When this desire manifests
itself, it is usually well to accede to their desires for psychological,
if not for academic reasons.

The same methods should be used in cursive writing as were
used in the teaching of manuscript. The children should be provided with a good model and taught the proper method and formation of letters. The method should include how to sit, the location
of the paper in relation to the writer, how to hold the pencil or
pen, and the most effective and easiest way to form the letters. Practice should again be provided through the use of meaningful materials. The children should learn to write words by actually writing
them. Producing pages of ovals and vertical lines teaches the children to make good ovals and vertical lines but there is no assurance
that these skills will be transferred to the production of legible
letters and words.

SPELLING

Spelling is another academic skill that has little or no intrinsic
value but is of value primarily in regard to increasing one's ability
to communicate through writing. As such, instruction should deal
with those words the child uses in his written material, such as

answering questions in relation to other academic areas, writing letters, and so forth. These are the words the children use and will be using. These are the words they should know how to spell. Many words contained in any arbitrary list are not designed for any specific child or group of children living in a particular environment and having unique needs. These lists will, consequently, contain many words of little or no value while omitting some of relatively common usage. It is known that a relatively small number of basic words (between two and three hundred) comprise approximately 50 per cent of all written communication. Every child should learn how to spell these words. Beyond this, much of spelling instruction becomes a problem of determining individual need.

Spelling is primarily a visual-motor, visual-memory activity, with the addition of the knowledge of some spelling principles. Only when spelling is introduced must a child know his alphabet and be able to recognize and reproduce specific letters by name. It becomes necessary at this time in order that he can organize the letters into words. The alphabet need not be learned in sequence until the child is ready to use references (dictionary, telephone directory, and catalogs), indexes, and so forth. Since spelling is primarily a visual-motor and memory activity used in conjunction with written activities, it should be taught in this fashion.

It is essential that a person be able to spell a word he desires to write correctly in order that the reader will comprehend his attempt at communication. It is not necessary or of any value to practice spelling words orally (except for such artificial situations as spell-downs and spelling-bees) in order to communicate. Practice the skill in the manner in which it will be used. For oral communication, correct pronunciation and clear enunciation are of importance, but spelling is not.

The development of spelling parallels and to some degree makes use of some of the same skills used in the development of independence in reading. Thus, the visual recognition of a word often enables the writer to determine whether or not it "looks right." A knowledge of syllabication, word analysis, prefixes, and suffixes is also an aid to spelling. Because reading and spelling are in many ways similar and yet follow somewhat different rules, they should not be taught simultaneously or in conjunction with one another except at the early, initial stages. The learning of one may, at a later date, interfere with the learning of the other. Many of the phonics rules learned for reading result in rather peculiar outcomes when applied to spelling. Certain basic rules of spelling are essential to competence. It must also be remembered that some words do not follow these rules and must be memorized.

SUMMARY

The language arts and communications skills are among the most important, lasting tools that can be taught children. Consequently, they must form an important part of any program for slow learners. Persons provided with a good foundation in these areas are much better prepared to continue the acquisition of essential knowledge and information throughout the rest of their lives than persons who have not attained a competence in them. An individual provided with the skills essential to the continuance of his education indefinitely and independently, is much more capable of making the necessary adjustments to a changing society and a changing economy. The language arts and communications skills are crucial tools in any plan for education.

No attempt was made in this chapter to provide the reader with a brief digest of how to teach the various skills contained under the inclusive heading of the language arts—speech, language, reading, and oral and written communication. The methods described thoroughly in many different volumes and the manuals accompanying reading series used with normal children are also appropriate for use with the slow learners. Instead of differences in methods, differences in emphasis and making use of the most appropriate ways of working with the slow learners must be the primary concern.

The characteristics common to most slow learners (slow developmental rate, reduced psycho-social stimulation, and a paucity of good speech and language experiences) require adjustments in the program if it is to meet their needs adequately. The entire program in language arts and communications instruction should be developmental in nature. It should be remembered that the retarded development of the slow learners will require an extended readiness program and a wider spacing of the introduction of successive skills than is true for normal children. Formal reading instruction should be introduced approximately one and one-half years later, on the average, for slow learners than for normal children. Other reading skills, such as the development of abilities necessary for independent reading and, later, the development of efficiency in reading, must also be introduced and developed proportionately later than is true for normal children.

Oral communication needs to be stressed for a longer period of time and to a greater degree with most slow learners than with normal children. Their speech and language skills are not as highly developed when they enter school as those of normal children. This is due partially to their lower intellectual developmental level. Environmental deprivation and lack of adequate language stimulation are also causative factors. As a result, a great deal of stress should be placed upon the development of this important area of communication.

Writing and spelling should be introduced as the need arises, after the slow learners have achieved sufficient intellectual development and background of experiences to enable them to benefit from the instruction. Since writing and spelling are important for communications purposes (and have little or no value in any other way), they should be taught within that context. Legibility in writing and accuracy in the spelling of those words used in written assignments should be continuously stressed. Every written lesson should be a lesson in writing and spelling.

SELECTED RELATED READINGS

California State Committee on Developmental Reading, "Reading Instruction for the Slow Learner in the Secondary School," *National Association Secondary School Principals Bulletin,* 35:11–53, February, 1951.

Epler, M. R. and O. B. Handley, "Third Group Pupil," *Elementary School Journal,* 59:451–55, May, 1959.

Featherstone, William B., *Teaching the Slow Learner,* Bureau of Publications, Teachers College, Columbia University, 1951, pp. 70–83.

Gates, Arthur I. and M. C. Pritchard, "Teaching Reading to Slow-Learning or 'Dull-Normal' Pupils," *Teachers College Record,* 43:255–63, January, 1942.

Gork, Edward R., " 'Switching' Slow Readers," *The Instructor,* 68:121, September, 1958.

Greene, Jay E., "A 'Slow English-Class' Investigates Community Living," *English Journal,* 40:339–41, June, 1951.

Hartung, Maurice L., "English for the Slow Learner," *School Review,* 54:198–99, April, 1946.

Hudson, C. A., "Experiment with Slow Learning Beginning Children," *American School Board Journal,* 101:18, July, 1940.

Justa, Sister Mary, "Meeting the Reading Needs of the Slow Learners," *Journal of Education,* 137:11–15, October, 1954.

Kirk, Samuel A., *Teaching Reading to Slow Learning Children.* Boston: Houghton Mifflin Company, 1940, 225 pages.

Konigsberg, Evelyn, "Speech for the Slow Learner," *National Association Secondary School Principals Bulletin,* 32:148–51, January, 1948.

Lessem, S. W., "Reading for Slow Learners," *English Journal,* 45:275–77, May, 1956.

Lobdell, Lawrence O., "A Classic as Reading Material for Retarded Readers," *English Journal,* 39:491–96, June, 1950.

McCarthy, Agnes, "Teaching Communication to Slow Learners," *English Journal,* 36:401–407, March, 1947.

———, "Teaching Slow Learners to Write," *National Association Secondary School Principals Bulletin,* 39:106–110, September, 1955.

Preston, Ralph C., "How English Teachers Can Help Retarded Readers," *English Journal,* 36:137–40, March, 1947.

Rickert, Mary O., "Motivation for Slow Learners," *English Journal,* 38:43–44, January, 1949.

Robinson, Esther A., "Reclaiming the Slow-Learning Boys and Girls," *English Journal,* 36:134–37, March, 1947.

Rothenberg, Julius, "'English Errors for Slow Learners," *English Journal,* 32:551–56, December, 1943.

Thornley, Wilson R., "Unlocking Resources of Retarded Students," *English Journal,* 39:302–306, June, 1950.

U. S. Office of Education, *Teaching Rapid and Slow Learners in High Schools,* Department of Health, Education, and Welfare, Bulletin No. 5, 1954, 97 pages.

Van Steenbergh, S., "Techniques Useful in Teaching Slow Classes," *High Points,* 22:71–73, November, 1940.

8

Mathematics and the

Content Areas

The entire curriculum for slow learners cannot be devoted to the development of proficiency in the communications skills, important as these may be. The emphasis changes from level to level. Communications skills may be the most highly emphasized area in the primary school but the children are also introduced to quantitative concepts and content in the social science and physical science areas. At the intermediate and junior high school levels greater emphasis is placed on mathematics and content but with continuing emphasis on communications skills. Communications skills and ability to manipulate numbers should be well developed by the senior high school level. At this time emphasis is placed upon the content areas and the application of skills.

SELECTION OF LEARNING EXPERIENCES

A section of chapter 4 was devoted to the development of a core curriculum for slow learners. This curriculum is founded upon the provision of meaningful and useful experiences for children based upon their physical, psychological, emotional, social, and environmental needs. These essentially define the slow learners' educational needs. It cannot be too highly emphasized that experiences, in order to be meaningful to the children, must be selected in reference to the present rather than in anticipation of some future need. Only if an individual learns to live and contribute effectively today can he be expected to make the appropriate adjustments and develop the necessary insights and understandings to deal effectively with problems as they arise tomorrow.

Following these principles, reading, writing, spelling, and effective oral communication skills are recommended as important skills (tools) to be taught because of their value in the development of effective daily communication. Certain other basic skills and content areas are also essential and should be included in an organized and systematic fashion. Among these are arithmetical or quantitative concepts, relationships, and usage; social science concepts (particularly those related to the children's personal and social relationships), civic problems and responsibilities, and state and national influences important in their lives; general and specific experiences and information concerning their own physical welfare and relationship to their physical environment; and other experiences that will improve motor skills and aesthetic appreciation.

ARITHMETICAL AND QUANTITATIVE CONCEPTS AND SKILLS

Arithmetical concepts and skills are used continuously throughout each day. They are related to the normal living activities of both children and adults. How useful, valuable, and effective they are is largely dependent upon the accuracy of the basic concepts involved, how well these concepts have been learned, and how well the skills can be applied.

Concepts involving size, shape, distance, amount, and time are essential to independent personal, social, and economic adjustment. Without an understanding of them the individual would be unable to carry on even the simplest activities or make the many decisions that are continually required in daily living. Selections of various kinds, such as those required in travel, keeping appointments, making purchases, homemaking activities, and most vocational activities are only a few of the many possible examples of daily activities in which quantitative and general arithmetical concepts are indispensable.

The development of basic quantitative concepts ordinarily have their initial beginnings prior to the children's entrance into school. Kindergarten and first-grade teachers must carefully assess the level of development of each child, however, since they will have diverse backgrounds of experience and levels of ability. Only following an evaluation is the teacher able to plan a systematic training program and provide the readiness experiences each child has need for. The program should progress steadily toward the learning of more complex skills as well as "filling in" any gaps or deficiencies the children may possess. Mistaken concepts must also be corrected. These initial stages do not include experiences of a formalized nature accompanied by drill on number combinations. They do, instead, provide the children with the background of experiences and information (the foundation) upon which the use of numerical combinations and manipulative skills will be based.

The various fundamental concepts that should be developed at the pre-academic level are those that concern motion, time, quantity, comparison, and location. These concepts have meaning and value to the children even before formal work with numbers begins. It is important to know "fast" and "slow"; "when," "what happened before," and "what is going to happen next" or at a later time; "all," "some," "many," as well as some common, specific measures; "bigger," "sooner," "thicker," "more"; and "up," "in," "on," "above," "across," and so forth. Since these are concepts used in daily living activities, they should be taught in relation to these activities. Taught effectively, they provide the sound foundation essential to future learning, to working with specific quantities and amounts, and to understanding arithmetical manipulations that can too easily become mechanical and meaningless.

Arithmetic probably demonstrates more clearly than any other academic skill the futility of teaching just the mechanics without providing the children with an adequate foundation of concepts and application. Few adults who have completed the elementary grades are not familiar with the exercise $\frac{1}{2} \div \frac{1}{4}$. Most of them, with a little thought, will come up with the correct solution, 2. How many of them, however, have an understanding of what they did, why they did it, or what the solution means? How is it possible to divide a fraction by a fraction and arrive at an answer that consists of a whole number? What does the 2 mean? Similarly, how can one multiply two fractional quantities ($\frac{1}{2} \times \frac{1}{2}$) and arrive at a solution ($\frac{1}{4}$) that is less than either of the original numbers? Don't these examples go against all the principles that were taught at an earlier date concerning multiplication and division as these processes are related to whole numbers? One of the first multiplication concepts developed by most children is that the product is larger than either of the numbers being multiplied together. Yet, when one or both of the quantities are fractions, this concept no longer holds. This is only one of many examples of possible confusion and lack of understanding, and one wonders how effectively many persons can *use* these manipulative skills that were "taught" in the grades. Fortunately, most normal or intellectually gifted persons achieve an eventual level of intellectual development that enables them to make the correct generalizations and then use these concepts correctly. Unforunately, this happy state of affairs cannot be depended upon to occur for many slow learners. If the school considers it desirable that the slow learners be able to use these concepts, the concepts must be taught in such a manner that the slow learners understand them and understand how to use them.

The area of academic learning in which the majority of the slow learners who are taught in undifferentiated programs are least retarded is the development of arithmetic mechanics or computational skills. The manipulation of numbers and recitation of arithmetic conbinations and multiplication tables can be, and unfortunately too often are, accomplished with little or no understanding of the processes involved. The children may have little or no ability to use or apply these skills to find the correct solution of a problem. It is often stated that children dislike the time that must be spent on mechanical practice in order to become efficient in their use. It is also assumed by many persons that slow learners have a short attention span and will not keep at a job for any length of time. Yet, every teacher who has worked with slow learners, particularly at the elementary level, knows that it is not unusual for slow learners to do pages and pages of arithmetic exercises and when finished to ask for more. Slow learners derive a feeling of accomplishment, a feeling that they are like the rest of the children, and a feeling of belongingness from this activity. It is usually the one academic area in which they can perform at or near the level of the majority of the children in the class. The success achieved makes them willing to put forth the continuing effort and devote the necessary time to master the mechanics.

This is a prime example of a factor important to learning that is often ignored by many teachers—the factor of success. Educators today devote a great deal of effort in an attempt to make learning experiences attractive to the children. This is important, but most children want to learn, at least initially. The desire will continue, regardless of the nature of materials and content, only if they feel they are learning something of value and that they are having success. While the completion of pages of arithmetic combinations and multiplication exercises may appear to be a deadening activity and thoroughly boring to many adults, high interest is often generated for the slow learners through the factor of having success in an activity that is apparently of importance in school. Too often this is the only activity in which the children see themselves as being successful, thus enhancing the activity in their eyes to even a higher degree. Accomplishments in this area often have tremendous extrinsic and prestige values, although there is little value of an intrinsic nature in that there is little or no comprehension of what is being accomplished. Little ability may be developed to apply these skills to the problems in which they are required. Arithmetic mechanics and skills should be taught and used at the child's level of comprehension and for the purpose of their application.

Arithmetic also demonstrates clearly the general principles that should be used in instruction, particularly for the slow learners. The three steps to be followed in sequence in the development of any concept or skill are: (1) develop a need for, and a basic understanding of, the concepts involved; (2) practice the skills involved sufficiently, so that their use becomes efficient—rapid and accurate; and (3) provide innumerable meaningful opportunities to apply the concepts and use the skills for the purpose of better learning their use, for re-enforcement of the learning, and for review to ensure retention. These steps are not completely independent of one another but indicate the emphasis that should be placed upon instruction at each of the successive steps. One cannot develop the need for, and understanding of, a concept without placing it in a context of practical application and at the same time giving some practice in finding the solution. Practice of the skill is thus included in the first step as well. If the basic concepts have been adequately developed initially, the second step of practice for the purpose of improving accuracy and efficiency will also have meaning and purpose. Some related application of the skills will also be recognized and understood. According to Brownell,

> The demands of modern living make arithmetic competence one of the real imperatives. The program of arithmetic instruction to which the present generations of adults were subjected did not produce this competence. The results of extensive testing by the Army and Navy have served only to highlight the prevailing adult arithmetical deficiencies, a fact which was known to teachers of mathematics in secondary schools and college. To remedy the evils of current mathematical deficiency what seems to be needed is not more of the same kind of instruction which produced these evils, but a fundamental reorganization in the subject matter and teaching of arithmetic.

> * * *

> The arithmetic programs of the past twenty-five years have been inadequate chiefly at two points. First, these programs have given children little chance to use ideas and skills already learned in solving their own personal problems. Second, these arithmetic programs have neglected the meanings and rational principles which make arithmetic a phase of mathematics.[1]

Where formalized instruction and practice of the mechanics are the first step, children are apt to develop facility in number manipulation without developing an understanding of the essential concepts involved, the need for these concepts, and the application of the skills to the solution of problems in needful situations. For this reason it is not unusual to find slow learners incapable of compre-

[1] William A. Brownell, "When is Arithmetic Meaningful?" *Journal of Educational Research*, 38:498, March, 1945.

hending what is desired or unable to find the solution to practical problems. They are unable to formulate the information in a way which will allow them to make use of their computational skills. The numbers involved in practical problems are often taken by slow learners and indiscriminately placed into computational form for addition, subtraction, multiplication, or division. Little or no regard is given to the content of the problem, the process appropriate for its solution, or the discriminate selection of the correct figures and quantities involved, based upon the information provided. If and when the correct solution is occasionally obtained, it is too often more dependent on chance than on design. The purpose of the second step of formalized instruction (practice or drill for habituation) is to provide the children with an efficient (rapid and accurate) method of problem solution. This should replace the earlier, more primitive methods used initially. These earlier methods (usually requiring the use of "crutches") include counting on the fingers, counting and grouping cubes or other objects, counting marks made on paper, and so forth.

Arithmetic and quantitative concepts, with their appropriate usage, should be taught developmentally. If the child has matured sufficiently to understand the concepts, and has also acquired sufficient skill and knowledge through either planned or incidental background experiences to be ready for their acquisition, they should be systematically introduced. Following the acquisition of the general quantitative concepts taught at the pre-school, kindergarten, and first grade levels (for children with normal intelligence) the children should be systematically introduced to more specific quantities and quantitative relationships. These should be introduced first through the medium of meaningful, concrete objects with which the children are familiar and commonly use. As a substitute, beads, cubes, or shoe pegs may be used, but the social value and consequent intrinsic purpose may be lost to some extent. It is imperative that children understand the meaningful, concrete relationship between name and amount before they attempt to deal with quantities abstractly. Eventually, the abstract understandings of quantities and relationships must be developed, because only by knowing these can the innumerable life applications be made as they are required.

Brueckner and Grossnickle list desired arithmetic outcomes under two phases—mathematical and social.

(1) Outcomes related to the *mathematical* phase of arithmetic:
    a. An understanding of the structure of the decimal number system and an appreciation of its simplicity and efficiency.
    b. The ability to perform computations connected with social situations with reasonable speed and accuracy, both mentally and with mechanical computing devices.
    c. The ability to make dependable estimates and close approximations.
    d. Resourcefulness and ingenuity in perceiving and dealing with quantative aspects of situations.
    e. Understanding of the technical vocabulary used to express quantitative ideas and relations.
    f. Ability to use and devise formulas, rules of procedure, and methods of bringing out relationships.
    g. Ability to represent designs and spacial relations by drawings.
    h. The ability to arrange numerical data systematically and to interpret information presented in graphic or tabular form.

(2) Outcomes related to the *social* phase of arithmetic:
    a. Understanding of the process of measurement and skill in the use of instruments of precision.
    b. Knowledge about the development and social significance of such institutions as money, taxation, banking, standard time and measurement.
    c. Knowledge of the kinds and sources of information essential for intelligent buying and selling and for general economic competence.
    d. Understanding of the quantitative vocabulary encountered in reading, in business affairs, and in social relations.
    e. Appreciation of the contributions number has made to the development of social cooperation and to science.
    f. Ability and disposition to secure and utilize reliable information in dealing with emerging personal and community problems.
    g. Ability to rationalize and analyze experience by utilization of quantitative procedures.[2]

A child should initially learn the gross meanings of quantity—more, many, less, and so forth. Following this he learns the small,

2 Leo J. Brueckner and F. E. Grossnickle, *How to Make Arithmetic Meaningful* (Philadelphia: John C. Winston Company, 1953), pp. 3-4.

specific quantities such as 1, 2, 3, etc. The next step is to relate the symbol to the quantity and begin to combine small quantities (simple addition). Only after the quantities are understood, the concept of combining quantities comprehended, and the relationship between the quantities and the symbols established can efficient methods of problem solving be developed. The last associations that must be made are between the quantity and the symbol and the printed word. The symbol and word ("2" and "two") are abstractions related to an abstract amount; they don't define the amount of *what*. The *what* may be any object or objects and thus the comprehension of the abstraction has universal application. The oral name, the printed symbol, and the written word all denoting a specified quantity or amount will thus have meaning in relation to the quantitative concepts already established. They are, therefore, also capable of being used in any and all needful situations. Children can respond by producing the correct amount whenever they are requested or required to do so.

The early introduction of rote counting, sometimes offered by parents or teachers, in no way ensures the understanding of the quantities involved. A child may learn to count to ten or more without comprehending the amounts involved. He may not even be capable of selecting a much smaller, specified number of objects. Counting is primarily related to sequence and order. As a child learns and understand sequence (first, second, the next one, and so forth) counting becomes a meaningful activity. Simply having the ability to name the number that precedes or follows a specified number name neither indicates a grasp nor ensures an understanding of either sequence or quantity. Actually, if sequence and quantitative concepts are developed initially, there is little or no necessity to teach rote counting as such. The concept the children must learn is the principle upon which the American number system is based—tens. Later, other systems will have to be introduced, as in measurement (12 inches, 1 foot; 36 inches, 1 yard; and so forth) and weight (16 ounces, 1 pound; 2000 pounds, 1 ton; and so forth).

Counting may also be of value in determining the specific number in a quantity of objects. There are definite and rather restricted limits to the number of discrete objects that can be specifically recognized at a glance. When the group of objects becomes too large, the specific objects must be counted or smaller sub-groups established that can be recognized and then combined. As the children acquire the knowledge and understanding of the amounts and relative positions involved, much of the necessary counting skill will follow of itself. Initially, time should be devoted to the comprehension of basic concepts, thus insuring better learning. In this way the amount of time it is necessary to devote to rote learning types of activities may also be reduced.

Present-day research related to learning in children does not indicate that slow learners have any unique learning problems as compared to normal children of the same developmental level. Slow learners do not comprise a unique population but are an integral part of the total population. As such, they follow the same continuum of characteristics, including learning, that is true for the population in general. No unique methods of teaching arithmetic are indicated. The key to instruction is a clear understanding of the developmental levels, the general readiness of the children, and the background of experiences the children bring with them to the learning situation. Where normal children have sufficient intellectual maturity and experiential background to derive benefit from certain instruction at a specific grade level, the slow learners at the same chronological ages may have neither. These experiences will have to be introduced to them at a later date, when they have matured sufficiently and been provided with the essential readiness experiences.

Addition and subtraction combinations should be introduced in much the same way as counting and sequence. The presentation to slow learners can be similar to that used with normal children but only at a later date, when they have achieved sufficient maturity and readiness experiences. The concepts, quantities, and combinations should be introduced through the use of concrete and, preferably, socially meaningful materials. No special techniques or methods for obtaining solutions rapidly should be introduced at this stage. "Crutches" of various kinds may be appropriate if they help the children "figure" or think their way through to a correct solution. As the children demonstrate the ability to understand and deal with small quantities and use combinations of them, larger and larger quantities should gradually and systematically be introduced. Finally, all of the basic combinations through the 9's are understood. As successively larger quantities are introduced and included in the various combinations along with the printed symbols, they should initially be associated with concrete materials. This is an aid to the establishment of understanding of the relationships. It is also an aid in achieving the ultimate goal of comprehension of the abstractions and symbolic representations of the quantities involved.

Once a child has really learned the concepts involved in combinations through the 9's and understands the number system, he can deal effectively with numbers of a quantity and size beyond his immediate comprehension. For example, if a child understands 10 and understands 5, knowing the number system he can work intelligently with 50, although he may not comprehend a quantity of that magnitude. He can understand that 50 is 5 tens or 10 fives. Adults must use the same kind of relationships or associative methods when attempting to understand the magnitude of municipal budgets or the national debt. With no direct acquaintance with quantities of those sizes, they nevertheless can be dealt with intelligently.

Following the development of concepts, sufficient practice or drill with the various combinations must be provided each child to eliminate the use of "crutches." He will then be able to arrive at the correct response accurately and rapidly. After a combination has been learned, periodic review is essential to ensure retention and efficient future use. Then, and then only, will children be capable of dealing effectively, rapidly, and accurately with the number combination abstractions and also apply the correct method to the solution of problems in the actual situations in which they are required.

In the past it was usually recommended that after a child understood and was capable of using small or simple addition combinations, subtraction, as a concept, should be introduced. However, since subtraction is not actually a new or unique concept, but an integral part of a larger concept of accession and deduction, it can be taught simultaneously with addition. The concept of a number such as "4" is more than just the quantity and may be better expressed by the term *fourness*. Children who understand the concept of fourness know that the quantity 4, as represented by $2 + 2$, $3 + 1$, 2×2, 4×1, $5 - 1$, $6 - 2$, $8 \div 2$, and so forth is, in all cases, the same quantity. This more useful, abstract concept of fourness is thought by many to be better developed if processes such as addition and subtraction are taught together rather than as discrete concepts and methods. Following this idea, the application of number combinations for the solution of addition and subtraction problems would be taught at the same time.

Other elementary, numerical manipulations and skills, such as multiplication and division, should be taught following the same three-step method. Since multiplication is a short method of adding or combining quantities of the same or equal size, it should be taught as it is related to addition. Similarly, division is the determination of the number of quantities of a specified size that are contained in a stated quantity. These basic concepts, which are all too rarely taught well, are essential if children are to make good use of the processes learned. Furthermore, these concepts should be taught as simply and directly as possible so as to minimize the learners' confusion. The children should be capable of using and applying the concepts prior to the attainment of proficiency in the mechanics and the complete memorization of tables. A number of new "methods" have recently received publicity, their authors stating that they improve arithmetic competencies. Where the method is designed to increase comprehension, it is worth examining more closely for possible use with slow learners. Where it is a method designed to speed up mechanics or accelerate work with large numbers, its values, at least for slow learners, might well be questioned.

Swenson, concerned with the interrelationships among the four fundamental processes states:

> If the processes are developed as simple matters of grouping and regrouping and if children are given ample opportunity to do the grouping and regrouping, there is no reason why the typical child should leave third grade without seeing these relationships: (a) Addition and subtraction are opposite processes—putting together and taking apart. (b) Multiplication and division are opposite processes—putting together and taking apart. (c) Multiplication is usually a faster putting-together process than addition. (d) Multiplication always deals with equal-sized groups, while addition may deal with either equal-sized or unequal-sized subgroups. (e) Division is usually a faster taking-apart process than subtraction. (f) Division always deals with equal-sized groups, while subtraction may deal with either equal- or unequal-sized groups.[3]

[3] Esther J. Swenson, "Arithmetic for Preschool and Primary-Grade Children," in *The Teaching of Arithmetic*, Fiftieth Yearbook of National Society for the Study of Education, Part II., 1951, p. 66.

When thinking of the fundamental processes in this manner, one can introduce addition, subtraction, multiplication, and division simultaneously through the medium of counting concrete objects. Using small, simple quantities, the concept of addition can be developed by counting the individual components of two quantities together to determine the total or sum. This could also be applied, if necessary, to more than two quantities. In subtraction, the smaller quantity (subtrahend) is counted out of the larger quantity (minuend) and the amount that remains is then counted to determine the answer (difference). Muliplication can be demonstrated and taught simply by first making the number of quantities that the multiplier indicates are present the size of the multiplicand. Then count the total number of units in all of the groups to determine the product. Division is no more difficult. Extract all quantities equal in size to the divisor from the total number of objects contained in the dividend, then count the number of groups to arrive at the correct solution (quotient).

It must be remembered that these are only bare outlines of possible methods to use in establishing the basic concepts involved in addition, subtraction, multiplication, and divison. New methods of presentation of arithmetic concepts and materials that seem to be much sounder and promise to be more effective than some presently in use are now appearing in basic texts. The previous descriptions do not describe the total arithmetic curriculum for slow learners; nor can they ensure that the children will attain full competency in the use of these various combinations, tables, and mechanics. The full curriculum must go much farther, carrying the application of teaching principles into instruction in the use of fractions, percentages, and decimals. The curriculum must also be extended to include measurement, time, and other arithmetical concepts found in common, daily usage.

While concept development must come first in instruction, sufficient practice must be provided to make sure that a high enough level of competency has been developed in the mechanics so that the skills are useful and efficient. One cannot go through life with a pocketful of beads, shoe pegs, or cubes in order to be able to figure out the answers to quantitative problems. Moreover, quantities soon become so large that the initial, concrete methods become cumbersome and impossible to handle. It is essential, then, to teach the use and application of abstract symbols to represent the actual articles. Practice should be provided to ensure the learning of various number combinations and tables, for the sake of accuracy and efficiency, and for the sake of solving problems that can be solved easily in no other way. Practice and more practice, drill and more drill is required to achieve this objective. But if the basic need has been established and the basic concepts developed prior to intensive practice, the practice has meaning and purpose.

During the establishment, through successive repetition, of the various combinations and tables as almost mechanically correct responses, continuous application of the skills should be required in many school experiences of the children. It aids in increasing ability to apply them in varied situations. It also acts to continue the reenforcing of the mechanics learned so that the use of the skills remains efficient.

The specific method used to establish accurate use of arithmetic mechanics is not of the greatest importance. Numerous methods, using different terminologies and approaches, have been proposed and are advocated by various texts and basic arithmetic series. Each series provides a teaching manual, which states a preference in regard to the best system for teaching addition, subtraction, multiplication, division, the application of these processes to fractions and decimals, and the development of concepts necessary to deal with large numbers and zero. The method advocated in the textbook that has been adopted is often one of the primary determinants of the method selected by a school system or teacher. Each system undoubtedly has its merits. Little or no research evidence is available that definitely indicates the superiority of one system over all others. The fundamental consideration is that the instruction for slow learners should be systematic, in sequence, consistent, and that no steps are omitted or merely touched upon lightly. Each step must be thoroughly mastered if a sound foundation for each succeeding step is to be established. The teacher cannot expect slow learners to eventually achieve sufficient intellectual power to fill in "gaps" from generalizations developed at some later date. From evidence previously cited, this level of ability is not reached by many normal adults, to say nothing of slow learners.

McConnell lists a number of guiding principles for teaching arithmetic in general that are applicable to slow learners. He states,

(1) Abtract ideas of number develop out of a great amount of concrete, meaningful experience, mature apprehension of number relationships can be attained in no other way. Furthermore, the
adequate development of number ideas calls for systematic teaching
and learning.

(2) Drill does not guarantee that children will be able immediately to
recall combinations as such.

(3) Habituation of number combinations is a final stage in learning
which is preceded by progressively more mature ways of handling
number relationships.

(4) Repeating the final form of a response from the very beginning
may actually encourage the habituation of immature procedures
and seriously impede necessary growth.

(5) Drill as such makes little if any contribution to growth in quantitative thinking by supplying maturer ways of dealing with number.

(6) Intermediate steps, such as the use of the "crutch" in subtraction,
aid the learner both to understand the process and to compute accurately. With proper guidance these temporary reactions may be
expected to give way to more direct responses in the later stages of
learning.

(7) Reorganization of behavior occurs as the child's understanding
grows, and results in the emergence of more precise, complex, and
economical patterns of behavior.

(8) Understanding the number system and the methods of operation it
makes possible facilitates both quantitative thinking and, ultimately, rapid and accurate computation.[4]

Aside from the acquisition of basic number skills, the content of
the arithmetic program should be taken from community experiences. It should be selected from the arithmetical concepts and
usages required of individuals residing in that community. Numbers
that need to be read and understood are commonly found in newspapers, advertisements, directories, licenses, and so forth. They are
very important vocationally as well as in ordinary day-by-day living
activities. Decimals are most commonly used in dealing with money.
Measurement (linear, quantity, and time) is used in too many activities to even begin to enumerate them. Fractional quantities are
important in the division of objects, change, time, and other measure-

[4] T. R. McConnell, "Recent Trends in Learning Theory: Their Application to
the Psychology of Arithmetic," *Arithmetic in General Education*, Sixteenth Yearbook, National Council of Teachers of Mathematics (Washington, D.C.: The
Council, 1941), p. 279.

ment activities. Percentage is primarily related to interest on money, although there are other common usages as well. These, then, largely determine the content of the arithmetic program. They should be presented in a meaningful context. Practice should be provided to help ensure accuracy and appropriate application. The community provides a wealth of opportunities to teach arithmetic in a meaningful way. Arithmetic is particularly susceptible to the inclusion of community-centered experiences.

The following is a broad outline of the skills and content one might normally include in an arithmetic program for slow learners at each of the four levels. The teacher may wish to (and should) supplement this brief list of competencies with the arithmetical needs he observes while working with the children. The list is not intended to be all-inclusive. It is intended to provide the reader with a fairly concrete indication of the arithmetic ability the average slow learners should achieve and an idea of the kind of content that might be appropriately included for most of the children at each of the four levels. Some of the slow learners will be unable to achieve all that is included within the allotted time. Others will progress farther. Since all programs should be developmental in terms of the rate and level of growth of each child, it is expected that this principle will be followed. Children who have not accomplished all that was expected at the previous school level should continue at their own achievement level. They should not start at the place the teacher or school has defined as the beginning of the new school level. Similarly, those children who have progressed more rapidly than the majority of the group should not be penalized for their growth by being required to repeat some of their learning experiences. Instead, they should be aided in continuing to learn at their appropriate rate by receiving instruction at their present level of performance.

Primary school

The average slow learners will be performing academically at middle second-grade level by the time they complete the program of the primary school. They may enter school with a mental age as low as 3 years-6 months. Even the oldest and highest of the slow learners will be intellectually below the school's expectations for the average kindergarten child. As a result, many of the concepts and skills normal children have learned prior to their entrance into school will be absent in the slow learners. Teachers must consciously plan to include activities that will develop them. Only in this way will the children be ready to benefit from the instruction of the more formal aspects of arithmetic when they are intellectually prepared for such a learning experience. Following, are some suggestions relative to the primary school arithmetic program for slow learners.

1. Instruction in a general arithmetic vocabulary should include words relating to concepts concerned with quantity, size, weight, height, time, and movement.
2. A specific vocabulary should be developed to include concepts related to time, numbers, processes, simple fractions, measurements, and money.
3. General concepts should be developed that involve amounts, zero, number sequence, ordinal numbers, grouping for processes (addition, subtraction, multiplication, and division), fractions, money, and measurement (lineal, dry, and liquid).
4. Processes that should be taught include:
   a. addition through sums of 10;
   b. subtraction through a minuend of 10;
   c. multiplication grouping, but with no memorization of tables;
   d. division using only groupings of small numbers; and
   e. signs of addition (+) and subtraction (−).
5. Basic concepts of money should be developed, including:
   a. recognition of all coins;
   b. knowledge of larger (more), smaller (less), largest (most), and smallest (least); and
   c. specific values and combinations of coins through 10.
6. Instruction should be provided to teach the reading of numbers; it should include the specific vocabulary related to arithmetical activities.

The skills and concepts being developed should be continuously related to the solution of problems requiring their use. Problems should be related to classroom and normal, daily living activities. At this level, particularly, many of the problems should be presented orally. The children should be required to make a choice of the appropriate process and select pertinent data or information. Where appropriate, visual and concrete materials should be made use of in finding solutions.

Intermediate school

At the completion of the intermediate school years, the average arithmetic achievement for slow learners should be at about the high fourth-grade level. The children will have a mean mental age of 10 years at this time. Some of the children will require primary school experiences while others will be performing at the intermediate school level at the time of their entrance. The arithmetic program for slow learners in the intermediate school should include an assurance of competency in the content of the primary program plus the following skills and concepts.

1. The children's vocabularies should be expanded to include all arithmetical processes, time (hours, minutes, seconds, days, and months), commonly used signs, and various common measurements. Standard textbooks often emphasize the learning of such technical terms as minuend, subtrahend, multiplicand, multiplier, divisor, dividend, remainder, numerator, denominator, common denominator, addend, quotient, and so forth. While the concepts are used continuously, the terms are seldom if ever used in practical, daily problem solving. The concepts can be taught without the use of the technical terms. Instead, descriptive terms the children readily understand should be used. Teach the concepts; the terms are seldom used or even remembered by most normal adults.
2. Instruction should include concepts related to the number system (place, zero, sequence, and ordinal numbers), grouping (addition, subtraction, multiplication, and division), carrying and borrowing (other terms are also in common use), fractional parts, measurement, tables and graphs, monetary system, and some common geometric forms.
3. Processes that should be taught should include:
    a. addition (of any numbers and with carrying);
    b. subtraction (of any numbers and with borrowing, excepting examples involving negative results);
    c. multiplication and division (tables through the 5's, carrying in multiplication, and remainders in division);
    d. all signs ($+$, $-$, $\times$, $\div$, $=$); and
    e. fractions through sixteenths, including the finding of fractional parts and performing simple addition of fractions.
4. The understanding of money should be developed to the point where the children can:
    a. apply processes learned;

b. understand parts and relationships through $1.00; and
c. read and understand a vocabulary that includes such terms as
   cash, interest, installment, payment, and so forth.

After completing the program at the intermediate school level, the children should be relatively competent in problem solving. They should understand the arithmetic processes taught through this level and be able to select the correct ones for the solution of two-step problems. They should be capable of using and figuring bills, order blanks, and sale advertisements. Most of the problems arising from industrial arts and homemaking activities should be within their ability to solve correctly. They should understand absurdities, recognize when essential data are missing, and in general have the ability to understand and discover basic relationships.

Junior high school

At the completion of the junior high school program, the majority of the slow learners will have attained their maximum mental development. Their average mental age will be about 12 years-7 months. The lowest of the group will have a mental age of 11 years-3 months and the highest a mental age of 13 years-11 months. It would be expected that the range of grade-level achievement would be from 5.9 to 8.5. The average achievement should be at the 7.3 grade level. Since this school level represents the last period in which the slow learners can be expected to show a meaningful increase in intellectual development, a planned arithmetic program to ensure their best ultimate performance should be provided them. The junior high school program should, therefore, include instruction in at least the following areas.

1. Vocabulary instruction should include numerous terms normally found in business and industry.
2. Measurement should be dealt with in precise terms.
3. The handling of money and the basic concepts related to earning, spending, borrowing, budgeting, and taxation form the foundation of the instruction.
4. Continued emphasis should be placed on processes to ensure their accurate and efficient use. The tables should be completed. Problems using any and all of the processes should be able to be dealt with.

Except for the completion of the tables for use in multiplication and division, most of the basic skill learning has been accomplished prior to the junior high school program. Many aspects of the higher-grade arithmetic programs for normal children (fractions, mixed numbers, decimals, and so forth) can also be taught to slow learners. In fact, they should already have an understanding of the essential basic concepts; beyond that, most of the activities are unessential and should not be included in the program. As previously indicated, much of the instruction at the junior high school level is planned to help the slow learners to use their skills and knowledges as effectively as possible. Thus, activities are planned to give them practice in problem solving using their previous learnings. The problems should be related to their daily school and out-of-school activities.

Senior high school

Slow learners enrolled in the senior high school program will usually have achieved their maximum intellectual development. If adequate instruction has been provided at the preceding levels, there will be little purpose or value in continued skill and developmental instruction. The only instruction of this type that should be provided in the senior high school program is of a remedial nature. This does not mean that no instruction in arithmetic should take place. Because a child has reached his intellectual maturity does not mean that he can no longer learn. Instead of skill instruction, however, the emphasis for slow learners at this level should be in terms of continuing emphasis and intensification of instruction directed toward application of skills and concepts learned.

During the senior high school years the slow learners are participating to a greater and greater degree in community economic experiences. It is from these and from the experiences encountered in the industrial arts and homemaking programs that the arithmetic problems should be taken. Whenever children indicate that they are having difficulty, the teacher should carefully analyze the situation and, provide immediate instruction in background experiences that will enable them to arrive at the correct solution. There is no formal arithmetic curriculum at this level. The curriculum is determined by the problems the children have to solve.

PHYSICAL SCIENCE

A person, in order to live effectively in his environment, must have a basic understanding of the physical world about him and ways in which he can use and control it to his advantage. At one time science in school was restricted to the study of general science, biology, chemistry, and physics in the senior high school. Today it is recognized that many scientific explanations and phenomena can be understood by elementary school children. As a result, science education has taken an important position in elementary and junior high school programs for all children, without necessarily becoming involved with highly technical terms, equipment, and experiments. The elementary program, instead, is concerned with developing understandings of the daily experiences of the children. This, rather than the senior high school approach, is the more appropriate for slow learners in terms of the objectives for them.

Facilities and equipment, of course, are determined by the type of science activities in the school program. Certainly programs of science should be in harmony with the purposes of the total program of education which, in the main, helps children gain values, understandings, and skills consistent with good citizenship in a democratic society. Each school must define its own objectives before making decisions concerning equipment and materials. Although many specific aims might be suggested, the following are representative of the general objectives found in most elementary school science programs:

1. Build science experiences around the solving of problems which are significant to boys and girls.
2. Provide activities which aid children to gain skill in the use of many methods of finding out things for themselves.
3. Enlarge upon children's ever-present curiosity and interest in the world around them, helping them gain an appreciation of the potential of science and technology for improving man's welfare, and alerting them to the dangers of misuse of scientific knowledge.
4. Select experiences which aid children to understand some generalizations and principles of science applicable to the solving of problems in their environment.
5. Show that advances in science require freedom of thought and inquiry.
6. Illustrate the relation of science to other areas of knowledge.[5]

The content of the science program is taken from the environment and experiences of the children. In carrying out the program,

[5] Albert Piltz, *Science Equipment and Materials for Elementary Schools*, Washington, D. C.: U. S. Department of Health, Education, and Welfare, Office of Education, Bulletin No. 28, 1961, p. 1.

the children should be encouraged to question and speculate. Activities employing investigation, experimentation, and reading should then be used to test hypotheses and find correct answers. Simple equipment is essential and visual aids have been found to be of great value. The activities may vary greatly in duration. Some require only a short time period, others may have to extend over several days, weeks, or even months. The following outline of instructional areas is only a short compilation of suggested content that may be appropriate for the various school levels.

Primary school

The science program for slow learners at the primary school level consists of teaching them to notice and become aware of their physical environment. Activities are directly related to the personal experiences of the children, many of them being an outgrowth of the "sharing" period. No formal approach is made to a study of science nor is a specific time for science set aside during the day. A great deal of science is nevertheless introduced. Such topics as the weather, communication, growing things from seeds and bulbs, the seasons, and pets are valuable. Through these topics and activities, basic concepts can be introduced and developed.

Intermediate school

Slow learners at the intermediate school level have learned how to read fairly well and have a background of investigation from their experiences in the primary school. They are ready for more formalized instruction and experimentation. Depending upon the facilities and locality, such topics as the following are appropriate: animals (wild, domesticated, useful, their young, and changes with the seasons), plants (useful, harmful, decorative, changes with the seasons, leaves, and seeds), and changes in the characteristics of water, the sun, birds, fish, insects, and basic machines.

Junior and senior high schools

Fairly difficult and complicated topics can be introduced at the junior high school level. The slow learners have not only developed to the stage where they can comprehend them but they are capable of carrying out studies themselves, usually under direction. Many of the topics at the junior and senior high school levels are the same as those found at the lower levels. The content and concepts are based at a much higher developmental level, however. Thus, they are fully as valuable and as meaningful as they were at the lower levels. Since good science laboratories are provided in most secondary schools, those activities that can be carried out or demonstrated more effectively in this setting should be done here. All students, slow learners included, should have equal access to these facilities.

While the junior high school program will, to a large degree, be based upon the experiences the children bring to school with them, this is not as true, directly, for the senior high school program. Much of the program of the senior high school consists of social and vocational, school-directed but out-of-school activities. These activities often provide excellent opportunities to introduce needed science topics. Again the suggested topics will vary according to the locality and needs of the children. The following should be considered: animals, plants, and their interrelationship and interdependence; the earth, rocks, soil, and changes; what things are made of; water and water supply; weather, air, rain, snow, and clouds; sound, heat, light, gravity; machines, magnets, electricity; health and hygiene; community health; and fire.

SOCIAL SCIENCE AND OCCUPATIONAL STUDY

At first glance the heading of this section may appear somewhat incongruous. Yet, as one observes the problems of slow learners during both the school and post-school periods, the two areas are seen to be inextricably related. The need for an understanding of the society and the community as well as competence in interpersonal skills is essential to maintaining oneself economically. Similarly, anyone who *can* but will not care for his own economic needs neither comprehends his role in the society nor can have achieved what is usually considered to be the desired level of personal adjustment. For these reasons the social sciences and vocational training and adjustment are grouped together. The emphasis may very well vary considerably at the different school levels, but the ultimate objective of development of effective personal independence remains constant throughout the program.

Modern education places great emphasis on "learning by doing." This does not mean undirected trial and error learning, for this only accomplishes its goal when the learner understands why he succeeded or failed. It is, instead, a method of instruction whereby important concepts are placed in a meaningful context in order that the learner may achieve the desired end by learning through directed, organized, supervised practice of them. The method usually recommended is the experience-unit organization of instruction. While instruction in all the skills and concepts may, theoretically, be accomplished through the use of experience units, the unit content is usually selected from the social sciences and occasionally the physical sciences. At the higher levels, it may be appropriate to plan the unit for slow learners around vocational choice and competency.

Primary school

The focus of the social science experiences at the primary level should be in terms of the past experiences of the children and experiences that are presently available to them. Since most of the slow learners reside in subcultural, low socio-economic areas of the community, and these areas are usually located near the center (industrial and commercial) of the community, this is the setting of the social sciences program.[6] Being located in this setting, these children are not only acquainted with their homes, neighborhood, and school area at an early date (like all children), they are often acquainted with the industrial and/or primary commercial area of the community as well. It is their neighborhood. Normal children, in outlying areas, often do not have this set of experiences until a much later date.

The home and various facets of the neighborhood, including the "down town," may well be appropriate experience-unit topics. Such topics as the policeman, the fireman, the postman, the grocer, the processing and packaging of foods, sale of goods, recreational facilities, helping agencies, and community health organizations are all

---

[6] In no area is the necessity for the curriculum to reflect the environment and experiences of the children brought out more clearly than in the social sciences. While most slow learners reflect very limited and poor cultural backgrounds, this condition is by no means universal. Some slow learners have well-educated parents and reside in the more highly desired sections of the community. Any program directed toward the former group of slow learners certainly does not meet the educational needs of the latter group. It is essential that the teacher be intimately familiar with the backgrounds of the children before selecting a specific experience unit for the purpose of developing certain skills, attitudes, and knowledges.

meaningful and valuable. Many of them will have already been encountered by the children or their families. Surprisingly few of these topics will be adequately understood especially in regard to the aid some of them can and do provide.

Throughout the social sciences program it must be remembered that it is not sufficient merely to discuss these potential experiences, emphasizing the concepts one hopes the children will accept and understand. Field trips should be taken in order that the children can both see and experience first hand those things it is thought will be of value for them to learn. Preparations must be made for these field trips so that the children will know why they are going, what they are looking for, and comprehend what they are seeing and doing. Following the experience, role-playing and other classroom activities should be planned to re-enforce the knowledges gained from the experience. Visual aids are of value but should be used only for re-enforcement and not as a substitution, except where the first-hand experience is impossible to provide.

Throughout the primary school program no direct emphasis is placed on vocations—at least as far as work the children will be performing is concerned. Mention may be made concerning people at work, why people work, and the work their fathers do. The children themselves, however, are not ready to observe the world of work seriously from a personal point of view insofar as their own personal employment in the future is concerned. Becoming an effective member of the home, neighborhood, community, and society has a real, although somewhat indirect, future vocational value. The development of an understanding of the young child's role helps to establish understanding of the future role as older child and, eventually, as adult. Change in children is a gradual thing—from early childhood into pre-adolescence, into adolescence, and finally into adulthood. Each change is an outgrowth of the former developmental level. How well and how easily one establishes his position and adjusts to the demands at any one level is at least somewhat dependent upon his effectiveness at the previous level.

Intermediate school

The social science experiences that should be provided at the intermediate school level are a repetition as well as an extension of those used in the primary school. It is necessary to re-emphasize the areas studied and experienced at the earlier level because the children are older, more mature, more knowledgeable, and their relationships with the home, neighborhood, and larger community are changing. Their behavior is expected to be different. They are expected to assume more self-direction and responsibility. In some areas they will be expected to do more than take; they will be expected to give, to make a contribution, helping to improve the lot of the younger, more immature children who are less able to take care of themselves. All of these expectations should be established in reference to their abilities and their maturity. They will be expected to "act their age."

Slow learners should be thoroughly familiar with the physical characteristics of their community (geography) by the completion of their stay in the intermediate program. They should also know about common methods of public transportation and how to use them. Wherever and whenever possible, trips should be taken using public transportation rather than school buses. In addition to a familiarity with the physical aspects of their environment, the children should be learning about the history of their area and community and the general characteristics of the local governmental structure or organization. Visits should be made to historical markers and buildings, museums, the courts, city hall, and other city and county buildings to learn firsthand more about the community and how it is run. At election time a study of the method of election and selection of governmental representatives and administrators should be made. General concepts and general understandings are the important things in this program, not how to mark a ballot or pull the levers on a voting machine.

Vocations, as such, still do not take an important place in the program at this school level. By observing people at work while studying the general social science emphasis, the children are steadily obtaining a clearer notion of the role of the employer and the employee in the society and community. A clear understanding of the characteristics and importance of their respective roles will help the children when they take their place in the economy.

Junior high school

The social sciences and vocational studies both receive specific attention in the junior high school. While current events have been discussed in a general way at the primary and elementary levels, they can form much of the foundation of the social science aspects of the junior high school program. Things the children see and hear on television, hear on the radio, and read in the newspaper provide reason and meaning for the study of geography, history, and civics. As current events are occurring, the subjects can and should be introduced in relation to them. By the completion of the junior high school program the slow learners enrolled should have an awareness and fairly good understanding of local and state government and even some general understanding of the national government. They should be aware of the United Nations and know something of how it operates. Geographically, they should have knowledge of their locality, state, and the United States, with a general understanding of the size and location of other important countries, oceans, and so forth. History study should also be centered in their locality but they should have some familiarity with the history of the state and nation.

Continued emphasis should be maintained upon study of the home and community. This emphasis should be primarily concerned with the slow learners' roles as pre-adolescents and adolescents. They should now be contributing materially to the home, not necessarily in terms of money but rather in service-maintenance, meals, cleaning, child care, and taking other kinds of responsibility. The home economics and general shop programs can do much to teach skills in these areas. The objective of development into contributing adults with the ability and desire to improve their environment should be emphasized; the achievement of it should be coming into view.

Achieving independence, including earning a living and maintaining oneself economically, is essential in the completion of personal and social growth. All training is directly or indirectly aimed toward this ultimate objective. Slow learners at the junior high school level are beginning to become interested in jobs. Thus, the general skills and attitudes essential to selecting, obtaining, and holding a job should be introduced systematically at this time. During the first two years of the junior high school period the children should be provided with numerous activities in the shops and laboratories that will give them two special kinds of experiences. One, they should have instruction in the correct use and care of basic tools and equipment and should also become acquainted with various common materials. Two, these school settings provide excellent opportunities to learn to participate in work-like situations both independently and cooperatively.

During the final year of the junior high school period, the area of vocations is introduced systematically. Blocks of time should be devoted to the topic of "How people earn a living," particularly in the local community and area. Broad job areas should be studied with the emphasis being placed upon the requirements of industry in relation to the jobs. When the children have a grasp of the general requirements, industries should be visited for the purpose of observing employees performing specific jobs. Classroom discussion should center around the requirements (skills, knowledges, and so forth) related to each position. Those children who have expressed an interest in this kind of work should then be encouraged and helped to evaluate themselves and their abilities in terms of the job requirements.

This aspect of the program is essential to the "turning out" of a satisfactory employee. If an employee is going to be willing to assume the necessary responsibility, perform the job satisfactorily, and be a "steady" worker, he must be employed in work that is satisfying to him. It is important that he aspire to the kind of work he can and should perform. If his aspiration level is too high, he becomes dissatisfied with lower-level positions. If his aspirations are too low, he is wasting some of his abilities. A major objective of the junior high school program is to help the slow learners harmonize their levels of aspiration and their levels of ability. They need to develop the ability of self-criticism as it is related to jobs and job aspirations.

Guidance also becomes an important factor here. It is not sufficient merely to develop the skill of self-criticism in the children. Help must be given that will aid them in making a better evaluation of all their abilities so that the choice of vocations is widened. Information is needed in regard to the individual skills required for specific jobs as well as the occupational potential in that community. Then, by selection of materials, direction of trips and observations, and directed discussions the slow learners' horizons may be broadened in regard to vocational opportunities. They will be ready to make more appropriate occupational selections.

Senior high school

The senior high school program for slow learners is fully as essential as any of the programs that have preceded it. Without it, the objectives of the total program cannot be achieved in the social science and vocational areas. Slow learners, by the time they enter the senior high school, should have an adequate foundation established in the social sciences (history, geography, and civics) insofar as their needs are concerned. This aspect of the program at the senior high school level should, as a result, be relatively informal and unstructured. It should be built largely around discussions of current community, state, national, and world affairs. As questions arise and events occur, answers and explanations should be found in references, visual materials, class discussions, trips, and combinations of these.

The area of vocations now becomes one of primary importance and a major portion of class time is devoted to it. Half the time is spent either learning about jobs or performing on the job. Most of the in-school time is taken up by study of community living and vocational skills. Assuming a normal 3-year senior high school program for most slow learners, the first year should be devoted to a continuation of the intensified study of jobs and job areas that was introduced during the final year of the junior high school. These studies are, again, community and area centered. Related skills and knowledges concerning employment agencies, social security, unemployment compensation, withholding tax, applications, job interviews, and so forth are all studied intensively, with a view toward their relevance and application within a relatively short period of time. The second year is one of sampling many varied positions in order to learn firsthand the role of the employee. The teacher (who is also the job supervisor) observes deficiencies in the potential employee's training and either provides appropriate school experiences to correct or alleviate the problems or makes arrangements for their provision by other teachers.

In contrast, during the third year these young adults should normally be encouraged to confine themselves to one or two job experiences. These experiences should be carefully selected with regard to both interest and ability. They should be jobs the students want to work on and can perform satisfactorily. One of the final trial positions, or one similar to it, may very likely become the individual's full-time employment upon the termination of his formal education.

SUMMARY

Mathematics, physical sciences, and social sciences and occupational education are important skills and content areas for slow learners. Planned, systematically presented experiences are essential at each of the school levels if the broad educational objectives for the slow learners are to be achieved.

Mathematical skills and concepts are used continuously throughout each day by all persons—measurements, time, money, dealing with quantities, groups, and quantitative relationships, fractions, size, and so forth. Without knowledge and understanding of these concepts and the skills essential to working with them accurately and efficiently, the individual would be unable to maintain himself in the complex society of today. These are skills, knowledges, and concepts well within the learning ability of slow learners and must be included in any program that is provided for them.

Mathematics, probably more than any other academic area, has been poorly taught in terms of ease and efficiency of use. The following basic principles of sequence of instruction have been too often violated. Their violation, in working with slow learners, leads to unsatisfactory results. The first step should involve the teaching of the basic concept, preferably through a situation where a social need has been developed. In this way the concept is taught using concrete, socially meaningful materials (e.g. combining of meaningful groups for additions). The second step is taken only after the basic concept has been developed. This consists of providing the child with sufficient practice (drill in the combinations, tables, and examples) until he can arrive at a correct solution rapidly and accurately. During and following the second step, the third step of instruction occurs—application. This continues throughout the remainder of the children's school life. They learn to use the concepts and apply the skills in any and all needful situations. There has been no value to the mathematics education until a useful, usable tool has been placed in the individual's hands.

Physical science helps the children to better understand and cope with their physical environment. They learn to understand natural phenomena and to make better use of their environment and materials as a result of better understanding. Weather, plants, animals, seasons, the sun, insects, machines, heat, light, gravity, magnets, electricity, and health are all included as part of the content of the science program.

The social sciences and occupational education were discussed together. Occupational education was dealt with as non-technical for slow learners until the senior high school program and as a result the two subjects are highly interrelated. The social sciences emphasis is related to the devlopment of understanding the history, geography, and structure of the community, state, and nation. Emphasis at each level should be in accord with the activities and community relationships the slow learners can and do develop at the time. The basic assumption underlying a meaningful, experiential, daily-living approach is that the tomorrow's adult will know only what today's child can learn. That is, if children are taught to deal effectively with their problems, as they and their environment gradually change, they will be able to make the necessary and appropriate day-by-day adjustments with a minimum of help and support.

Many of the school experiences concerned with travel skills, ability to adjust socially, and understanding the structure of the community have indirect value vocationally. The study of vocations, as such, should not be introduced until the children are well into the programs of the secondary schools. It cannot be introduced and be expected to have material value until toward the close of junior high school. It cannot be satisfactorily completed without a senior high school program. If carefully planned programs are provided, the slow learners that only conclude their education when they are ready to take an independent place in the community should prove to be an asset to that community.

At the conclusion of the senior high school program (but not before), slow learners should prove to be satisfactory employees who can work effectively in a number of occupational settings. They should have acquired the social skills essential to "getting along" with fellow employees, with their families and neighbors, and in the community. They should be capable of handling money, spending it wisely, and budgeting to meet regular financial obligations. In times of stress or of unemployment they should know how and where to seek aid. They should have avocational skills and be familiar with available recreational facilities in harmony with their interests and abilities. Finally, they should have sufficient under-standing of the laws of the community and state, and the operation of the society that effects them, to be able to live within these requirements.

SELECTED RELATED READINGS

Bolzau, E. L., "Adapting American History to Slow Learners," *Social Education*, 14:115–17, March, 1950.

Cutler, H. S., "A Program for Slow Learners," *National Council for Social Studies*, Fifteenth Yearbook, 1944, pp. 55–62.

D'Ambrosio, L. M., "Adjusting the Social Studies to the Non-Academically Inclined Child," *High Points*, 34:13–18, January, 1952.

Ennis, J., "Course in Applied Science for Non-Academic Pupils and Slow Learners," *High Points*, 32:50–55, February, 1950.

Featherstone, William B., *Teaching the Slow Learner*, Bureau of Publications, Teachers College, Columbia University, 1951, pp. 83–87.

Greene, Jay E., "A 'Slow-English' Investigates Community Living," *English Journal*, 40:339–41, June, 1951.

Herman, A., "Current Events for the Slow Learner," *High Points*, 35:31, November, 1953.

Holinger, Dorothy, "Helping the Non-Learner in Grade One," *Arithmetic Teacher*, 5:15–24, February, 1958.

Miller, J. and G. L. Weston, "Slow Learners Improve in Critical Thinking," *Social Education*, 13:315–16, November, 1949.

McFeely, R. H., "Faculty Planning to Meet Individual Differences: For the Slow Learner," *National Council for Social Studies*, Fifteenth Yearbook, 1944, pp. 63–71.

Orr, Kenneth N., "Helping the Slow Learner," *Social Education*, 19:107–108, March, 1955.

Sobel, Max A., "Providing for the Slow Learner in the Junior High School," *Mathematics Teacher*, 52:347–53, May, 1959.

U. S. Office of Education, *Teaching Rapid and Slow Learners in High Schools*, Department of Health, Education, and Welfare, Bulletin No. 5, 1954, 97 pages.

Weiss, M. F., "Mathematics for the Slow Pupil," *High Points*, 23:61–64, April, 1941.

Weitz, Leo *et al.,* "Social Studies and the Slow Learner," *High Points,* 31:13–26, September, 1949.

Willarding, Margaret F., "The Use of Graphs for Retarded Children," *Arithmetic Teacher,* 4:258–60, December, 1957.

9

Special Subjects

The slow learners are by definition somewhat retarded intellectually as compared to normal children. Since the language arts, arithmetic, science, and social studies programs are primarily concerned with and dependent upon skills and concepts highly correlated with verbal intelligence, it is in these areas that the slow learners have the greatest difficulty. It is in their achievement related to these areas that they deviate most widely from the normal and are faced with their major frustrations and failures. The special subjects areas of the school, industrial arts, homemaking, art, music, and physical education, are much less dependent

255

upon high verbal intelligence. Many slow learners can participate
on a more nearly equal footing in these areas as a result. Broadly
speaking, the educational experiences planned for and provided
slow learners in these areas can often be quite similar to those
provided normally at the elementary and secondary school levels.
Moreover, many of the slow learners can be integrated into regular special subjects classes because the criterion of relatively equal
ability and participation can be satisfied.

When one discusses the need for unique kinds of learning experiences required by certain children, the image that is immediately found in the mind of the reader or listener is the self-contained
classroom. He seems to think that special curriculums and experiences can be provided only in this manner. The special subjects
areas are excellent proof that this notion, even under present school
organization and structure, need not necessarily be true. In actual
practice, many experiences needed by the children in related special
areas may be able to be provided more effectively and efficiently in
ways different from special, self-contained classes.

The following discussion will be concerned not only with the
special subjects *per se* but will also include suggestions concerning
organizing the school for the most effective instruction at the various
levels.

PRIMARY AND INTERMEDIATE SCHOOLS

The primary and intermediate school programs in relation to the
special subjects have been grouped together because the broad educational approach, subjects included, and objectives are relatively
the same for both levels. While the academic subjects and skills
continue to be of fundamental importance, receiving the major
portion of the time and stress from the teacher, the special subjects
have definitely taken their place in the programs. Where once the
classroom teacher was responsible for their presentation, he now
confines his efforts largely to instruction in the academic areas, with
specialists taking over much of the responsibility in these areas.
Physical education, art, and music teachers or supervisors are an
integral part of most of the larger and many of the smaller elementary school programs.

Two approaches to instruction in the special subjects are commonly found. In one case, supervisors have developed courses of

study and curriculum guides (often including instructional suggestions) to be used by the classroom teacher. Occasionally the supervisor visits the classes and demonstrates instructional techniques for
the benefit of the teacher. Teacher meetings may also be held at
which the supervisor discusses and explains various aspects of the
program. In the other instance, specialists are employed and made
directly responsible for the instruction. These teachers have numbers of classes, often housed in more than one school. The daily
schedule has specified times set aside for instruction when the
special-subjects teacher can be present to work with the class. Some
elementary schools have even become departmentalized, with the
teachers of the special subjects having their own specially equipped
rooms to which the children come for instruction.

One of the most commonly found forms of school organization
today consists of partial departmentalization. Under the system
some of the special-subjects teachers go to the regular classroom
(art and vocal music); others have their own rooms (physical education, instrumental music, and library) and the children come to
them. If these methods are in practice in a particular school, the
slow learners can benefit from the instruction on much the same
basis as the normal children. Teachers of slow learners, in order to
provide appropriate kinds of educational experiences for the children, must have an understanding of them, their characteristics,
and their educational needs. This understanding is required of the
teacher of the special areas in much the same way that it is required
of any other elementary school teacher. The special teacher who
acts as a consultant to the regular teacher or who takes over the
actual instruction of normal children in the special subjects should
be willing and able to do the same in regard to the slow learners.
Since the special-subjects teacher may have experience and training
directed toward work with normal children, he may have some difficulty in planning instruction for slow learners. The teacher of slow
learners can be of service by helping the specialist to better understand the children. As a result, the program provided normal children can and will be changed, if such changes are necessary to make
it more suitable and valuable for the slow learners.

Basically, the concept that must be kept in mind when one is
planning for slow learners is that, although they may be able to
perform quite normally insofar as their physical and motor devel-

opment is concerned, they may not be able to grasp the intellectual requirements essential to adequate performance. Also, it is probable that a greater incidence of below average physical and motor development will be present among the slow learners than among normal children.

Physical education

The physical education program for slow learners at the elementary school level is quite similar to that provided normal children. The majority of the slow learners will be within the average range in regard to their physical and motor development. Most of the individual activities will require little or no change. The group and team activities may present some problems because of the slow learners' inability to understand the requirements and rules of the games. Where physical education is provided for more than one classroom at a time, the majority of the slow learners can compete on relatively equal terms with their age-group. It may be necessary to place some of the slow learners with a group of children who are slightly younger. Their game and play interests tend to harmonize more closely with their mental ages than with their chronological ages. Hence, grouping with slightly younger children or providing them with the program designed for younger children is often appropriate.

Generally, the home and community or neighborhood background of the slow learners will have placed less stress upon good physical development than is true for normal children. They will usually have had less opportunity to develop their motor skills, as a result of crowded living conditions, lack of recreational facilities and equipment, and provision of fewer toys and playthings. Consequently, the physical education program of the school becomes of even greater importance for the slow learners than it is for normal children. Everything possible should be done to improve their skills and general physical development, using both individual and group activities. The program should also include activities that can and will carry over into out-of-school life so as to encourage maximum growth and development both in school and after formal schooling has been terminated. Only if the teacher is intimately familiar with the children's environment will it be possible for him to provide instruction in the most appropriate games and activities.

Art

The art program should, for maximum value, be more closely integrated with the academic program or experience unit than is usually true. If the regular teacher and the art teacher will briefly discuss the classroom topic presently under consideration, they will usually find it possible to select new art activities from this topic that will have great meaning for the children. The level of skills found among slow learners should equal that found among normal children of the same age. The one difference may be that it will be somewhat difficult for slow learners to grasp such abstract concepts as composition and color relationships.

Slow learners should be carefully and systematically taught in this area in much the same way they are taught in the academic areas. It should always be remembered that trial and error learning only takes place when the child is able to generalize from his successes or failures as to why he succeeded or failed. Nothing should be left to chance. Children should be *taught* some of the major aspects of art: how to observe accurately; the characteristics and correct methods of working with various materials, tools, and media; composition; design; figures; landscapes; perspective; mixing colors; and so forth. In this way the teacher can be assured that they will be able to use art as an effective means of expression and derive satisfaction from their efforts. Without careful, planned instruction they tend to become discouraged. The result is that they soon learn to dislike art and art activities as much as they have learned to dislike other school-centered activities. Remember, these are learned attitudes that the teacher is largely responsible for. Since slow learners have had many frustrating and dissatisfying school experiences, they are more prone to quickly develop antagonistic attitudes toward any school-related activity than are normal children.

Much that is generally stated concerning the artwork and figure drawing of children may be true for the normal child but does not hold for the slow learner. Poorly produced figures and objects are not necessarily indicative of the way in which the slow learners see or feel about these objects. These poor results are more apt to be the result of a lack of instruction and guided experiences. Too often, they have never been taught to observe accurately. They have never learned relationships and perspective. They have not learned the characteristics of various media and how to use them most effectively. It is the responsibility of the instructor to become fully aware of the background deficiencies of the children. It will then be possible to provide them with comprehensive, systematic instruction that will enable them to express themselves as effectively as possible.

In those schools where children do not remain with a single teacher and in a single class group all day, many of the slow learners can work in art activities with normal children. This placement must be made on an individual basis because slow learners, like normal children, have varying talents and abilities. They should be placed individually with groups performing at about the same level. In this way they will derive the greatest benefit from the instruction. Slow learners can and should also be included in other art-related activities with the rest of the children (e.g. trips to museums and art galleries where the experiences will be interesting and of value to them).

Music

Many of the statements made in relation to art are also applicable to music. *Good* music appreciation and vocal programs have the same values for slow learners as they have for normal children. The music period is not a time to sleep or play, it may be a time to relax, but above all it is a time to enjoy and learn. Like the art program, it should not be left solely to the classroom teacher. The music teacher or supervisor should include the slow learners in the total school music program. The one area that may present some difficulty is learning note and scale singing at the same age level as normal children. These skills can be learned by slow learners but often it must be at a later date. Similarly, they can also learn harmony and part singing.

Many schools have provided instrumental instruction at the elementary school level. Numbers of slow learners can and do play instruments. They should be encouraged to participate in this program, again on the same basis as normal children—interest, ability, and application. Because the majority of the slow learners come from homes where the income is limited and sporadic, it will probably be necessary for the schools to provide a larger percentage of the instruments than is usually true.

Schools often provide, or are provided with, community musical experiences. Since all experiences have value only insofar as the child is ready for them, the slow learners should be presented with selected musical experiences. Forced attendance at musical events usually does more harm than good.

Library

Some elementary schools provide libraries for the children under the direction of a full or part-time librarian. Where this is true the slow learners should be provided with instruction in the use of the library and encouraged to make use of it. In order that the experience will be a valuable one, the librarian must be familiar with their ability levels and the topics under study. In this way the children can be helped to use the library to acquire information and for recreational purposes. In conjunction with this program, a trip to the local library (branch or main) will help them in making continued use of this important facility.

JUNIOR AND SENIOR HIGH SCHOOLS

The special subjects are much more highly emphasized in the secondary school than at the elementary school level. Rooms with special equipment and facilities are provided. Teachers confine their instruction to a single school. Often several teachers in each area are required to fill the demand. Many more materials are provided and the children have opportunities to deal with the area much more extensively and intensively than is true for the elementary school. Ordinarily, at the junior high school level, all children are required to have some experience in each of the areas. Those that are interested can continue with electives throughout their attendance in the senior high school.

Not only are the special areas provided in the elementary school expanded in the secondary school but additional areas are usually added. Practically all secondary schools provide special programs in homemaking and industrial arts. In large schools each of the special areas may be divided into a number of sub-areas. Under art one may take painting, composition, design, ceramics, jewelry, and so forth. Numbers of choral and solo experiences as well as various instrumental groups may be offered in music. Industrial arts and homemaking may offer specific courses in cabinet making, printing, machine shop, auto mechanics, dressmaking, cooking, and so forth.

Physical education may offer such specialties as football, basketball, swimming, and other games as well as a program in corrective physical education for those who have need for it. One additional special-subjects area that deserves mention for slow learners is the program in driver education.

The first two years of junior high school, and sometimes all three years, are devoted to giving all the children a broad, introductory experience in all the special-subjects areas. Physical education is usually required of all children for the entire three years. The other areas usually restrict the experience to a half or full semester. Slow learners enrolled in the junior high school program should participate in these special subjects in much the same way as other students. At this time it would probably be advantageous for most (if not all) of them to attend all classes with their own group, with the possible exception of physical education. This is not unharmonious with the usual practice of the junior high school. While the children move from class to class and teacher to teacher for their various subjects, they usually move as a group so that the same children tend to remain together throughout the day. Where a child has a particular ability or disability in one subject, he may be placed with another group for that period. There is no reason why the same kind of arrangement cannot be made for the slow learners.

There are two primary reasons for planning classes for slow learners in secondary schools; social considerations and the availability of special facilities and shops. In order to provide the experiences that will be of greatest value to the slow learners in the special-subjects areas, it is essential that the school personnel become well acquainted with each child's skills and disabilities. Only in this way can the most effective counseling be provided. By having them attend the classes in the special subjects as a group, it is possible (1) to make the necessary arrangements for instruction so that the experience will be of greatest value to them and (2) for the teacher to carefully observe each child in order that recommendations can be made regarding future work. In this way there is an assurance that each child's abilities will be developed in that area to the level that will be most advantageous to him.

In the senior high school program more flexibility in terms of class placement should be planned. Since the population of senior high schools is considerably greater than is usually found in elementary schools (and this population is confined to 3 rather than 6 or 7 grades) more slow learners should be in attendance at each level. With a number of classes for slow learners available, the desired flexibility necessary to the best programming for each child should be possible. Classes largely restricted to slow learners should be provided in many of the special subjects, but numbers of the slow learners should also be enrolled at the various levels with the children in regular classes. This will be discussed in somewhat mor detail under the specific special-subjects areas.

Physical education

It was previously stated that physical education is required of practically all normal children throughout the junior high school and much of the senior high school period. This should also be true for slow learners. Usually physical education classes are fairly large and the boys and girls are segregated. As a result, children from two or more classes or groups receive physical education instruction simultaneously. The children are usually organized according to grade level, regardless of size or physical and motor development. Instead of using this method of grouping with slow learners, it is recommended that each one be placed according to his ability, regardless of the grade-level designation. In this way they will be able to participate in the activities with the rest of the children and receive the greatest possible benefit from the program. Special classes for slow learners are not recommended under ordinary circumstances. Where a slow learner has some physical or motor disability that makes it impossible for him to participate in the regular physical education program, he should be enrolled in a corrective physical education class if one is available.

Another facet of the physical education program in many secondary schools is hygiene and sex education. With the kinds of environmental backgrounds experienced by most slow learners, these are very important areas for their consideration. At the primary and elementary levels they should have been taught good hygienic practices appropriate to their level of development and an attempt should have been made to establish habits of cleanliness in their normal living activities in school. It was anticipated that as these practices became habitual in school many of them would carry over into their home and community living. Children at the secondary level are now old enough to learn "why" good hygienic practices are necessary so that they will continue to use them purposefully and intelligently. They should also learn about public health agencies and the services that can be obtained from them.

Sex education is also of greater importance to slow learners than to normal children generally. They receive little or none at home but pick it up from loose talk in the streets. The rate of illegitimacy is much higher in the subcultural areas of communities than in other areas. While children living in this part of the community may be much more knowledgeable concerning sexual activities (and more outspoken) than most children, it doesn't mean they have more understanding and, consequently, less need for sex education. As a result of this knowledge, extensive misinformation, and poor attitudes their need is probably much greater.

Art

The art program of the junior high school has many of the same objectives as the program of the elementary school. More facilities are usually provided and more instructional time is made available to the children. As a result, the children can go into various art activities somewhat more intensively. The program, however, remains fairly general in nature and should be provided as part of the program for all slow learners. For most of them it will be their last formal instruction in the field of art. But, for all the children it can have very real value in the areas of communication, appreciation (or pleasure), and recreation.

Those slow learners who show a very real interest and ability in art should be encouraged to develop their skills in this area to as high a degree as possible. This can be most easily accomplished by having additional art courses "built" into their senior high school programs. While these students may never become great painters or sculpturers, the field of art has a number of potential vocational outlets where some slow learners can perform effectively. Examples of these areas are commercial art and the graphic arts. Persons at a number of different levels of artistic talent or ability can find activities they can perform satisfactorily in these fields. Those students who have sufficient potential may be referred to the vocational school for supplementary, more technical experience either as a

part of their senior high school program or upon following graduation.

Music

Slow learners should participate in the junior high school music
program in the same way as any other children. They should be
encouraged to try out for junior and senior high school choruses,
bands, and orchestras. While vocational outlets are somewhat limited in the music area, some slow learners will develop sufficient skill
to perform with dance bands. The music programs for most of the
slow learners will be for appreciation (or enjoyment), recreation,
and the opportunity to participate in all-school activities thus helping them to feel that they are an integral part of the total student
body.

Industrial arts

All slow learners (boys and girls) should have planned industrial
arts experiences in a general shop, probably at the junior high
school level. They should learn the selection, use, and care of basic
tools and the characteristics of commonly used materials. In the
general shop the children can be introduced to work with wood,
plastics, metal, electricity, and so forth. The emphasis, as previously
indicated, should be on the selection of correct tools and materials
to perform a particular job. The jobs or projects should be related
to everyday needs, mostly in the area of repairs or simple construction—repairing a screen, putting a plug on a lamp, or constructing
a stool. In some areas, such as electricity and plumbing, it might
be well to also emphasize appreciation of those tasks that are too
difficult for the average person to attempt.

The boys should receive more intensive work in the industrial
arts at the senior high school level, in at least one course. This may
be best taught in a general, all-purpose shop. Numerous values
should accrue from this program in addition to the "pure" industrial arts skills too often thought of as being the sole purpose of the
program. In the industrial arts activities the slow learners can learn
practical conservation and economical use of materials, planning,
interpreting drawings and sketches, certain applications of mathematics (measurement, costs and so forth), how to follow directions,

how to work along with others in a near-industrial situation, and reading, as it is applied to work.

A number of slow learners will show good ability in the industrial arts areas. These boys should be encouraged to continue this part of their education by taking more advanced courses in more highly specialized areas, often with the regular classes. Provisions should even be made for some boys in the vocational school, where they will receive technical training to perform in a semi-skilled or skilled job area upon completion of the program. In one of the most effective programs the students actually perform on a job as a part of the course. Some industrial arts programs build and sell a house each year, others place students in industry on an apprentice-type basis. These kinds of experiences, for children who can benefit from them, are invaluable.

The industrial arts program has a close and important "tie-in" with the whole school approach to vocational selection, training, and placement for slow learners. The teachers responsible for the programs for slow learners must work very closely with the industrial arts teachers.

Homemaking

The initial homemaking experiences should be offered to both boys and girls. All the children in the program should be capable of preparing some simple foods and making simple garment repairs, such as sewing on a button. Beyond these elementary experiences, most of the homemaking activities should be provided almost exclusively for girls. Occasionally a boy will display an interest and ability in cooking, baking, or sewing. These experiences should be given him, supplemented by available courses from a vocational school, because there are potential vocational opportunities available here in which some slow learners can and do work.

Following the general, introductory homemaking activities provided all slow learners, the girls should take a number of courses that will enable them to become effective "homemakers." These courses should provide the girls with the desire and the ability to have better kept and operated homes than the ones they came from. The homemaking program (along with the industrial arts program and the attitudes related to home and community living emphasized in the classroom program) can do a great deal to improve the general living conditions and environment for the next generation, the children of these slow learners. In many instances these programs can even have a positive influence on the students' present living conditions.

The developing social conscience of the society and the state has been reflected in a number of activities designed to improve the living conditions of the sub-cultural, low socio-economic groups of the community. Public health and public housing programs are only two of the more obvious governmental activities. Huge urban renewal programs have been instituted, designed to abolish slum dwellings and replace them with modern apartments. Social workers, settlement houses, and other groups have striven valiantly to help people residing in these depressed areas to arrive at some satisfactory solution to their problems. Unfortunately, while society has been able to do much with the exterior, physical aspects of slum living, it has been able to accomplish very little with the basic cause of the slums, the people. It is easier to move a family from a ramshackle, filthy, cold-water flat with out-door toilet facilities into a modern apartment with complete bath facilities than it is to change what goes on inside the dwelling. Because a family is living in a modern apartment does not mean that they will keep it clean or that the quality of the meals or level of child care will improve. Because they have a modern bathroom with hot and cold running water does not mean they will take baths. The residents must be educated to the need for, and in the practice of, this kind of behavior. This can be done through education of the children in school, at least insofar as the next generation is concerned. And there is some evidence that schools with meaningful programs are accomplishing this objective.

Most of the girls in the slow learners group are going to become homemakers. It behooves the schools to provide them with training in the kinds of homemaking activities that will be of most value to them. The cooking program should consist of activities that are practical and realistic for persons living on a limited income. They should be taught how to prepare substantial, wholesome, attractive, tasty meals. Little or no time should be devoted to counting calories or learning the categories of foods. Generally balanced meals can be achieved using the more common concepts of meat, potatoes (or potato substitutes), vegetables (yellow and green), salads, and desserts. They can easily learn which foods or combinations of foods should be included in a dinner. Similarly, they can learn to make good breakfasts and lunches. These meals should be prepared by the children, using stoves, refrigerators, sinks, utensils, and appliances that are common enough for there to be a good chance of their having them or being able to get them. Baking should be done in the same use-oriented manner. Rather than requiring cakes, cookies, puddings, and so forth to be prepared from "scratch," the children should be encouraged to use mixes and other simplified methods. In actual practice, these are probably more economical, because there is much less chance of failure and consequent waste.

Sewing instruction should follow the same principles of practicability. The girls should be taught hand and machine sewing. The objects worked on should be their own or for their families. Stress should be placed upon care and repair. What original sewing is done should be of a relatively simple and practical nature. The girls should also be introduced to knitting, crocheting, and needlework, all of which are good recreational or avocational activities.

The homemaking unit of the school, to be of greatest value, should include the rooms and facilities to carry on all the activities normally performed in maintaining a home. The girls should be taught to launder clothes, including the preparation (sorting, presoaking), which materials or kinds of clothing should and should not be washed, various kinds of laundering (hand, machine), and how to use a washing machine. Simple dry cleaning and methods of spot-removing should be introduced as well as the safe use of cleaning fluids. They should also be taught ironing and pressing.

As the result of having a complete homemaking unit, the girls can be taught general cleaning techniques and family living skills. How to sweep, scrub floors, wax, dust, and use vacuum and carpet sweepers should all be included. Among the family living skills they should learn are playing games, carrying on conversations, and serving meals. Serving meals is one activity that is often mistaught in the schools. This does not mean inviting a group of faculty members or VIP's for lunch to be served by waitresses (the children) dressed in fancy tea aprons and headbands made in sewing class. It means having the children sit down together at a family-type meal, practicing the everyday manners the family should be using during their meals at home.

One additional area of study in the homemaking program is child care. This is a most important area both for the present and for the future. Many of the girls will have younger brothers and sisters they must care for. Opportunities also arise for them to earn money as baby sitters. They have need for these skills. In the future, most of them will have children of their own. It will be of great help if they know how to bathe, dress, and feed young children and how to generally take care of their needs.

Thus far, the stress has been placed upon knowing how, or the learning of homemaking skills. A concept that must go along with knowing how is an understanding of *why*. Why should clothes be washed and cared for in the ways indicated? Why should an adequate diet be prepared? Why should houses and people be clean? Why should accepted table manners and social graces be learned and commonly practiced? Why should children be cared for in certain ways? Only as the children understand and accept the "whys" will these skills and methods become meaningful. Only then will they be willing to learn and attempt to put them into practice. Their acceptance and understanding of the necessity of these ways of homemaking will often be reflected in changes occurring within the homes in which they are presently living. Many girls are required to help with homemaking activities and can have a great deal of influence by introducing better ways of doing housework or by preparing more adequate meals. Even greater changes will be apparent in the future homes that they establish, as compared to the ones in which they were raised or "allowed to grow."

Driver education

Every slow learner, whether or not his family owns an automobile, should be highly urged if not required to take driver education training. Most, if not all of them, are or will be driving an automobile. Some of the boys will obtain positions in the trucking and delivery vocations. If they are going to be on the streets and highways (and they are), it is essential for their own and everyone else's welfare that they become safe, knowledgeable drivers.

The emphasis of the driver education program should be upon safe driving. The students should learn how to operate an automobile safely, the dangers of driving too fast or too slow, road and atmospheric conditions that effect safe driving, highway and driving laws and regulations, to avoid unsafe driving practices, and so forth. They should be taught to be aware of the things that cause an automobile to be unsafe to drive and the necessity for them to have appropriate repairs made. Certain road repair, such as changing a tire safely when on a trip, should be taught. Such concepts as how an internal combustion engine works, how the carburetor works, and what the ignition system consists of are unessential to safe driving and a waste of time for most of the slow-learning children. If understanding of these concepts were essential to becoming a good driver questions about them would be included in state driver examinations. They are not.

Vocational agriculture

Numbers of secondary schools in rural and semi-rural areas provide programs in vocational agriculture. Slow learners growing up on farms and interested in farm work should be encouraged to participate in the program. It will be rare that a school has a sufficient number of slow learners to organize a separate class. Since the materials that have been developed for use in these programs are planned for use with children having normal intelligence, some instructional problems are presented. But these are not insurmountable. Where the reading and other materials used are at too high a level or are too complex in nature for the slow learners, the special teacher will find it necessary to provide supplementary instruction. The materials must be either simplified so that the slow learners can understand them or they must be interpreted for the slow learners. Thus, the slow learners may essentially receive double instruction, one period from the teacher of vocational agriculture, supplemented by a period of study with and assistance from the special teacher.

The majority of the slow learners who have been raised on a farm and participated in the performance of farm work and chores will have sufficient background (readiness) to benefit from the course of instruction. It will help them, as it does normal children, to become better farmers and farm workers.

Library

The discussion concerning the value and use of the school and public libraries at the elementary level is also applicable to the secondary level. Libraries are found more commonly at the secondary school levels than at the elementary school levels. The special teacher should familiarize himself with the contents and regulations of the library. Where materials appropriate to the needs of the slow learners are not available, arrangements should be made for their inclusion. Instruction concerning the use of the library and assignments requiring its use should be made to ensure that the children will become familiar with it. The librarian should also know who the slow learners are and what help they may require in order that she can provide services appropriate to their needs.

Extra-curricular activities

The extra-curricular program of the secondary schools is very important for slow learners. It is an opportunity for providing them with numerous experiences that cannot be given them in their regular curriculum. Slow learners should be encouraged and helped to participate in those activities insofar as possible. They should attend athletic events and school dances on the same basis as any other student enrolled in the school. Intramural athletics for both boys and girls are an excellent means of helping them improve their physical and motor skills as well as offering contacts with a wider group of children on an informal, natural basis. Those boys who have the ability and inclination (and are doing satisfactory work in the program) should be encouraged to try out for the school's athletic teams. Some slow learners become excellent athletes and can receive healthy attention and praise in this way when it has been almost impossible to obtain it in any other way.

Dramatics clubs and school plays may provide an outlet for other slow learners. It is not always necessary to have dramatic talent to belong to and become a valued member of one of these groups. Students are needed to take care of the lighting and to act as stage hands. Those with abilities in art or industrial arts are needed to build scenery. Another school activity that has been previously mentioned but should also be included here is membership in one or more of the school musical organizations; choruses, glee clubs, bands, or orchestras. Membership in various clubs, particularly of a recreational nature, should be encouraged in those areas in which slow learners can participate on relatively equal terms. These activities give them opportunities to learn valuable leisure-time skills, give them important social skills, and help them (as well as the rest of the student body) to feel that they are a part of the school community, in much the same way that the school tries to teach them to accept themselves as a responsible part of the greater community in which they live.

SUMMARY

The special-subjects areas of the schools have been expanding and taking an increasingly important place in the total program of the school during the past three decades. The depression years of the early 1930's saw some schools reduce the emphasis on these experiences and some popular educational sensationalists writing today decry the inclusion of some of these activities within the public schools. Nevertheless, they have come to attain a position of importance and can provide valuable experiences for the children that would be difficult to include in any other way. The special subjects do not replace the academic instruction or even reduce its importance. They do add to the total education of the individual and can help to make the academic instruction more meaningful.

The special subjects usually included in the primary and intermediate programs are art, music, and physical education. Slow learners have need for these kinds of experiences, provided in much the same way that they are provided to normal children. Most schools have employed special teachers or supervisors to plan and/or instruct in the special areas. The slow learners should also have the benefit of the skill and training of these specialists. In order that the instruction will be most beneficial, some pre-planning is essential. The specialist or supervisor should consult with the classroom teacher and become familiar with the program being conducted for the slow learners. In this way, the special subjects will have meaning in relation to the total program. He needs to learn about the developmental levels, interests, and backgrounds of the children. He also needs to know the topics or areas of study that are being conducted. Only in this way can the total instruction be integrated and made most meaningful to the children. As a result, the children will learn more in relation to the special subjects than they would if there were no correlation or relationship between these subjects and the other facets of their educational program.

Homemaking, industrial arts, driver education, and the area of extra-curricular activities should be added to the slow learners' programs at the secondary school level. All slow learners should have the physical education, art, music, industrial arts, and homemaking activities of the junior high school, where they are largely exploratory in nature. Some industrial arts (particularly for the boys), homemaking (particularly for the girls), and driver education should be required of almost every slow learner at the senior high school level. The rest of the special-subjects program (with the exception of physical education) should be used on a selective basis for students who have a particular aptitude, ability, or need for them. Many of these subjects can be related directly to the broad vocational training aspects of the program, providing the basic skills to which any industry can add the specific skills required. The special subjects also provide many opportunities to teach the application of arithmetical and reading skills in needful situations. They also give the students many opportunities to practice, under supervision and direction in a near-life setting, cooperative skills and work habits essential to good adjustment to an industrial situation.

The extra-curricular program of the secondary schools can also provide innumerable experiences of value to the slow learners. Participation in all activities of this type has high social value and is an opportunity for the children to learn social skills and to understand their necessity and value. Athletics, clubs, school plays, and student government can all help to broaden and enrich the individual's education.

The educational programs of the elementary and junior high schools are much the same for all children. The programs elected by normal or superior students in the senior high school may deviate widely, depending upon the interests and abilities of the student. One student may select a program that will enable him to enter business shortly after graduation. Another may select a program that will enable him to enter a college or university to continue his education. Even the college preparatory programs may differ according to the subject area the student wishes to emphasize.

This general pattern of education is also true for slow learners. Education for slow learners should become more selective and more individualized as the student progresses. At the senior high school level certain common *areas* should be provided all slow learners; communications, arithmetic, social and physical sciences, and physical education. The special-subjects areas, however, are carefully selected, the selection being based upon the interests, needs, and characteristics of each individual.

SELECTED RELATED READINGS

Backofen, C., "Reaching the Slow Learner in a Junior High School," *Pittsburgh School,* 23:163–66, May, 1949.

Denton, L. H. and L. E. Hoffman, "Family Arts: A Course for Slow-Learning Junior High-School Girls," *National Association Secondary School Principals Bulletin,* 25:81–85, April, 1941.

Gahimer, H. S., "The Problem of the Low-Ability Student," *Education,* 62:172–79, November, 1941.

Gaitskell, Charles D. and Margaret R. Gaitskell, *Art Education for Slow Learners.* Peoria, Illinois: Charles A. Bennett Company, Inc., 1953, 46 pages.

Haft, H., "The Activity Method in High School," *High Points,* 24:53–57, June, 1942.

"High School Methods with Slow Learners," Washington, D. C.: *NEA Research Bulletin* 21, No. 3, October, 1943, pp. 60–86.

Orr, Kenneth N., "Helping the Slow Learner," *Social Education,* 19:107–108, March, 1955.

Stone, Mary E., "Let's Help the Slow Learner," *Practical Home Economics,* 32:13, April, 1954.

U. S. Office of Education, *Teaching Rapid and Slow Learners in High School,* Department of Health, Education, and Welfare, Bulletin No. 5, 1954, 97 pages.

part IV

Reporting and
General Program
Principles

10

Grading, Reporting, and Promotion

The reporting of children's progress to parents and policies of promotion are so interrelated and interdependent that they cannot be dealt with separately. The methods used will be dependent upon the over-all philosophy of the school, which also determines the objectives of education, and many of the methods selected for the achievement of these objectives. The fundamental problem is to find a method whereby parents are informed clearly, accurately, and concisely of the exact educational status and growth of their child. A policy must be established to indicate clearly when a child should be promoted, retained, accelerated, and, eventually, graduated. Finally, a determination must be made concerning the organizational structure of the school in order that instruction can be provided efficiently and promotional policies carried out without undue strain on instruction or on the teachers' time and energy.

GRADING AND REPORTING

One of the first questions teachers ask about the slow learners that are enrolled in their classes is, "How do I grade them?" This question arises because there is a basic confusion concerning the purpose of grading. To some teachers a grade is an evaluation of the work of the individual as compared to some arbitrary standard or level of competency. This is usually thought of as the degree of knowledge or ability the individual possesses. Thus, a grade of 90 means that he knows 90 per cent of the material included in the course. A second concept commonly followed is to use the grade to indicate how well the individual is doing as compared to his group or to children at his age and grade level. The teacher assumes that the children's abilities, and consequently their test scores and project and homework marks, will follow a normal distribution. A "C" grade is average. Since most children are of average ability, this is the most commonly given evaluation. A grade of "B" is slightly above average and "D" slightly below average. Since they represent, to an equal degree, the parts of the distribution on the high and low side of the average, "B's" and "D's" are given equally often. The same is true for "F's" and "A's" except, since they represent the tails of the distribution, they are given least often.

There are a number of fallacies in this latter grading concept. First, few if any classes represent a normal distribution of the population. Second, since the populations of classes are skewed, a normal child enrolled with children of below-average intelligence will receive spuriously high grades. The reverse is true if the child is enrolled in a class of children with above-average intelligence—his grades will be spuriously low. If the teacher attempts to base grades on a larger population than the present class, he must resort to relying upon his memory concerning the performance of other classes of children (assuming the characteristics and content of the course remain identical from one year to the next. Or, he must use the results obtained from the administration of standardized tests. This is essentially what is done in the use of Regents Examinations in the state of New York, where the individual is compared to the performance of the children in the entire state who also have completed that course of study and taken that test.

The last fairly commonly used method of grading is to evaluate the performance of the individual against what the teacher thinks he is capable of doing. This method is used more often with slow learners and mentally retarded children than with average, bright, or gifted students. Usually the teacher attempts to determine the achievement level at which the person should be performing according to his mental age. He then compares the child's actual achievement to this projected level. The teacher, however, usually places a number of restrictions upon the use of this method. It is usually almost impossible for a slow learner to achieve an "A." Even when he is working at, or even above, his ability-expectancy level, the teacher has "pangs or conscience" and cannot give him the same grade as he gives a brighter student who is a higher achiever. However, many more slow learners are apt to receive "C's" and "D's" with a sprinkling of "B's" and only an occasional "F" under this system than under either of the other systems. It is also rare for a teacher to give a bright student who is an under-achiever in terms of his ability, but nevertheless performing above grade level, less than a "B." More often than not he is likely to receive an "A." Of the three methods of grading, the last is usually the least consistently applied to all the children, even by those teachers who "believe" in it.

Historically, grading presented few if any problems to the teacher. Grade-level achievement standards were theoretically fairly well established for each grade level. Those children who could not perform at or above this level were given failing grades and retained in that grade for at least another year. There was somewhat more difficulty in assigning grades to those children who were performing satisfactorily compared to their group when grade expectations and evaluations were made. Those who were performing significantly above the average of the group were usually accelerated so that they would be placed with a group with whom they could be compared. The interpretation of a child's grade was relatively simple. He either was or was not performing satisfactorily at the grade level in which he had been placed.

With a changing philosophy in education came a changed meaning to grades. Greater emphasis was placed upon the individual needs of the children. Some of the emphasis was removed from development in the academic areas. Emphasis was also placed upon the development of personal, interpersonal, and social skills. The characteristics of report cards and methods of reporting changed. After many years, educators still appear to be far away from anything approaching a universal solution. Early report cards consisted of a listing of subjects with a number grade being given for each. Some arbitrary point, such as 65 or 70, was designated as failing. One of the first changes to occur was the substitution of letters for number grades. Each letter was usually interpreted to cover a range of approximately 8 points on a hundred point scale, "A" being a grade ranging from 92 to 100, "B" from 84 to 92, and so forth.

The more progressive educators thought this method was also unsatisfactory and tried a system of two grades, "S" (Satisfactory) and "U" (Unsatisfactory), or "P" (Pass) and "F" (Fail). One step beyond this point was taken by a few schools, particularly at the primary level and in some special programs. That step was a complete abandonment of the traditional report card. Reports were made to parents on a more descriptive basis in a letter, a face-to-face conference, or a combination of both.

During this period, report cards (including letters and conferences) took on other new characteristics. One seldom sees, except at the senior high school level, a report containing only the minimum information common in the past—days absent, times tardy, height, weight, list of subjects, and a grade for each. Most reports now include, in addition to these things, an evaluation of the child's social adjustment, with some occasional attempts made to evaluate his emotional development as well. One kind of grading may be used for one part of the card, letters or numbers being most common for academic grading, and another for the other part of the card, "satisfactory," "showing improvement," or "unsatisfactory" for example.

Many changes have occurred over the years in the methods used to report to parents. Different methods are often used within the same school system at the various grade levels. Committees of teachers and parents have devoted many hours in attempts to develop satisfactory devices. The adoption of a new method or technique for reporting means that many more hours must be spent by teachers, principals, supervisors, directors, and other administrators attempting to educate (explain to) parents concerning the characteristics, interpretations, and the purposes to be achieved under the new system. Nevertheless, parents tend to remain confused.

Causes for confusion

There are many reasons why parents are confused by the schools' reports concerning their children's progress. They tend to look at the reporting form superficially, interpreting it in terms of the reports they had known when they were students—and in many instances they had not understood these either. As was previously indicated, educators often devote a great deal of time attempting to interpret the meaning or purpose of the reports to parents, primarily through PTA meetings. Unfortunately, the majority of the parents do not attend these meetings and much of the effort is wasted. It sometimes appears that educators are much more proficient in educating the community regarding the need for a new building than they are in their ability to explain the purposes of education and how reports indicate how specific children are achieving these objectives.

Teachers and administrators are also often confused as to the purpose of reports. New reporting methods are developed by committees, submitted to the administration, and adopted. If one makes an attempt to learn about the characteristics of the report and how to interpret it in reference to an individual child, several different versions may be heard from several teachers approached. In other words, a single reporting system may mean different things to different teachers and the grades or evaluations a child receives are dependent upon the interpretation made by that teacher. Every parent must, therefore, understand the orientation of each of his child's teachers if he is to be able to accurately interpret the evaluations sent home. This kind of communication is most difficult to maintain effectively.

Letters and parent-teacher interviews have proved to be little better. Too often the teacher hesitates to be frank concerning a child, paricularly a child with learning problems. Instead of describing the problems, telling the parents about the corrective steps that have been taken, and evaluating the success of these steps, the teacher tries to indicate the issues by a method of circumlocution; in the end no one is any wiser than they were in the beginning. It is difficult to explain to a parent frankly that his child has limited intelligence and will be unable to perform academically at the same level as other children. Where the parents are intelligent and well educated, their personal involvement precludes their emotional acceptance. On the other hand, if the parents have limited intelligence and the family is one of the lower class, the child appears relatively normal to them as compared to his siblings and the children in the neighborhood. The parents also, in all probability, had difficulty in school, so it is not an unusual, unexpected, or even an important matter. Yet, accurate reporting must be done clearly, kindly, and in a fashion which leaves no room for doubt.

Probably the greatest source of confusion in this area is lack of a clear understanding of the purpose of reporting by the school personnel. This is reflected in the obvious deviations of reports on the same forms by the various teachers of a single school, to say nothing about the discrepancies that appear within a total school system. Another application of reporting that brings this out clearly is the extreme difference that can be noted at a glance between the various reports used at the different levels; primary, elementary, junior, and senior high school. Too often there is no consistency and no common educational objective apparent in these various reports. As a result, the conscientious parent is required to study reports and reorient his thinking as the child leaves one school and enters another.

With these difficulties being true for children and parents in general, the understanding of the reported evaluations of slow learners too often becomes impossible. Have they been given marginal passing grades merely to "get rid" of them, to let some other teacher wrestle with the problem for a time? Are the parents interested enough, sufficiently educated, and not so emotionally involved that they are capable of an appropriate interpretation? Those slow learners who come from subcultural homes (the majority of them) have parents who usually have had limited success in school and place small value on formal education. These parents seldom attend school meetings and pay scant attention to evaluation reports. Un-

less the report is simple and direct, they have little or no understanding of its complete meaning. A different kind of problem is
present when reporting to parents who have had some education
and/or place a high value on education. Their aspirations for their
children are high. It is difficult for them to accept the idea that the
child may be a slow learner. When reports from different teachers
are inconsistent, the parents' hope for normalcy is reinforced. Any
problems the child may have in school are due to poor instruction
and the fault of some teachers. If the child receives good grades,
based upon a comparison of his achievement and his apparent
abilities, this supports their hopes and aspirations.

Purpose of reporting

The purpose of reporting is to inform parents clearly, concisely,
and accurately how well their children are performing in school.
This purpose is true for any grade level whether it be primary or
senior high school. Parents have a right to know how well their children are achieving the established purposes of the school. Only with
this information can they develop realistic aspirations for their
children and plan their future education wisely. This is also important for the children directly, since children's aspirations will
tend to reflect the aspirations adults in their lives have for them. It
will be much easier to help slow learners accept the programs provided them and the educational objectives that are appropriate for
them if their parents have understood and accepted these programs
and objectives. Stated in another way related to evaluation and reporting, reports should help parents to better understand the intellectual and learning abilities and potentials of their children.
Reports should also help parents understand the present academic
level and the potential of their children. This is a difficult job to
accomplish even with regular, realistic, consistent reports sent home
several times a year, year after year. It is impossible to achieve with
a single report or a single conference. It is essential that all the help
possible be given parents. They cannot achieve the necessary level
of understanding without help because of their closeness to, and
emotional involvement with, the problem.

Characteristics of a good report

The examination of a good report or report form should indicate clearly the characteristics of the curriculum for that grade or level. This also shows, indirectly, the general educational objectives for children enrolled in that school system and the more specific educational objectives of that particular program. Thus, if teaching the children reading, arithmetic, and other skills is a part of the curriculum, it should be included in the report or on the report form. The same is true for those aspects of personal and social development considered to be important and for which provisions are made to ensure, insofar as possible, their development and improvement in the desired direction. Unless some method is used when making an evaluation to indicate the particular aspect of social studies, health, physical science, natural science, mathematics, and so forth being studied, who is to know what the children are learning or supposed to be learning? This should be indicated clearly on the report. Today, this is common in the senior high school, where science is more aptly called biology, chemistry, or physics; mathematics is designated as algebra, geometry, or trigonometry; and social studies is taught under such specific titles as civics, economics, ancient history, modern history, American History, English History, and so forth. In the elementary and junior high schools the broader, "catch-all" terms are more likely to be used. The report should indicate clearly what the child is being taught and what he is expected to learn.

A good report should be short, simple, and concise. Few parents will take the time to carefully examine a long, complicated report that is difficult to read and interpret. Consequently, they will not understand all the implications of the information they have obtained from the report and will often even misinterpret the information they have noticed. Many of the slow learners' parents have little or no more intelligence and education than the children (of older ages). They are incapable of understanding a complicated report.

A report form or report card probably fulfills the need most adequately in terms of the above criteria. Both interviews and written reports require that the teacher have a basic form with listed areas if all of the important factors are to be discussed. The written report then becomes quite formalized but remains complicated and difficult to comprehend. The same is true for the conference report, except that the parent may selectively hear those things he desires. When a problem becomes so acute that the parents can no longer ignore it, they can and do complain bitterly that the schools have never informed them about this matter. And, they actually believe what they are stating. They were not informed in such a fashion that they comprehended the information and the implications of the report.

Reports will, of necessity, vary in content and format from level to level in order to reflect those aspects of the curriculum that are stressed at any one time. Thus, there are particular reports that are most appropriate for children at either the primary, intermediate, junior, or senior high school levels. These reports must be consistent, however, so that the same broad, general educational objectives are apparent throughout. Having reports designed for children working at specific levels is not sufficient insofar as the individual is concerned, however. The report must also indicate the specific level at which *the* child is working within that broad level. For example, a child of eleven in the intermediate school, reading at the second grade level, may have learned most of his number combinations but be unable to use most of the tables well. This should be clearly indicated.

It is not sufficient that just the level of the child be clearly described. Parents observe growth in their children, but usually have no accurate basis of comparison, not having the normal development of numbers of children readily available to them. The child's performance may be compared to past performance and his development may seem to be satisfactory. If his performance is compared to what the parents remember of what they were able to do the child's performance is either satisfactory or unsatisfactory depending upon the recollections of the parents. Or his performance may be compared to the performance of older and younger brothers and sisters as well as neighborhood children. The evaluation of his performance will then be determined by the levels of performance of these children.

It is not easy for parents to accurately evaluate a report containing only a description of the child's behavior and growth. If the parents are well educated, residing in an urban community composed largely of professional people and executives, they (the parents) have one special kind of comparative population. The mean I.Q. of children attending schools in these communities is often 110, 115, or higher. Comparatively, the "normal" child becomes a slow learner and the slow learner becomes mentally handicapped. Even teachers may become so used to working with bright children that unless they consciously "back away" periodically in order to obtain a better perspective of the situation they also think of the slow learners as being more retarded than they are.

The reverse, of course, is true for persons residing in the low socio-economic and subcultural areas, whether urban or rural. In some of these schools the mean I.Q. of the children is 80, 85, or 90. The slow learners are the average. They compare favorably with their siblings and neighborhood children. The "normal" child is "bright" or superior. After a relatively short period of time teachers, too, base their expectations and instruction upon the ability and achievement of the majority of the children in the class, unless some method is used to help them maintain a broader perspective. An accurate reporting of the present performance level of the child and a record of his school development is not sufficient. Good reports can also help here.

The report must also provide a comparison of the individual's performance and development to that of the population of children of his general age level. Note that the comparison must be made to the population of children, not just the children of his class, his school, or his neighborhood. Probably the easiest way to indicate this is according to grade level. Children of his age are normally expected to be performing at a specified grade level and he is performing (satisfactory or unsatisfactory) work at the indicated grade level. The parents know, and the school records show clearly, the level at which he is performing and the kind of work (quality) he is doing at that level.

One of the reasons consistency of reporting has been emphasized so strongly is that a report of the type just indicated, sent home to the parents for the first time after a child has been in school for a number of years, may come as quite a shock. The parents may question the report, and rightly so. It is the first one of that type that they have received. Why haven't they been informed previously? Everyone except the child may be blamed for his poor performance, if the fact of relatively poor performance is accepted at all. Pressures that may or may not be appropriate are often placed upon the child to encourage him to earn a better report, to show a better performance. In the case of slow learners, the pressures usually would not be appropriate especially where programs of a specific nature, designed to meet their needs, are not available. Slow learners tend to be working at or near their ability level.

Parents have little or no basis for aspiring to unrealistic goals for their children if, starting with kindergarten, realistic and accurate reports are made. Reporting just the level at which the child is operating is not sufficient, however. This type of reporting tends to be negative in nature and discouraging to both parents and children. It also tends to encourage in educators attitudes that are all too prevalent today. Such attitudes hold that the children are lazy, they are inherently disinterested, they need more discipline (punishment), they will learn if given more homework, schools and parents should insist on higher standards for *all* children; children should be forced to perform at a higher level; no allowances for or recognition of individual differences should be made insofar as learning abilities are concerned. These attitudes cannot help the teacher working with slow learners.

The report must also contain two additional ingredients. These are (1) the ability level and developmental rate of the child and (2) his performance as compared to an estimate of his achievement potential.

A child may be performing very poorly when his achievement is compared to children of his age and physical development. But he may be doing satisfactory work when his achievement is compared to the level that he is potentially capable of reaching at this time. In recent years there has developed among many educators a belief that children should be evaluated against their own abilities or potentials. Although, in practice, this principle of evaluation and reporting has not been too widely used or strictly applied, it can and has created a number of problems. Children may receive satisfactory grades even though their performance is considerably below grade level. These reports are given to their parents, who may continue to have many misgivings concerning the performance and ability of their children. Nevertheless, the reports continue to support their aspirations for normalcy of the child. As a result, if a higher education for the child is considered desirable, the parents may make plans for college and insist upon a college preparatory program. It is then a distinct shock and disappointment when they receive an impersonal notice from a registrar to the effect that these satisfactory grades are insufficient to qualify the youth for college admission. By this time the aspirations are so firmly imbedded that many parents will search for a college to which their child will be admitted. They may eventually succeed with certain small, private, liberal arts or religious colleges or junior colleges where admission standards are somewhat lower than is ordinarily true. Here the child may remain for a semester or a year. Few last longer. But what is worse, this kind of post-high-school education is no more appropriate than the public school college preparatory program in which they had participated. Another year has been wasted for the child.

The foregoing discussion is, in many ways, more appropriate for those slow learners who come from middle and upper-middle class homes than for the much larger group coming from the low socio-economic areas. It does, however, also apply to numbers of the latter group as well. These children and their parents may also have aspirations of bettering themselves, particularly economically, through higher education.

Reports based upon the children's performance as compared to their ability as well as upon their level of performance as compared to the level normally achieved by children give parents no basis for holding unrealistic goals. Repeatedly re-enforcing these concepts through successive reports helps parents to become ready to work with teachers and counselors and to realistically discuss the problems related to future training and education. They will be ready to benefit from the interviews and to act appropriately.

One of the clearest methods of indicating a child's intellectual and learning potential as compared to the population of children his age is to use a percentile ranking. Thus, slow learners would rank in the lowest quartile or in the lower 20 to 25 per cent of all children. Slow learners would not all be ranked the same, the slowest being in about the fifth percentile with the fastest being in about the twentieth percentile. Unfortunately most parents would not understand this type of reporting, although it could still be used for school records. Reports being sent home should describe the children's present level and potential in terms that are more generally comprehensible. This can be done in reference to school achievement. For example, a slow learner who is 12 years of age and has an I.Q. of 80 should be achieving at 4.3 grade level. Normal children of his age are expected to be achieving at 6.7 grade level. He may actually be achieving at 3.5 grade level. He therefore needs help to achieve up to his ability level (4.3) but is not expected to achieve at 6.7 grade level at this time or age. His growth will be at about four-fifths the rate of that expected from normal children. His ultimate maximum academic achievement can be expected to be at about 6.7 grade level.

A straightforward, accurate, realistic, and complete report has greater value than merely showing parents the level at which the child is presently performing. They need to know the entire story, including the expected development of their children. Children also read their reports. Thus, because the slow learners will have access to this information it should be of such a nature that it will aid them in the development of more realistic levels of aspiration. It is also apparent that a complete report, which gives a total picture concerning a child's abilities, is neither pessimistic, leaving no place for hope and growth, nor overly optimistic, encouraging the children to aspire to things they cannot achieve.

PROMOTION AND GRADUATION

Promotion from one grade to the next and from one school to the next, ultimately resulting in graduation, is generally considered to be tangible evidence of children's adequate performance and successful accomplishment. Retention in a grade is usually considered to be synonymous with failure.

In the early part of the century, when promotion was based upon academic achievement, the teacher needed only to average the scores a child had received on his various tests and assignments to determine whether or not he was to be promoted. Changing philosophies of education have been reflected in promotional practices that are far less arbitrary. They are also more difficult to define in reference to grade-level/achievement-level. This has led to a great deal of confusion in the schools. A marked amount of ambivalence is apparent as one discusses modern promotional policies with teachers and tries to determine upon what bases specific children were promoted.

Theoretically, most promotion is based upon a social concept.

The child is placed with, and continues through school with, that group of children who are at about the same social developmental level as he. In other words, he is placed with the group of children that will provide him with the kinds of social experiences he is capable of understanding and learning. This social development is usually equated with chronological age. The exception usually noted is for those children who fall too far behind the average of the group in their academic achievement. Then, despite their normal social development (in many instances), they are occasionally retained; i.e., required to repeat a grade. This is the problem that faces the teacher who has slow learners in his class.

The method of social promotion has also, in some states, led to obvious dual standards of promotion and graduation. New York State, with its Regents Examinations and Diplomas, is an example of this. At specified grade levels and in specified subjects, State Regents Examinations are given to all children who want to take them. If the child passes the examination, his Regents score is recorded and he continues into the next course. The child who fails the Regents Examination but has done satisfactory work as far as the school is concerned may elect to repeat the course in order to take the examination over again and remain in a Regents Program, or he continues with the next course. Upon the completion of the high school course of study, if the child has taken certain courses and passed the Regents Examinations for them, he receives a Regents Diploma. If he has passed all the Regents Examinations but not followed the specific course of study, he receives a school diploma. He also receives a school diploma if he has received passing school grades in a sufficient number of courses (but failed one or more Regents Examinations) and has included a few specified courses in his program, such as civics and English. Thus, the Regents Diploma indicates the completion of a somewhat rigidly specified college preparatory program. A person with a school diploma, however, may also be eligible to enter college. How, specifically, does one determine who passes and who fails?

Criteria for promotion

The present concept of promotion most generally followed is based upon social development. In practice, most children are promoted annually if they are performing fairly well in their academic learning and the criterion is usually applied only to those who are performing poorly—remedial problems, emotional and behavioral problems, and slow learners. The children who are doing superior work are seldom given a second thought beyond their normal, annual promotion. This method is unrealistic. The objectives of education and what is known concerning the development of children is often ignored. It has not and cannot prove to be a satisfactory solution.

A concept of *developmental promotion* must replace academic, social, or annual promotion methods and combinations of these methods commonly used today. Under a principle of developmental promotion a teacher would examine the record of *each* child carefully to determine whether or not he would be promoted at the end of the year, and to decide what the appropriate placement would be for each child during the following year. Insofar as possible an attempt should be made to place each child in the group that would promote his total growth to the greatest extent. Grouping should be based upon the Gestalt or total development of the individual. Physical, emotional, social, intellectual, and academic development of all the children must *all* be taken into consideration before appropriate groupings can be determined.

Most of these data are readily available although seldom used, at least in this context. Physical developmental information can be obtained from the periodic medical examinations, physical measurements that are regularly taken, and general teacher observation. Social and emotional development information is often contained in the anecdotal records and can be supplemented with careful observation in the classroom. The children's behavior should be observed and noted during participation in general school activities. When serious doubt exists, the school psychologist and school social worker or visiting teacher can usually provide the essential supplementary information. Intellectual developmental information is readily available from the results of routinely administered psychological examinations. This can be supplemented by observations of the children's behavior in learning situations. Again, the school psychologists can provide supplementary information when this is necessary. Academic development should present no problems. The teacher should be intimately familiar with the specific level of each child in each subject area from day to day. This knowledge can be verified with an examination of cumulative records, day-to-day work, and the results of standardized achievement test.

When all these factors have been taken into consideration, the teachers are in a position to recommend appropriate regrouping from the groupings presently in existence. Since most children develop in most of these areas at about the same rate, they will tend to remain together throughout their public school lives. Gifted children tend to develop in all areas at a somewhat faster rate than is true for the general population. Most of them should, therefore, complete their public schooling in one or two years less than average children. The reverse is true in regard to the development of slow learners, in general. It would be appropriate for many of them to be required to spend a year or two more in school than is true for the average.

The concepts of promotion, acceleration, skipping a grade, retention, failure, or repeating a grade should not be present in the educators' consideration of grouping or recommending a child's placement within a group. These concepts, unfortunately, are well established in the thinking of parents and the public in general. This is just one more area where good educational leadership and public education are required. It is the responsibility of the educator to assume this leadership, and the necessary change in attitudes will never be accomplished unless it is forthcoming. A good place to initiate these new concepts of grouping is with the organization of a program for slow learners.

Criteria for graduation

Graduation is a form of promotion. It is promotion from school to the community. Consequently, the same criteria apply to graduation as were described as applying to promotion. When any pupil has satisfactorily completed the course of study appropriate to his interests and abilities, he should be graduated. Graduation is essentially an indication that the school has completed that phase of its job. The individual is now as ready to take his appropriate place in the society and economy of the community as he ever will be. The diploma is merely the school's formal statement of that fact. Graduation has and still does mean many things to many people. One popular misconception is that graduation is the ticket to college admission. This is only partially true. It signifies that a student is ready to enter college only if he has completed a college preparatory program and met other necessary criteria. As a result of the college preparatory emphasis, some kind of relatively fixed value or standard has been placed upon the concept of graduation by many persons. This has been broken down to some extent by students graduating from commercial and other non-college preparatory programs. There still is, however, a great deal of resistance to the idea of graduating a slow learner from a somewhat less well understood program, with different criteria being applied concerning what constitutes satisfactory performance.

Whenever the issue of graduation for slow learners is raised a number of questions are immediately asked. What kind of a diploma should be given? What will the community and employers think of the diploma if it is given to everyone? When (at what age) should the slow learners graduate?

If graduation is conceived of as previously described, the questions have largely been answered. On the other hand, if graduation means the achievement of a specified level of competence, skill, and knowledge, there is no answer. There is no graduation for most of the slow learners. There should not be a common high school diploma, nor just two diplomas (a college preparatory and a non-college preparatory certificate). The diploma should indicate by a name or title the course of study in which the individual was enrolled and from which he graduated. It must be remembered that the diplomas, except in a very broad sense, do not indicate the persons' specific competencies or predict the kinds of adjustments they will make in the community.

Employers who seek employees who merely hold high school diplomas are apparently looking for no specific competencies in the persons they hire. The job requirements must be such that they are not based upon school-trained skills and knowledges. If they were, employers would begin to use the same methods used by colleges and universities, requiring credentials, recommendations, and transcripts to determine the specific learning experiences of the candidates for the position. In addition, they would want to know how well the candidate had performed in these various experiences. This is now being done in certain areas, especially in regard to graduates of commercial courses. Here, employers require direct appraisal of the applicants' abilities in typing, shorthand, bookkeeping, or whatever office skill is needed. They do not base their selection upon high school graduation. Any employer who states merely that he will employ only high school graduates, offering no more well-defined training prerequisites, literally deserves to get anyone, no matter how he finally obtained his diploma—including the slow learners and the mentally handicapped.

Slow learners, like any other students, should be given an opportunity to graduate from high school and receive a diploma if they so desire. Young people in school and those about to complete their education place high value upon these things. This is also true of many adults, particularly their parents. If graduation is unattainable insofar as the slow learners are concerned, it merely re-enforces any feelings they may have that they are different and do not belong. It also takes away one of the strong reasons, as far as they are concerned, for remaining in school and completing the program. Those that have completed the program have a right to participate in the graduation exercises as a part of the graduating class and should receive their diploma along with the total group.

When should the slow learners graduate? They should graduate upon their satisfactory completion of the program based upon their teachers' evaluation of their work. Their ages will vary because they will not all be able to accomplish the work in the same length of time. By the age of twenty, most slow learners should be ready to graduate. A few may require a slightly longer time, others may be ready to participate as independent members of the community at 18 or 19 years of age. Generally, unless there are mitigating factors such as irregular school attendance, lack of appropriate school programs, illness, emotional problems, and so forth, the longer it is necessary to keep slow learners in school after the normal period of time the less chance there is that they will ever be able to complete the prescribed course and assume an independent role in society. Prolonged education cannot make up or compensate for all the deficiencies an individual may have. Those slow learners that do not or cannot complete the program should not graduate.

SUMMARY

Reporting and promotion are among the more acute problems relating to the presence of the slow learners within the public schools. They are often unsolved problems because of the lack of an accepted, well-defined, common philosophy and a program that follows it. As a result, a great deal of ambivalence and contradiction is obvious in the daily approach to these problems. At present they are seldom solved to the complete satisfaction of anyone. Children may receive "passing" grades on assignments if the grading is based upon their abilities to perform. Yet, it is conceivable that these same children may be required to repeat the grade. Later, they may be "passed" on a social promotion basis but never permitted to graduate.

Reporting is a method of clearly and concisely informing both parents and children the evaluation made by the school (usually the teacher) concerning the children's achievement. A report, in order to be of maximum value, must be simple, easily read, and easily interpreted. Yet, it must be so complete that there can be no doubt in the minds of the readers concerning the academic and learning status of the child. The report should (1) contain the areas of study and behavior that the school considers important for that child and which the school is attempting to help the child learn or improve. It should (2) indicate clearly how well the child is performing in relation to the population of children his age. It should also (3) indicate clearly how well he is performing in relationship to both his past performances and to his ability.

General educational objectives are largely the same for all children. Specific objectives and emphases may differ materially among children with different abilities and/or different backgrounds. Specific objectives will also change for children at different levels; primary, intermediate, junior, and senior high school. Reports must also differ for children in the various programs and at different levels within these programs. Thus, reports for slow learners may contain items not included in the reports provided other children and may also omit some items usually considered important for most children.

Promotion, in the true sense, should never occur. It is, rather, a reflection of the school organization found most commonly today. With developmental grouping there is no need for the concept of promotion. It is replaced by a concept of growth and of development. Children should be continuously evaluated. When too great a disparity develops within the existing groups, the children are regrouped more appropriately. This may occur at any time of the school year and preferably not at the end of it.[1] In this way each child is always housed with that group of children who have educational needs similar to his own. He will, as a result, receive meaningful instruction at his developmental level for a greater proportion of the day than under a system of age grouping or annual or social promotion.

Promotion, if the concept is to continue to exist, should be thought of in reference to the children's move from the primary into the intermediate school, and so on from level to level. Promotion occurs when the child has completed the program designed for him at one school level. It occurs when he will derive greater total benefit from a more advanced program level than the one he has been attending.

The same principles apply to graduation, since this, too, is a form of promotion. Slow learners, like all children, should be able to graduate and receive a diploma signifying that they have completed, to the satisfaction of the school, the program that has been provided them. Graduation signifies the obtaining of an objective and helps place value on education. These values are especially important for slow learners because they need to be kept in school until they are ready to participate independently in society. They should not be encouraged to leave school just because an education law says that they may do so. A program designed to fill the slow learners' needs will make them want to continue their schooling, hopefully until graduation.

SELECTED RELATED READINGS

Featherstone, William B., *Teaching the Slow Learner,* Bureau of Publications, Teachers College, Columbia University, 1951, pp. 29–32.

Goodlad, John I., "Some Effects of Promotion and Non-Promotion Upon the Social and Personal Adjustment of Children," *Journal Experimental Education,* 22:301–28, June, 1954.

"High School Methods with Slow Learners," Washington, D. C.: *NEA Research Bulletin* 21, 3:74–75, October, 1943.

[1] By failing to regroup at traditional times, the end of a semester or a year, the concepts of "passing" and "failing" that are associated with regrouping at these times are de-emphasized.

Karnes, Merle B., "The Slow Learner—Administrative Plans that Help," *N. E. A. Journal,* 48:22–23, October, 1959.

Meade, Mary E. and Raymond A. Green, "What Program of Education for the Slow Learner?" *National Association Secondary School Principals Bulletin,* 35:17–32, March, 1951.

11

Principles for Organization
of Program and Instruction

The following are a compilation and summary of the basic principles that should be followed in organizing a sound educational program for slow learners. The purpose of this chapter is to provide the reader with brief, concise statements of these principles in order to provide a convenient guide. It is hoped that the chapter will prove to be a handy reference by clearly delineating the various steps that must be taken when organizing a program and the principles to follow in providing the most effective instruction.

No attempt has been made to place the various principles either in an order of importance or in the order in which they should be followed. The chapter organization is, instead, planned in relation to content and areas. There are numerous starting points and routes that may be taken that eventually lead to the same conclusion or objective, a program that meets the educational needs of the slow learners. Most school systems are already following many of the principles, at least for their normal children. They must only add those that have not been incorporated into the school program and organization and make them applicable to the slow learners as well.

RESPONSIBILITY OF THE SCHOOL

A unique and differentiated program for slow learners is predicated on the principle that *every child has the right to an equal opportunity for an education.* This does not mean that all children shall receive the same or identical educational experiences. It means that the educational experiences provided each child will be those that will promote learning for him in the best way and to the highest degree possible.

It is very easy to recognize that the visual instruction normally used in education is inappropriate for a blind child. It is also understandable that until a deaf child has been taught speech reading and language, oral instruction is inappropriate for him. The need for differentiated instruction for children who deviate physically or sensorily is easily understood. To do the same kinds of planning for intellectually and psychologically deviate children is much more difficult. Perhaps it is because they look too normal. Nevertheless, the need for educational programs carefully planned to meet their needs is fully as great as the need of children having physical or sensory handicaps. Planning programs for children with intellectual and psychological disabilities is a much greater and more fundamental break from tradition than planning for children with other disabilities. In this area one is concerned with the basic fundamentals of education. Understanding of child development, how or under what conditions learning takes place, and understanding causes of behavior and how it can be influenced and controlled are all essential ingredients that the educator must understand to develop programs for slow learners.

DIAGNOSIS

An adequate diagnosis of the children to be placed in the program is essential. Prior to the advent of intelligence testing and the development of other diagnostic instruments and techniques, it was impossible to organize a program specifically for slow learners. As a result, classes were often described as being for problem children, or for children who were having difficulty in school.

The diagnosis is also of direct value educationally. It provides the teacher with the kinds of information he needs to plan an instructional program immediately rather than having to spend time attempting to determine the level at which each child is performing. From the diagnosis, he can tell the reading, arithmetic, and language level of the child. He can also obtain information concerning the approximate rate at which the child will probably develop intellectually, his level of social adjustment, and his emotional adjustment. The intelligent use of this information can save a great deal of time for both the teacher and the pupil.

Only slow learners should be placed in the program. Many children present educational problems that on the surface appear to be similar in nature. Among these are slow learners, remedial problems, social deviates, and the emotionally maladjusted. Each of these groups of children, however, present unique problems that require a specific treatment or program. It is impossible to deal adequately with such a diversity of problems within a single classroom. Each group requires its own program, including the slow learners.

PLANNING FOR A PROGRAM

Programs for slow learners should be planned to begin as soon as they enter school and should continue until the school believes that they are ready to take their place in the community. In other words, planning should be for a total program. Slow learners usually become acute problems to the schools in the upper elementary grades and in the junior high school. It is at this time that their behavior becomes so deviate that it causes disruptions in the regular classroom. Truancy becomes common and delinquency far from rare. As a result, the value of school, insofar as the slow learners are concerned, is very limited. The school programs are too often another example of "too little too late." The behavior that becomes apparent at this time is caused, to a large degree, by what occurred at the earlier grade levels. Furthermore, where schooling is provided only until the child may legally leave school, the school certainly is not in sympathy with, nor committed to, a program for slow learners. This is less educational time than is ordinarly provided children with normal intelligence. When a school makes a decision to organize a program for slow learners it should start at the primary level and have it continued until the children are ready to take their place in the community. A survey should be made regularly of the kindergarten and first grade populations. The slow learners discovered should be placed in primary classes. Following the primary school program, programs should be provided in the intermediate, junior high, and senior high schools. The program, to be of greatest value to the children, must be complete at all levels.

TEACHERS

Teachers employed to work with slow learners must be interested in working with children who have these kinds of problems. It is not essential that the teacher have had previous successful work with normal children before receiving this assignment. There is no evidence that teachers who theoretically understand normal development of children better because they have taught normal children for a period of time consequently understand slow learners better. Logically, the reverse might be expected to be true. After having worked with children with normal intelligence, who develop rapidly intellectually as compared to slow learners, it must be very difficult for a teacher to adjust to the slower developmental rate of the slow-learning children. Secondly, the curriculum of the regular class is ordinarily oriented toward preparation for higher level instruction and eventual preparation for college. Thus, teachers who change from the instruction of normal children to the instruction of slow learners are required to reorient their entire educational philosophy. They must establish new educational objectives. This is a most difficult thing to do, particularly for the teacher who has taught under one philosophy and with one set of objectives for a number of years. Yet, without changed objectives, the kind of instruction required is impossible.

Schools may have some difficulty, initially, in finding teachers on their staff with both the ability and attitudes desired. Nevertheless, programs should not be started until staff is available. More harm than good can be easily done. The teacher who takes a class with the attitude, "Well, I guess it is my turn. But next year I will have a group of normal or bright children again," should never be allowed to work with slow learners. This should not necessarily be held against the teacher except that the attitude, as expressed, is not a healthy one. Some teachers are most effective when working in a particular area with gifted children. Others may work most effectively with normal children or slow learners. Insofar as possible, a teacher should work with that group of children with whom he can do the most effective job. New teachers should be employed with an eye toward the specific educational needs of the school.

Much of the problem of selecting teachers who can perform well with deviate children reverts back to the teacher-training institutions. Today, most elementary teacher preparation programs require students to take courses that theoretically include child development, learning theory, dynamics of behavior, and educational philosophy. The educational course requirements for secondary teachers are usually somewhat lower. Unfortunately, these courses are most often taught at a very superficial level. All aspects of psychology are often included in a single course under the catch-all title of Educational Psychology. Yet, any person who proposes to become a teacher must have a basic understanding of the learning process and why people (children) behave as they do. A better understanding in these areas alone will make for the training of better teachers. The thing that seems to be forgotten too often is that the basic function of the teacher is to teach. He is not employed to baby-sit, entertain, or run a popularity contest. The teacher must also have clearly defined objectives of education. Adequate development of these knowledges and concepts would eliminate many of the problems facing education and give direction to the fumbling attempts that are being made to provide appropriate education for all children.

CURRICULUM

The curriculum for slow learners should be developmental in nature. It is, therefore, essential that a good understanding of the development of slow-learning children be achieved before the curriculum can be defined. This does not include just their intellectual development. Development in the emotional, social, physical, motor, and achievement areas must be considered as well. Only when these are understood and incorporated into the curriculum can the desired experiences be provided at the time the children have need for them. Only in this way will they derive maximum benefit from them. There is an optimum period when instruction can be provided most effectively and most efficiently. A developmental program will introduce the experience at that time.

The curriculum should reflect the background or environment of the children. Most school curriculums reflect a middle and upper-middle class bias. This is not appropriate for the majority of the slow learners who come from sub-cultural homes in the lower socio-economic areas of the community. In order that the experiences have purpose, meaning, and value for these children, it is essential that they reflect the environment with which the children are familiar. This does not mean that the schools must accept the values generally held by persons residing in this environment. Appropriate values must be developed by the children, through the school program, that will enable them to live as effectively as possible in this environment. As they attain adult status these experiences should have been of such a nature that the persons educated under them will gradually exert the necessary influence to improve their environment.

It is obvious, then, that there is no one curriculum for slow learners. Different communities and environments will dictate that specific kinds of experiences must be included. In addition, those slow learners who come from homes reflecting a higher cultural and socio-economic level require experiences that are different from the majority. Their experiential backgrounds and value systems are much like those of most normal children. Because of this background, numbers of these slow learners may not need a special program or require dramatic changes in the curriculum. The mental hygiene aspects of a special program, where the children can have successful, satisfying experiences may be the primary factor influencing the development of differentiated programs for them.

GROUPING

Children should be grouped in school upon the basis of similarity of characteristics and similarity of educational needs. Many groupings of persons occur in the community, based primarily upon mutual interests and common abilities. When children wish to play a game, they look for others who can play or who can learn to play the game. Church groups (congregations) are formed on the basis of commonly accepted tenets. Social groups are usually composed of persons of about the same maturity (not necessarily the same age), who have about the same education, are engaged in somewhat the same kinds of employment, and have similar interests. Effective school grouping should be formed in much the same way in order to provide instruction effectively and efficiently. Within a school there may be housed classes of children of many ages and many needs, a heterogeneous community. Within each classroom the children should be grouped as homogeneously as possible in regard to their educational needs. Since there is nothing sacred or permanent about a group, as a child's educational needs change the composition of the group with whom he is placed changes. Slow learners should be placed in an educational setting that is designed in terms of each child's characteristics, background, experiences, and level of development. Grouping of all children on this basis will tend to group slow learners together.

Slow learners should be integrated with other children for those activities in which they can perform on a relatively equal basis. Since the slow learners' disabilities are primarily in the verbal, intellectual area, the possibility of many of them participating with normal children in art, music, industrial arts, homemaking, and physical education is very good. The probability that effective integration can be accomplished in the skill and academic content subject areas is highly questionable.

Classes for slow learners should be housed in schools servicing the neighborhood in which the children reside. Some school systems have taken what appear to be extreme measures in an attempt to accomplish complete integration of the children in the community. Busloads of children are transported to schools located in neighborhoods, geographically and culturally, far removed from their own. This may be appropriate when the purpose is an attempt to acculturate a group of relatively intelligent children being raised in a foreign culture (due to many foreign born families living in the same area) into the American culture. However, when the children are incapable of adjusting and maintaining themselves in a more complex culture, which is true of the slow learner, this kind of effort is self-defeating. The children are actually being provided inappropriate experiences in groups with which they have little or nothing in common except that they are all children of about the same chronological age.

Schools tend to reflect the environment of the area in which they are located. If they are good schools they will provide the kinds of experiences that have meaning and value to the children who live in that environment. Only when classes for slow learners are housed in schools catering to children with similar environmental background and, consequently, broadly similar needs in the social area, can the concepts of integration discussed in the previous paragraph be accomplished.

DEFINING EDUCATIONAL OBJECTIVES

Many schools want to establish programs for slow learners but never seem to be able to quite achieve the end result. They become so "bogged down" in details that they lose sight of the goals. Or, when they begin to work on it, the problem takes on such gigantic proportions that solution seems impossible and they become satisfied with half-way, inadequate measures that are expedient for only a small, specific, acute aspect of the total problem. Actually, there is no "program for slow learners" that fits the needs of all slow-learning children or the characteristics of all school systems. Basic principles are common to all programs. How these principles are put into action depends upon the whole complex of the local situation.

In establishing a program for slow learners, *the general, broad objectives of education must first be clearly defined and accepted by the faculty and school administration.* Only then can specific objectives related to the various facets of the program for the slow learners be defined. There is a definite hierarchy of objectives to be established. If they are studied and defined in an orderly, systematic fashion, a clear definition of the program for slow learners at every level and in every area results. The teachers, as a result, are aware that each experience contributes not only to an immediate objective but understand it as it is related to the broader objectives as well. Each teacher understands his relationship to the total program and how he is contributing to it. Furthermore, in order that the objectives be understood and accepted, committees of teachers, supervisors, and administrators should develop them. The order and rank of these objectives are shown in Table I in the Introduction.

SCHOOL ORGANIZATION

The most meaningful organization of the school is in terms of broad developmental levels rather than the existing grades and sub-grades. A number of schools have attempted this organization at the primary level with the creation of ungraded primary programs or primary schools. More recently, some schools have attempted to abandon the grade concept entirely at the lower levels by organizing the ungraded elementary school. Following known principles of child development, the school should be organized into four broad, developmental levels, primary, intermediate, junior high, and senior high. Groupings within these levels should be flexible and regrouping should occur when needed rather than at the end of a semester or year. No grade levels should be attached to the groups. A child may belong to several groups, depending upon his development in the various defined areas. Thus, he may be with one group for reading but a different one for arithmetic or the special subjects. The length of time a child remains at one level would depend upon his development. Three years would be the average but two or four years for a specific child would not be rare.

The same kinds of groupings can also be provided at the secondary level, with blocks of time being planned for the academic areas. This would permit the teacher to become better acquainted with each child and would also permit a great deal more integration of learning activities than is possible under a highly departmentalized system.

The program for slow learners would fit naturally into this type of school organization. Their program would become an integral part of the total school program. The self-contained classroom, where all activities for a group of children are provided within the confines of four walls, is a false concept. *The slow learners should have full access to all the facilities and should have instruction available from all the specialists.*

It is further recommended that *teachers of the slow learners should stay with the majority of the group during the entire time they remain at one school level.* The term majority is used advisedly because an occasional child will require regrouping and will remain at one level for a longer or shorter period than the average. Others will have achieved a degree of ability and maturity sufficient to shorten the time that must be spent in the special program. Keeping one teacher with a group of children has a number of advantages. The primary advantage is that greater continuity of program can thus be provided.

RELATION OF TEACHERS AND CHILDREN TO THE TOTAL SCHOOL

The teachers of slow learners should be considered an integral part of the school faculty. No salary differentials, except as they are related to additional training, greater competency, or supplementary responsibility should be provided. Attendance at meetings, committee assignments, and general school responsibility should be required upon the same basis that these activities are required of all teachers. The teachers must be considered a part of, not apart from the rest of the teaching personnel.

The classroom assigned the class should be of equal quality and location to other academic classrooms. It should not be off in a corner, in the basement if no other classrooms are there, or next to the boiler room. The desks, tables, chairs, and other equipment should also be of equal quality to the furnishings found in the rest of the school. This program must not be considered to be of secondary importance.

The slow learners should be considered an integral part of the student body. They should be included in all all-school activities on an equal basis with other children. They should participate in student council, auditorium programs, social activities, open houses, and P.T.A. parent-child functions. Grossly deviate behavior should no more be condoned for them than for any other child. They are not a group apart from other students.

Slow learners should be permitted and encouraged to participate in extramural and athletic activities on the same basis as other students. If they are performing satisfactorily in their program, they are eligible. In the same fashion, the various club activities are open to them in those areas in which they can participate effectively.

The total program must be accepted by the faculty and students if it is to have maximum value. Both the instructional and administrative personnel, who may or may not be directly involved, must understand and accept the program. Attitudes reflected in such disparaging remarks as, "If you don't behave yourself you will be sent to so and so's class," are soon accepted and echoed by many regular students. Student and community attitudes are largely a reflection of the acceptance, tolerance, or rejection felt and expressed by the faculty and administration. The preceding principles are helpful in developing the kind of acceptance essential to a successful program.

CHARACTERISTICS OF THE CHILDREN

Children who deviate from the norm intellectually are often thought to have other major deviate, innate, and developmental characteristics. *There is no available evidence to indicate that slow learners learn any differently from normal children who are at the same developmental level.* Since behavior of a social nature is also learned, the causes for observed behavioral differences can be explained for slow learners on exactly the same basis as for normal children. The same type of statement also applies to the negative attitudes toward school and learning often attributed to slow learners. While they often express a dislike for school and anything connected with school, they do so largely because of a long history of frustration and failure. Much of this has been the result of inappropriate school placement, being forced to follow a curriculum designed to meet the needs of other children, and poor instruction.

The major deviation of slow learners is in their general cultural and socio-economic background. *Most slow learners come from deprived homes where they receive relatively little psycho-social stimulation of a desirable nature as compared to most children.* Whether the amount that they do receive is appropriate for their slower rate and somewhat retarded level of development is problematical. Even more questionable is whether or not it will stimulate them to develop accepted behavioral patterns. Evidence indicates the environmental stimulation is inadequate both quantitatively and qualitatively. Further evidence also indicates that many of them would be able to operate at higher intellectual levels if early stimulation were provided. This places a heavy responsibility on preschool and primary programs.

A popular concept among lay people as well as among many teachers is that the slow learners will come to "no good"—that they are potential delinquents. Often this delinquent behavior is interpreted as emotional maladjustment. *Slow learners are susceptible to the development of severe emotional problems in the same way and due to the same causes as other persons.* The delinquent behavior often noted (and it is far from being universal) is not necessarily related to an emotional problem; no more than a bright student's behavior that results in high grades or another student's behavior that results in his becoming an outstanding athlete may also be reflections of emotional problems. Delinquent behavior is more apt to be planned, purposeful behavior that is not only accepted but actually approved by the "community" of which the individual is a part.

INSTRUCTION

Psychologists have studied the laws of learning extensively for half a century. Educators should be familiar with them in order that they may follow them as principles that are essential to providing effective instruction. These laws and principles of instruction are as applicable to slow learners as they are to normal children. There are no new, unique, or dramatic principles of instruction that are applicable specifically to slow learners. There is no easy method that will suddenly solve all the educational problems for this group. While methodology may be changed somewhat to enable slow learners to derive the greatest amount of benefit from the instruction, no completely new or unique practices are likely to be discovered.

When instructing slow learners, *it is essential that the children are ready to learn the particular concept or skill being taught.* Instruction should be provided only when the child is ready for it. He must have an appropriate background of experiences and sufficient mental, emotional, and social maturity. Studies available indicate that a certain level of mental development is required for the acquisition of specific academic skills, knowledges, and concepts. Since the slow learners grow more slowly intellectually than do normal children, they will be ready to benefit from instruction in the same skills at a later date than are normal children. Prolonged pre-academic and readiness periods are required to provide the slow learners with meaningful introductory experiences. Later, as the result of these experiences and sufficient mental development, they will be able to profit from the more advanced, formalized instruction in the academic areas.

There are more disadvantages than advantages in presenting new materials or concepts too soon. Children have little chance of success if they do not have the necessary background and psychological readiness. As a result of the frustrations and failures encountered, they may develop unhealthy attitudes toward school and the acquisition of academic skills. If, however, the readiness period is continued beyond the time at which the child has the necessary maturity and experiential background little harm has been done. Studies of children learning to read, for example, indicate that in cases where reading instruction has been delayed, those children acquire the skills more easily and soon catch up to children who were taught at an earlier date.

Readiness is an extremely important phase of instruction in the development of any skill or concept. Time spent preparing children for instruction will be more than repaid in the rapidity with which the learning will be acquired. Healthy attitudes will also be developed toward learning and socially more acceptable overt behavior will result. The children are having success. There is no necessity for the development of socially unacceptable, compensatory behavior.

Another way of stating the principle of readiness is that *instruction should be at the child's level*. Everything that is taught the child, he should be able to learn—with the application of some effort. He should find it necessary to apply himself to the lesson, because learning is an active rather than a passive process. The teacher must be continuously aware of exactly how, and at what level, each child is performing. Then instruction can be provided systematically by giving him successively more difficult and more advanced learning activities. One of the very real dangers in categorizing children is that it tends to stereotype the teachers' thinking. Teachers, not expecting much growth from slow learners, may provide instruction that does not stimulate the slow learners to develop as rapidly or to the highest degree possible.

Instruction should always start with the familiar and proceed to the unfamiliar. Even kindergarten children have had a wealth of experience upon which to base their learning activities. This background, particularly in the area of academic skills, becomes infinitely broader as the children continue in school. If new concepts and skills are presented in relation to material already familiar to the children, they feel secure because the learning situation has not been radically changed. They are interested because they understand and are having success. The new concepts and skills have value and meaning because they are related to material that is already familiar and that is well understood.

By teaching at the child's level, the teacher takes advantage of one of the most potent interest factors available to him—success. *Nothing contributes to interest in an activity to as great an extent as does legitimate success.* This success is not just a "pat on the back" for doing simple activity correctly or for receiving "100" on a paper containing examples previously performed many times. It means that the student has grown and learned as the result of striving to perform a task correctly, and he has achieved his goal. The important part of the success concept is that he was successful in achieving a meaningful, desired goal.

Therefore, *the learning activities must have value and meaning to the child.* School activities should be a part of rather than apart from the total, daily living experiences of the children. The things they are taught in school should have application outside school and should make their adjustment in the community easier and more effective. The students' entire environment and background of experiences must be taken into consideration when planning learning experiences.

Repetition and practice should be used extensively to ensure learning and retention. In order that practice will be of value, the children must first understand the concepts involved and these concepts must be meaningful. Recent learning studies with mentally handicapped children indicate that the retarded need no more repetition than the normal if the two groups are at the same developmental level. When the intellectual growth of slow learners is compared with the intellectual growth of normal children, the normal children are seen to grow mentally one year during each calendar year while slow learners grow only 9 to 11 months mentally during the same period of time. It requires from 13 to 16 months for slow learners to develop intellectually the same amount normal children develop in one calendar year. Learning experiences for slow learners must be paced at a somewhat slower rate. Merely increasing the number of repetitions does little or no good. The reason many teachers have assumed that slow learners require more repetitions is because skills and concepts have been introduced too soon. The slow learners have not been ready either in terms of experience or maturity. The repetitions used prior to readiness have been a waste of time and effort for both the teachers and the students.

Skills and concepts should be taught, insofar as possible, through the use of concrete, socially meaningful situations and materials. This is the purpose of the use of experience units and integrative instruction. When instruction is attached to a familiar, meaningful situation, evidence indicates that the learners will understand the instruction more completely and more rapidly.

Instruction should be planned to encourage transfer. From psychology, it is recognized that two types of transfer occur, transfer of identical elements and transfer of principles. Much of the instruction that has been planned for retarded children has been based solely upon transfer of identical elements. Teachers have literally attempted to provide the children with all the experiences in school that they will face outside school, even to the teaching of specific, simple-level jobs for future employment purposes. This is impossible. One can neither incorporate all the possible community experiences within a school program nor predict the experiences a person will be having during the rest of his life. Teaching must be done for transfer of principles.

A mark of superior intelligence is superior ability to deal effectively with abstractions. An intelligent person can understand high-level abstractions and principles and perceive the ways in which they are applicable to concrete situations. The lower and more immature the intellectual level the poorer the ability to use and apply high-level abstractions. The slow learners will be limited in their ability to use abstract principles by their somewhat limited level of intellectual development. They can, nevertheless, learn to use principles effectively. They can transfer and use abstractions at their developmental level. Careful planning of experiences is required to teach them to understand the principles involved. Then instruction should stress the application of these principles.

Instruction should be highly organized and taught systematically. The children should miss no essential steps. As the result of understanding the preceding and succeeding related experiences, they will have a better understanding of each step involved.

This principle carries beyond the instructional methods and materials and into the daily classroom routine as well. Children feel insecure if they are not familiar with what is expected of them and what is going to happen next. The younger and more intellectually immature the child, the higher the degree of organization and the more consistency he requires. As compared to normal children, slow learners of the same chronological age require a higher degree of organization of classroom routine to aid them in feeling secure. They need to know more specifically than do the normal children what the next classroom activity will be. This also helps to establish a "mind-set" or readiness for the next learning activity.

This does not mean the teacher must adhere to a rigid time and sequence for all activities and study. The children can withstand some disruptions in the regular routine, but in general, a sequence should be followed. Even though concepts are developed through the use of units of experience, specific experiences can and should be organized to follow in a fairly consecutive order from day to day.

When a new concept or skill is to be introduced, the initial step to be taken is to develop a need for it. It can then be developed through the use of socially meaningful, concrete materials. The second step is to provide the child with sufficient practice or repetition to make its use accurate and efficient. Third, numerous situations should then be introduced where the skill is required. This helps the child understand its broad application and also provides sufficient review to reduce the factor of forgetting.

A number of instructional methods are used by teachers today based upon their orientation, the subject matter being taught, and the level of the children in the class. One of these methods employs the primary use of verbal abstractions. In another, the instruction is accomplished with concrete materials. A third method organizes the instruction around the developed social needs of the children. Each of these methods has definite value and can be important when instructing children, depending upon their background of experience (what learnings have preceded the present instruction) and their level of intellectual maturity. Each method is not equally applicable to the slow learners, normal, and intellectually superior children at any specified age. In order that instruction will be most effective, the method or methods most applicable for that group at that time must be selected.

The verbal abstraction method is probably the most commonly used single method of instruction found in the classroom designed for normal children. Primary teachers and teachers of special subjects use it less than teachers of academic subjects, but throughout the schools it is ordinarily used extensively. Instruction using this method is accomplished through the use of verbal or written discussion and explanation. A teacher explains a concept to the children verbally. General classroom discussion and further explanation follow in an attempt to ensure the children's understanding of the concept. Another way the concept may be presented is through assigned readings selected from textbooks or prepared by the teacher. Following the reading, the children may be required to apply the skill or concept, but again in an abstract way, by answering questions or providing an oral or written explanation in their own terms.

Many teachers use the verbalization and abstraction method of instruction almost exclusively. Some commonly used examples of this method are found in the area of arithmetic, although the principles apply as well in social studies and the other areas. The use of such arithmetical manipulations as "$4 + 3$," "$8 - 2$," "17×4," "$358 \div 16$," "$7/8 + 3/4$," "$1^{15}/_{17} - 1/5$," and "$1\frac{3}{8} + 1\frac{1}{3}$" is dealing with the quantitive and functional concepts in an abstract way. Using this method of instruction, it is assumed that the children have the quantitative concepts necessary. It is also assumed that they know the function of the processes involved and are capable of using them correctly in arriving at the correct solutions of problems. Unfortunately this does not necessarily follow. It is quite possible for children to manipulate the numerical quantities correctly without having the concepts firmly established or to be able to put the skills to use.

The fact that manipulations and verbalizations do not ensure the development of concepts or the ability to use the manipulative skills is demonstrated by the results achieved on standardized tests. It is not unusual to find a child who scores considerably higher on the arithmetic mechanics than on the arithmetic comprehension parts of the tests. This is particularly true of slow learners. The ability to apply principles to or derive principles from a number of experiences and then apply them to specific, applicable situations is a mark of high intelligence and/or instruction designed to accomplish this. Slow learners and younger normal children are usually somewhat deficient in this ability. This may be, however, largely due to the type of instruction they received.

Concrete materials are more widely used by primary teachers than by other teachers at the elementary level. They are also used more extensively by special-subjects teachers than by teachers of academic subjects at the secondary levels. Using this method, the teacher develops concepts through the actual handling and manipulation of objects by the children. These objects may have no specific, related meaning or intrinsic value to the children. They merely *represent* objects that they will actually come in contact with when they do apply these concepts to meaningful situations. For example, the primary teacher may use shoe pegs, beads, or cubes of wood to develop quantitative concepts and the initial understanding required in performing addition, subtraction, multiplication, and division. Instead of having to visualize the quantities and concepts involved, the children actually handle the quantities and groups and manipulate them in order to arrive at the mathematical solutions.

Art teachers regularly use the various media, materials, and tools to demonstrate methods, techniques, or such abstract concepts as design or composition. Industrial arts teachers supply the students with materials and tools, requiring them to perform tasks that will require the use of concepts and techniques they are attempting to develop. The same is true for instruction in homemaking. Science instruction is usually filled with the use of concrete objects, objects to observe and dissect in biology, chemicals to combine in chemistry in order to observe reactions, and various machines to work in the laboratory to observe the laws of physics. While furniture may be constructed in an industrial arts class or cookies made in a cooking class, the activities themselves are, unfortunately, not always built around a desire, a need, or a needed experience of the children.

This method of instruction is neither universal nor the only one used in the primary grades or the special-subjects areas. It largely depends upon the orientation of the teacher and the willingness of the administration and school board to provide the materials. Yet, there is experimental evidence that shows this method to have greater value for some kinds of instruction than the verbal method, particularly for the intellectually retarded and immature children. Slow learners will develop more understanding of the basic concepts involved, will develop a superior understanding of the academic skill, and will be able to use the skill more intelligently in life situations in which it is applicable through the use of this method of instruction.

Teaching, using activities related to the children's social needs, is the most desirable and most effective method with children who are retarded intellectually. The same is probably true for young, intellectually immature children with average intelligence as well. It is the method most widely advocated by modern educators. Its application, unfortunately, is too often of a poor quality or only a superficial overlay built upon a traditional, subject-matter approach.

The social needs from which the concepts to be taught are developed arise through the normal, daily living experiences of the children. The alert teacher takes advantage of these situations and incorporates them into the classroom experiences of the children. This has the additional advantage of making the school experiences truly a part of the child's living experience. It provides social meaning to the school activities. Where this is difficult or impossible, units of experience are organized within the classroom to provide life or near-life learning situations for the children. These units may incorporate the development of concepts and skills in one or more of the academic areas.

The methodology of instruction follows closely the methods used with concrete objects. The children have an opportunity to handle and manipulate materials in accordance with the principles the teacher is attempting to develop. The primary difference between the two methods (concrete and social need) is that where the object or concrete method of instruction often uses intrinsically meaningless objects, the social method utilizes objects that have meaning for the child, experiences that are related to his desires and background. The children have a need for the concepts and skills. They want to learn them in order to achieve a certain desired objective. They learn them through the use of the materials that are included in their normal social activities. They learn to apply the concepts and skills with the materials from and in a life or near-life situation. Thus, the transfer required from principles to actual practice is facilitated.

These are the reasons for the inclusion of all kinds of units of experience, usually centered around the areas of health, social science, and physical science within the classroom. Through these activities and experiences, basic reading, writing, spelling, arithmetic, and other skills can be developed and the children will understand their purpose and value. Knowledge and concepts in the social and physical sciences are also learned as they are related to the lives of the children. They learn to use them as they are learning them.

Instruction must be planned to ensure eventual understanding of principles. Because teaching related to social need and using the objects related to that situation (thus incorporating all of the values of the concrete method) is recognized as the superior method for slow learners, the use or introduction of abstractions is often left to chance. Before any skill or concept attains its ultimate value to the individual it must be understood abstractly, or as a principle. The purpose of relating instruction to familiar activities is not primarily to teach the children how to react in *that* situation, although they do learn that as well. The fundamental purpose of this type of instruction is to help the children to understand the concepts better and more quickly by relating them to already familiar activities. These activities also serve to provide purpose to learning. Once the children have grasped the concepts as they relate to this situation, instruction must be planned to help them understand the concepts abstractly. With an abstract understanding of principles, the principles can be applied to needful situations. The education the children are receiving is becoming a useful tool.

Children who eventually attain the level of mental maturity found in normal adults have sufficient ability to arrive at correct abstractions from "learnings" included in their programs at a much earlier date. The slow learners' eventual level of intellectual maturity cannot be depended upon to guarantee the completion of their education independent of the school. Instruction (methods and techniques) must be planned at all levels to ensure the understanding of the skills and concepts that are desirable and necessary.

GRADING AND REPORTING

When grading or evaluating a child and reporting the grades for the information of others (usually the parents), the following four basic principles should be followed.

The report should be a clear reflection of the objectives of the program. By examining the report or report form (in most schools this is a card) it should be possible to make a fairly accurate description of the curriculum in which the child is enrolled and the educational objectives that have been defined for him or the group of which he is a part.

Each child's performance should be evaluated (graded) in relation to as accurate an estimate of his potential as possible. The frame of reference is the individual. He, and anyone else, should know whether or not he is performing at the level he should be achieving. If he is not, measures should be taken to help him improve. If he is performing significantly above his estimated potential, the data used in making the estimate should be examined closely, questioned, and additional information obtained in order that a more accurate estimate may be made.

Each child's performance should be evaluated (graded) in relation to the population. This indicates how well he is doing as compared to others. However, if a child who is a slow learner is rated only on this basis, it is impossible for him to receive anything but a low evaluation and he may become discouraged. On the other hand, if he is rated only against his own ability, his rating may always be high and he and his parents may develop unrealistic aspirations for him. By including both ratings in the report there is no excuse for discouragement or unrealistic aspirations.

Finally, the report should be clear, concise, and easily read and interpreted. The report should be simple, so that parents with little education can read and understand it. It should be short, so that a great deal of time need not be spent endeavoring to understand it. Finally, it should be so clear that it is impossible to misinterpret the statements and evaluations made in it.

PROMOTION AND GRADUATION

Promotion of slow learners should be on a developmental basis. After considering carefully the intellectual, physical, motor, social, emotional, and academic development of the individual, a decision regarding promotion can be made. If, considering all the developmental areas, the experiences provided at the next school level will be of greater benefit to him than the experiences provided at the present level, he should be promoted.

Graduation is recommended when a child has satisfactorily com-

pleted the program defined for him and is ready to take an independent place in the community. Since students enroll in a number of different public school programs, there should be a number of different diplomas given out at graduation. Some diplomas may indicate that the students have completed a college preparatory program, some that they have completed commercial courses, and others that they have completed a program of a less academic nature. The latter type would be appropriate for most of the slow learners and the mentally handicapped. If a company seeks to employ a high school graduate, it should be looking for certain competencies. Recommendations and school records will show whether a student has these competencies, his diploma will not.

SELECTED RELATED READINGS

Harper, F. S., "Slow Learners Learn By Doing," *Clearing House,* 16:223–27, December, 1941.

"High School Methods with Slow Learners," Washington, D. C.: *NEA Research Bulletin* 21, 3:60–86, October, 1943.

Lerch, Albert M., "What Can You Do With Them?" *School Executive,* 74:58–59, April, 1955.

Moskowitz, Myron, "Teaching the Slow Learner," *School Review,* 56:476–83, October, 1948.

Smith, G. M., "When I Teach Slow Learners I Try to Remember These Points," *Clearing House,* 24:177, November, 1949.

Wright, M. A., "Teaching the Older Slow Learner," *Exceptional Children,* 12:42–46, November, 1945.

Index